This outstanding book addresses the challenges of chronic disease in children from multiple viewpoints with a great deal of practical knowledge. Given that diabetes is one of the most common chronic diseases of childhood, this work will serve to guide families in navigating the sometimes challenging journey to ensure the best possible outcomes for all.

—**Robert Gabbay, MD, PhD,** Chief Scientific and Medical Officer, American Diabetes Association

The journey with a chronic illness can be overwhelming, and often calls for education, support, and self-empowerment. Parents and caregivers of children with chronic diseases often take on the critical role of preparing their children for the journey toward—and often extending into—adulthood. Every parent wants to ensure that their child is well-equipped to manage their own care when that time comes. The Crohn's & Colitis Foundation recognizes this guide's value in helping parents along this challenging road. This book is a great resource to help families manage mental health, school accommodations, social activities, medical management, and everyday experiences for all with a chronic illness.

—**Crohn's & Colitis Foundation**

Frank J. Sileo's and Carol S. Potter's book is a heartfelt and candid look at the emotional journey as a parent and full-time caregiver for a child with chronic illness. Frank offers practical advice and personal insight from the experience of dealing with his own invisible disabilities diagnosed in his early 20s. Carol offers her experience with caregiving for her husband who had terminal cancer. Their tips and wise counsel for accepting the "new normal" and having a PLAN (Putting Life into Action Now!) are life-giving, as is their advice for speaking up ("If you don't ask, you don't get") and maintaining your own health and welfare. This book is a must-have for parents in a caregiving role for a child with chronic illness and pain or any disability.

—**Jess Stainbrook,** Executive Director, Invisible Disabilities® Association

When your child is diagnosed with a chronic illness like Type 1 diabetes, your world stops. You have days, perhaps weeks, to learn and master life-sustaining care for your child. *When Your Child Has a Chronic Medical Illness* is a comprehensive guide to help parents as they embark upon a life different from what they had expected. This book is extremely thorough, and you will find advice, guidance, and comfort regardless of your family's situation.

—**Jeff Hitchcock,** President, Children with Diabetes

As a physician, I have often been in the position of delivering the diagnosis of a child's chronic illness to their parents and family members. In those moments, I often wish I could provide them with support and resources beyond just medical care. This lovely and poignant text does just that, and I will be using it as a reference for patients and their families as I develop my practice for years to come.

—**Miriam E. Goldblum, MD,** Psychiatry resident, Weill Cornell Medicine/New York Presbyterian Hospital

Sileo and Potter bring parents a timely road map for how to navigate raising a child with a chronic illness. The book is jam-packed with practical information and guidance about topics that affect children and their families—everything from coping with hospitalization to schooling, and even taking a vacation. The authors translate medical and educational concepts into layperson's terms, making the information highly accessible and understandable.

—**Deborah Vilas, MS, CCLS, LMSW**

Sileo and Potter have created an instrumental guide for parents caring for a child with a chronic medical illness. Within the challenges and complexities of the health care journey, you will learn the importance of taking time to reflect, connect, and honor their feelings with a sense of hope and support. This book demonstrates how you can recognize your capacity for self-care and self-compassion, choose renewing emotions, and create a plan to greet the challenges before you with a new perspective of possibilities.

—**Kelly Briggs, RN, NE-BC, HNB-BC, RYT-500,** Director of Integrative Health & Medicine, Hackensack Meridian Health Network

This book is an essential resource for helping families overcome the daily obstacles and uncertainties of caring for a child with a chronic medical illness. With sheer compassion and a desire to help, the authors bring hope as well as effective techniques to navigate through the day-to-day challenges. Along with practical advice for everyday living, readers are empowered to understand and uncover their own personal needs, desires, beliefs, attitudes, and feelings. Sileo and Potter bring the physical and emotional well-being of the caregiver to the forefront, with resources and tools such as mindfulness, spirituality, and humor.
—**Allison Morgan, MA, OTR, E-RYT,** Founder, Zensational Kids

An extremely informative guide on navigating pediatric chronic illness for anyone involved in a child's care, from parents and teachers to medical practitioners. This comprehensive book provides an insightful perspective on the emotional and logistical challenges for families in navigating chronic illness from diagnosis through treatment and beyond. The authors' personal and professional experiences provide a deeper appreciation for the many aspects and impacts of chronic illness, and enable me to be a more compassionate practitioner with children and their families when I am lucky enough to be involved in their continuum of care.
—**Julia S. Buckley, MS RDN,** Owner, Julia S. Buckley Nutrition

Sileo and Potter have inspired me with their work. This book is crucial for parents as well as for all of those who care for or know someone with a chronic medical illness. As an adult who was once a child with a chronic illness, I wish this book had been around to help my parents in our journey. As a professional, I will use it to help my clients navigate their own journeys.
—**Lisa B. D'Acierno, LCSW,** Founder and Director, D'Acierno and Associates Psychotherapy

When Your Child Has a CHRONIC MEDICAL ILLNESS

When Your Child Has a CHRONIC MEDICAL ILLNESS

A Guide for the Parenting Journey

Frank J. Sileo, PhD & Carol S. Potter, MFT

Foreword by Lawrence D. Rosen, MD, Founder of The Whole Child Center

Published by
American Psychological Association
750 First Street, NE
Washington, DC 20002
https://www.apa.org

Order Department
https://www.apa.org/pubs/books
order@apa.org

In the U.K., Europe, Africa, and the Middle East, copies may be ordered from
Eurospan
https://www.eurospanbookstore.com/apa
info@eurospangroup.com

Typeset in Sabon by Circle Graphics, Inc., Reisterstown, MD

Printer: Sheridan Books, Chelsea, MI
Cover Designer: Melissa Jane Barrett, Provo, UT

Library of Congress Cataloging-in-Publication Data

Names: Sileo, Frank J., 1967- author. | Potter, Carol S., author.
Title: When your child has a chronic medical illness : a guide for the
    parenting journey / by Frank J. Sileo and Carol S. Potter.
Description: Washington, DC : American Psychological Association, [2021] |
    Includes bibliographical references and index.
Identifiers: LCCN 2020032002 (print) | LCCN 2020032003 (ebook) |
    ISBN 9781433833816 (paperback) | ISBN 9781433833823 (ebook)
Subjects: LCSH: Chronically ill children. | Parents of chronically ill
    children.
Classification: LCC RJ380 .S55 2021 (print) | LCC RJ380 (ebook) |
    DDC 618.92—dc23
LC record available at https://lccn.loc.gov/2020032002
LC ebook record available at https://lccn.loc.gov/2020032003

https://doi.org/10.1037/0000229-000

Printed in the United States of America

10 9 8 7 6 5 4 3 2 1

*To Mom and Dad—For your love and support on my professional
and personal journeys. I'm sorry for throwing my vitamins
behind the couch and giving you a hard time at the pediatrician.
To Dr. Mitchell K. Spinnell—Much gratitude for the expert,
compassionate medical care you provide to my family and me.*
—Frank J. Sileo

*To those who shared their time and stories with us.
And to all the parents raising children with a chronic illness—
You are my heroes.*
—Carol S. Potter

CONTENTS

LIST OF WORKSHEETS

FOREWORD

Every parent begins their journey with expectations. Despite all personal and universal experience that might suggest otherwise, we envision our future children as physically and emotionally happy and healthy, free of illness and struggle. When our child is diagnosed with a chronic illness, we are thrown off course. Lives are immeasurably changed, in a moment. That "perfect future" we've imagined is gone, poof, forever altered. The idyllic vision is now replaced by a million urgent fears . . . "What now? What do I do? Who do I ask? What will happen to my child . . . and to me?" As a pediatrician for nearly 30 years and a parent for many of those, I am keenly aware of the groundlessness families face when confronted with the diagnosis of a serious health condition for their child. I have found families require two equally critical things at these times—a dose of compassionate realism and a dash of realistic hope. In your hands, you are holding a book that artfully and gracefully provides both.

Relying on evidence-informed literature and lengthy clinical experience, psychologist Dr. Frank Sileo and marriage and family therapist Carol Potter offer so much wisdom that you may not want to read this invaluable guide cover-to-cover but, instead, find what is needed at the right time, for you. There is a wealth of practical guidance, covering communication tips, school and medical system guidance. You will also find an ample supply of emotional support and coping strategies for those inevitable times hope and faith are most needed. In particular, Chapter 9 ("The Cone Zone") includes truly important mindfulness tips. Parenting a child with a chronic illness is a rollercoaster of a journey. Just when you think you've found some solid footing, the ground shifts. For certain, in my experience, all parents set out to do what's best and right for their child. But what's often overlooked in the struggle to do everything possible so your child can have the best life possible is, well, you. One of the many aspects I love about this book is the attention devoted to self-care. Kindness and compassion must start within, for only then can we sustainably offer what we have to give to our loved ones without losing ourselves in the process.

There is no single story. All children are unique, special in their own way. It is rare that a parenting resource provides so much to so many—and, luckily for you—you have one in your hands. May this book serve you in the way you need. I, for one, am overjoyed to have such a comprehensive and compassionate guide to recommend to families who will benefit tremendously.

Lawrence D. Rosen, MD
Founder, The Whole Child Center

ACKNOWLEDGMENTS

There have been many people who have helped and supported us in realizing the vision of this book. You could almost say, it takes a village to write a book! First, we want to thank Eileen Kennedy-Moore, PhD, for sharing her knowledge about creating a proposal, and Linda McCarter for believing in our vision and bringing us on board at the American Psychological Association (APA). Brianne Dickey gave us invaluable assistance in the research process. Marj Kleinman, Deb Vilas, and Kelli Carroll provided needed insight into the role of the Certified Child Life Specialist. Friends and family cheered us on and gave us a pass when deadlines meant missing meetings, get-togethers, and so on. Elise Frasier headed up an incredibly supportive and enthusiastic editing team at APA, all of whose involvement we have greatly valued. Special thanks go to Susan Herman, our development editor, who helped us turn a sprawling manuscript into a book keyed to our particular audience. Of course, the greatest thanks go to the patients, families, and professionals who have shared their stories with us. The understanding they have imparted always kept us focused on what would be most helpful to the parents we hope to reach.

When Your Child Has a CHRONIC MEDICAL ILLNESS

THE UNEXPECTED JOURNEY BEGINS

When your child was diagnosed with a chronic illness, your life turned upside down. Your picture of the life you thought you would have turned upside down too. And now, whether you are mere days from learning of the diagnosis or several years down the road, you probably have some days of smooth sailing and some days when you're nothing but stressed out. You know that at some point you will find a new normal, and you know that your struggles will develop your strengths. But in the meantime, you're asking yourself: "Where will this journey take me next?"; "I wish I knew all the possible detours so I could plan for them"; "Are we there yet?" You knew you were in for a ride when you became a parent, but you weren't counting on this many bumps in the road!

What is obvious for you now is your calendar of appointments. Does it look something like this?

- Monday, 3:45: Take child for a blood draw
- Tuesday: Meet with child's teacher to discuss making up assignments
- ASAP! Call insurance company to make sure they'll cover the next procedure

On Saturday you had scheduled a coffee date with a friend—but you have to skip it. You need to take an extra shift at work because your coworker covered for you last week when you had to miss so you could keep your child at home during a flare-up of the illness.

Most likely, you are already a pro at navigating certain parts of the chronic-illness journey. You've learned that your child's health needs often dictate where you will be and when. You also have a set of map coordinates, so to speak, that keep you focused when you perform procedures you never thought you'd need to do—for example, monitoring your child's blood sugar and treating urgent highs and lows, or executing airway clearance techniques you learned from the respiratory therapist. You can tick through a symptom checklist in seconds to determine whether a nurse consult over the phone or a visit to the emergency room is in order.

You are doing an amazing job. You are parenting the very best you can—even if the view through your windshield looks different than you thought it would. Your amazing love for your child is enough to power you through most days.

Other days, you feel lost.

Where are all these emotions coming from? Why am I suddenly angry for no reason? Some days, I am so exhausted it is hard to get out of bed. It kills me to see my toddler crying when I can't help him. And why can't my teen take this more seriously? At times it seems like she doesn't care!

If you are feeling lost in uncharted territory, know that you are not alone: You are part of an enormous community. Estimates of the numbers of children with chronic illness range from 15%[1] to 31%,[2] with some estimates as high as 43%.[3] Estimates may vary depending on which conditions are included; autism, for example, may be counted as a chronic illness even though it is a type of neurological condition that we do not address in this book. Still, this means that in your child's class of 20 there may be two to eight other children with some kind of chronic illness or condition.

Many of these illnesses and conditions were once fatal, or condemned children to a very short life, often full of suffering. The good news is that, with the amazing advances of medical science over the past decades, new treatments have been found that greatly prolong the life and enhance the well-being of children with chronic illnesses. The challenge is that these new treatments can't always cure the disease, and the additional work of caring for children has shifted from the medical community square onto the shoulders of their parents. That's you.

You've probably seen firsthand how, as a society, we keep our sick on the sidelines, out of our everyday awareness. We even act as if they are some other species of human. This makes them and their families invisible. In the parallel universe of chronic illness, you may feel there are no familiar markers. You're meeting a new, strange cast of characters. People you thought would be with you through thick and thin have disappeared, while others you may barely know have stepped up in ways you never imagined. Your relationships seem to be changing every day! You feel like you're cutting a path through the wilderness.

In reality, though, there are some paths, well-worn ones. You don't have to stumble around in the dark. Maybe you've met other families who have been through a chronic illness journey. Their path won't be exactly the same as yours; each family's journey is unique. Still, the paths are there. Others have felt how you are feeling right now. Others have gotten stuck in the same ruts as you. Others have traveled the rocky relationship road, too. And guess what—some of them even left a few notes in the logbook to help you out.

WHY WE WROTE THIS BOOK

Chronic illness isn't a journey we expect or plan to take with our child, but sometimes that is what life hands us. We wrote this book because we, the authors, know from our own experience how confusing and challenging this journey of chronic illness can be, but we also know that families can meet those challenges, and even thrive in the face of them. Frank has an autoimmune disorder called Crohn's disease. Carol cared for her husband through his cancer, until she had to say goodbye to him. In our professional lives, we both work with children and families to help them learn how to deal with the emotions and relationship challenges that chronic illness can bring. One of the things we've both learned is that it's impossible to chart a course for this journey on any kind of map—not even the kind that computes real-time data and works on your smart device. The other thing we've learned is that there are options for finding your new normal and navigating your life besides having to feel your way through the narrow places and over the bumps all on your own.

On the chronic illness journey with your child, there are potholes aplenty, but there are also some excellent pit stops and scenic vistas. Your emotions, your relationships, and your needs for self-care are all real—just as real as the medical facts you see in black and white. They are as real as the physical needs your child has. We wrote this book to help you see these hidden parts of the journey.

So many things drain your energy: strong feelings, tough choices, not to mention the sheer volume of calls you make and texts you write daily to maintain your support system. Our hope with this book is to help you save some of that energy. The learning curve is steep, but we hope to level it out a bit for you. In this book we share some need-to-know facts from the scientific research on parenting and chronic illness. We also share the wisdom from journeys of other families with childhood chronic illness. We want you to be able not only to cope but also to feel confident, engaged— and, yes!—happy, as your parenting life continues to unfold.

WHAT'S IN THIS BOOK

This book is intended primarily for parents who have a child age 3 through 17 with a chronic illness. We say age 3 instead of infancy because many of our tips are about talking with your child and setting expectations and boundaries that go beyond such basics as sleep, eating, and diapering/toileting (though these life tasks are always relevant in different ways and at different developmental stages). Many excellent resources are available to parents with an adult child who is living at home or who is transitioning to independent living. We recommend starting with websites of pediatric hospitals and care facilities to learn more. Some helpful websites include **https:// luriechildrens.org** (search for "Transitioning to Adult Care" under the "Specialties and Conditions" tab), **https://arnoldpalmerhospital.com/ content-hub/how-to-transition-your-child-with-a-chronic-illness-into- adulthood,** and **https://childrens.com** (search for "Transitioning to Adult Care").

In putting this book together, we wanted to mirror the process of a journey, starting with the immediate effects of your child's diagnosis. We offer the information in a somewhat chronological order, starting with your first knowledge of the diagnosis and the steps we recommend taking first. You might be surprised that the first several chapters are focused on you, the parent. This is because your first responsibility—even in parenting or a couple relationship—is to take care of yourself. If you've ever been on an airplane you know what the flight attendant says to do with the oxygen mask, should it deploy: Put one on yourself before trying to assist others. If you can't breathe, you are no good to anyone else.

In Chapter 1 we discuss the range of emotions you might be feeling now or in the future, and we offer a few healthy tips for coping. The same emotions will arise again and again, often in roller coaster fashion, so being able to recognize, deal with, and express them appropriately will be key to reducing your stress. In Chapter 2 we demonstrate how to be compassionate to yourself, and we guide you through some self-care options to help build your resilience.

Chapter 3 is all about channeling that resilience and the dreams you have for your family into getting what you need, whether that be a support group or respite care. We also address some of the rubber-meets-road decisions you may need to face, such as whether or not quitting your job might be in your family's best interest. We expect that, as your journey unfolds, your needs as a parent and as an individual will change. At some point you may want to use therapy for psychological support, either for yourself, particular individuals in the family, your couple relationship, or the family as a whole. So, in addition to positive coping strategies, we also highlight in Chapter 3 some red flags that could indicate the need for psychological support, and we describe how and where you can find it.

As you learn more and more about your child's diagnosis, you will not only need to talk with your child about the illness, but you may also need to learn new ways of listening to your child. Chapter 4 covers this in detail. Chapter 5 then turns to your copilots on the journey. Whether you are parenting alongside your spouse, an ex, your own parents, in-laws, or others, effective communication skills come in very handy, especially when emotions run high. In Chapter 5 we explore how to have good, productive conversations, and we present ideas for strengthening your emotional connections with others close to you. Chapter 6 covers important conversations to have with siblings and other family members as well as tips for maintaining a family focus even when many of your daily activities are oriented toward your child.

Chapter 7 is all about working with medical professionals to make your child's journey as smooth as possible. They play a crucial role in keeping your child well and happy. We show what advocacy and self-advocacy can look like for your child, both in the clinic and when treatment continues at home. We also discuss helping your child with swallowing pills and coping with needles.

In addition to medical personnel, families often need to communicate with school personnel: teachers, aides, school psychologists, and others. Chapter 8 describes how to obtain support or special-needs services at school, how to work through other school-related issues (such as bullying), and when to consider whether homeschooling might be the best route.

Chapter 9 offers boundary-setting skills that you can practice with coworkers, acquaintances, or others with whom you don't regularly share details about your family's situation. For example, how can you be both honest and civil when others offer their support in the form of unwelcome advice?

Perhaps the most challenging aspect of having a child with a chronic medical condition is hospitalization. In Chapter 10 we address the potential disruptions of a hospital stay. We also provide helpful coping tools for easing your child's discomfort during difficult procedures.

Chapter 11 explores the ways the family changes when a child dies as a result of chronic illness. Here we offer some practical guidance for end-of-life conversations and resources for dealing with grief.

Chapter 12 provides a brief summary of the book and some encouragement as you continue on your parenting journey.

Toward the end of the book we include a part called Resources for Your Journey, which lists children's books, organizations, and apps that may be helpful.

Throughout each chapter we provide practical tips, geared toward your child's age or developmental stage, for managing emotions, communicating effectively, and building relationships. We end each chapter with a list of actionable ideas to help you think about next steps you will take toward making the best of your family's journey. In many chapters we've also included stories or quotations from real life. We hope that hearing what our patients have said, and learning how they found solutions or ways to feel better, will inspire you to keep reading. Where we describe or quote individuals, please note that we have changed names and other identifying details to protect their privacy.

We have used as our foundation both the scientific research literature and our own clinical training and experience. Fortunately, the research now includes, in addition to more formal quantitative research, valuable qualitative studies, which highlight major themes in the actual lived experience of families with a child who has a chronic illness. Quantitative research, which deals with groups as a whole and shows us patterns of what interventions affect which outcomes, is also valuable. Please note, however, that no intervention or treatment described in the research yields a 100% response; that is, although well-designed studies tell us a great deal about groups of people, they cannot tell us definitively what is happening for a particular individual or a particular family. Even in studies where large effects are found—say, 30% or 40% or more—that means a difference was made in only 30% or 40% of families. The other 60% to 70% were unaffected.

In brief, when considering treatments for your child, you have to rely on your own knowledge of your family and of what is best for everyone. Your family's culture and background, your resources, and your context will influence how you see the issues and what you determine is the best course of action. All that we offer here, although solidly based, are possibilities. We ask that you read what we offer with an open mind and then reflect on what makes sense for you. We trust your judgment to determine the right course of action for your family.

You'll notice that throughout the book the pronouns we use shift. Sometimes we refer to "they and them," sometimes to "she and her," sometimes to "he and him." This was intentional! Language matters, and we want ours to be inclusive, so that many readers can relate to the material and see a bit of their own situation in the stories we describe.

OUR STORIES ABOUT CHRONIC ILLNESS

All chronic illnesses have their own unique characteristics. Some may have a trajectory with many ups and downs, ranging from acute symptoms to remission to a return of even more acute symptoms. Some people may eventually develop a terminal illness. Others' condition remains pretty steady, with a greater degree of predictability and consistency of symptoms. Two people with the same illness can even have vastly different experiences—for example, in the way their bodies respond to medications or to a special diet.

We point this out because it can sometimes be hard to listen to others' stories if the specifics are different from your own. "Well, *they* have partners who can come home early to cook!"; "Well, kids with *that* condition don't have to worry about missing months of school!" It's tempting to react this way sometimes, but we want to encourage you to open yourself to others' experiences. Look for what is similar in their stories. Some feelings are universal. Take what is helpful to you, and shelve or discard the rest. Stay on your own path. For a little insight into our personal journeys, read on.

Frank's Story

A little over 30 years ago, my life changed in two ways. First, I was accepted to the psychology graduate program at Fordham University in New York City; I was on my way to a career as a psychologist. Second, I started to have gastrointestinal problems.

I was 22 years old at the time—younger than most of my classmates—and although I was excited, and honored, to be admitted to a program that admits a limited number of students each year, I was equally petrified about the mountains of work and time that came along with graduate studies. I also had to get acclimated to commuting into New York City, taking buses and subways. Believe it or not, despite living in nearby New Jersey, I had little exposure to the stress of public transportation.

About halfway through my first year, I started to have gastrointestinal problems. Any time I ate, food ran through my system like a rocket ship. I could not keep any food in my system. I lost a tremendous amount of weight, and I looked, and felt, ill. Everyone, including me, thought my symptoms were from the stress caused by beginning graduate school.

Eating seemed to become my enemy. Meals were always followed by a sprint to the bathroom. There were several instances when I was on the public bus going to school when I would feel sick and no bathroom was in sight. This caused me tremendous anxiety. I was in constant fear that I would soil myself. I couldn't leave the house in the morning before feeling completely emptied out. There were many instances where I left only to return minutes later to use the bathroom. I was "bathroom stalled."

Although people in my life were supportive, I was often met with, "It's all in your head," "You're just stressed out," and "My gosh! You're so thin! Put some meat on those bones!" I also dealt with a lot of insensitive diarrhea jokes. I wasn't laughing. I was feeling hopeless, defective, and depressed.

What followed next was a series of appointments with several doctors for various opinions. Was it irritable bowel syndrome? Inflammatory bowel disease? With the doctor appointments came many different tests and procedures. I had blood drawn over and over. I felt like a pincushion. I had multiple upper and lower GI (gastrointestinal) tests done. I had numerous sigmoidoscopies, colonoscopies, CT (computed tomography) scans, parasite tests, stool tests, and MRIs (magnetic resonance imaging scans). I drank barium solutions that tasted like chalk and made me gag. The prep for the colonoscopy was dreadful. I even had a pill camera test in which I swallowed a pill with a miniature camera in it. I had to wear a vest that was hooked up with electrical equipment so that pictures can be taken as the pill traveled through my body. I looked like a terrorist. All of these tests and medical appointments meant taking time off, sitting endlessly in waiting rooms, driving all over the New York City region, being probed in uncomfortable places, and repeating my story over and over. Some of the medicines prescribed actually made my symptoms worse or just made me feel worse in general—more exhausted, more stressed out.

As time went on, I lost more weight and continued to feel horrible. I would look at myself in the mirror and not recognize my own reflection. I was appalled at my appearance. Clothes hung off my body. Despite being sick, I never missed school and continued to work diligently on my doctoral degree. Nothing was going to stop me.

After about a year or so of back and forth with doctors, tests, and medications, I finally received the diagnosis of Crohn's disease. Crohn's is an autoimmune disease that affects the gastrointestinal tract anywhere from the mouth to the anus. My Crohn's was at my terminal ileum, which is the point at which the small intestine meets the large intestine. Because I had so much scar tissue in that area due to Crohn's, my terminal ileum became narrowed. If I ate certain foods, like raw vegetables or nuts, it blocked the opening, which caused tremendous pain, nausea, vomiting, and emergency room visits. Although I was relieved that I now had a name and a treatment option attached to what was happening to me, I still was not myself. I struggled with diarrhea, low-grade fever, fatigue, and weight loss, among other symptoms.

I popped antidiarrheal medication like Tic Tacs. I found that turkey was easy on my digestive system; however, I ate so much turkey I swore I was going to grow feathers. At times, I pureed my food and ate baby food to give my bowels a rest. This helped, but it made going out for dinner and socializing extremely challenging. I watched my diet, and at times restricted my intake of food: No food, no diarrhea. This was not a healthy approach to my disease or to living, but I didn't know what else to do.

In 1995, after 6 years of studying, doing externships, an internship, writing, defending a dissertation, and a multitude of other hurdles, I graduated from Fordham with my PhD in counseling psychology. At that time, I was the youngest person to graduate with a doctorate from Fordham's counseling psychology program. I had started working in my field and began a small private practice. I started working therapeutically with children, adolescents, and adults. I loved my work as a psychologist but continued to have periodic flare-ups with Crohn's disease. I went to my doctor regularly. I also sought out treatment from alternative doctors. In the early to late 1990s, alternative medicine and treatments were rare and not as well respected as they are today. Still, I would do anything to feel better. I kept persevering in my career and worked full time while maintaining a part-time private practice of about 15 patients a week. I was busy.

At that time, my professional work mainly involved helping children deal with issues related to divorce, feelings of anxiety and depression, or bullying incidents at school, among others. I wanted to do something for myself and others who had Crohn's disease. I joined the New Jersey chapter of the Crohn's and Colitis Foundation and started getting involved as a board member. I participated in walks and fundraisers. I was also starting to get asked to speak to various chapters across the country about the psychological aspects of chronic illness.

I eventually began to get referrals in my practice of children, adults, and families struggling with chronic illnesses, in particular gastrointestinal diseases. The kids started to call me "Dr. Gutsy." In working with the children in my practice, I use a therapeutic technique called "bibliotherapy." Child bibliotherapy involves reading a story about a particular problem to a child. The story helps them understand the problem, validates their thoughts and feelings, and offers healthy coping tools and solutions. During a session with a young girl who had Crohn's, she said to me, "How come there are no books on Crohn's disease for kids?" This got me thinking.

I started writing a children's book, and in 2005 my first book was published. It was called *Toilet Paper Flowers: A Story for Children About Crohn's Disease.*[4] This book launched further speaking engagements and became the genesis of my writing career as a children's book author in addition to being a psychologist. The speaking engagements across the country, and that first book, are what I view as making lemonade out of lemons.

Being diagnosed as an adult was difficult. Having gone from being a healthy individual to one who was ill with restrictions really presented me with challenges. I have learned a lot from my patients, however. I love listening to and helping my patients, especially when the young ones share their stories of what it was like to be diagnosed as a child. I remember a boy I met at a walk for Crohn's and colitis. His name was Joe, and he was about 5 years old. He had a tremendous spirit and an enthusiasm for life. When I asked his mother how Joe felt about having Crohn's, she told me, "It's all he has ever known. He doesn't know any different. He had to accept it from the day he was born." That put things into a different perspective for me. I still think about Joe from time and time and hope he is doing well.

When I am doing speaking engagements across the country, it is amazing to me to discover that although my disease and the disease the audience members have is the same, our journeys may be completely different. So many factors in one's life can change the journey. What is constant in my therapeutic work and through meeting people across the United States is that everyone struggles with the same feelings and has similar questions. We all share the same humanity. We are all vulnerable and brave. We are tired but we continue to fight. We feel hopeless, but somehow we continue to put one foot in front of the other. We feel alone and want to connect with others.

All the parents I meet want to be the best parents to their children, to give them everything in life, with the ultimate goal of being well. Every day, I meet courageous children and adults fighting for a better day, a cure, a breakthrough. This book, about parenting children with chronic illness, has been something I have wanted to write since I began my therapeutic work with children and families who are affected by health conditions. I fervently hope that you and those in your life can not only learn from the pages that follow but also discover things from each other and realize that we are not alone on our journey for our kids and for ourselves. Never give up. I wish you health and peace in your lives.

Carol's Story

I remember vividly the moment when my life split in two. It was late morning on Monday, October 19, 1987. For many, it was called Black Monday because of a sudden drop in the stock market, but it has an entirely different meaning for me.

I had been visiting my agent, talking about going back to work now that my son was 3 months old. My husband had been having some medical issues, and we had spent a harrowing weekend waiting for the results of a test he had done Friday. I met him for coffee down the street from my agent's office, so he could tell me what was going on. And I heard the words no one wants to hear from someone they love: "It's lung cancer," he said.

A sob of anguish and disbelief sprang out before I could stop myself, and he immediately let me know that he needed to be able to lean on my strength. I pulled myself together, offered him some words of encouragement, and watched as he drove off with a friend to see the oncologist.

When I looked up, my whole world had changed. Everything looked the same, and yet nothing was the same. The streets, the cars, the trees and street signs, even the sun shining in the open southern California sky—suddenly, nothing felt familiar. In the weeks and months that followed, I found myself in a parallel universe of doctors' offices, pharmacies, and hospitals, a world that exists side by side with our everyday world but that is invisible to most of us, until we find ourselves dealing with the unthinkable.

I remember the stress of having to fill a prescription at the last minute, one of those triplicate prescriptions that could not be filled by phone but required a trip to the doctor's office to retrieve a hard copy and a wait at the pharmacy while it was filled, assuming they had the medication on hand. With all the other aspects of life to manage, I was often unaware that the medication had run out, but it needed to be filled *today*.

There were long, painful conversations with doctors about what treatments were available, and misunderstandings galore. When my husband and I would go over what the doctor said, we often had entirely different versions. His pessimism unnerved me, and I am sure my stubborn optimism left him feeling unseen in some important way. Juggling the needs of a new baby and a sick husband stretched my capacities to the limit, and although I appreciated the concern of our friends, the constant task of keeping people up to date exhausted me, to say nothing of the pain of having to repeat bad news to one friend after another.

The illness of a family member affects everyone in the family and has ramifications for how each family member engages with her world. Relationships are altered, interrupted by medical emergencies, and sometimes put to the side to tend to the needs of the ill person. These lost periods may be difficult to reclaim.

There was, however, another aspect of this time that surprised me, fulfilled me in a way I never would have imagined: a sense of mission. I felt something like a calling to be caring for my husband at this time. My life had a very particular, significant—and yes, I would say, sacred—meaning that helped me persevere despite the sadness, the fatigue, the unpredictability. Not only did he need me to do for him what he could not do for himself, but also everything I did served as balm to soothe him, relieve his pain, help him sort out his own meaning. It felt like a tremendous honor.

OUR HOPES FOR YOU

This may sound strange, but one of our hopes for you, the reader, is that you can skip over some parts of this book completely! Perhaps you are already good at self-care, or at managing sibling relationships; your child may never need hospitalization or many of the procedures we talk about. We also hope that this book can shorten the learning time around the emotional and interpersonal processes you haven't had as much chance to practice. There will be times you'll feel proud of yourself and your family for how you are able to thrive and other times when you'll fall flat on your face. The worst part of that is feeling that you may be failing those you love. But then you'll get up again and keep going.

We are honored to share the findings of research and our own training and experience with you. We want to give you the tools you need, first to understand that what you are going through is real and that your feelings are to be expected, and then to meet head on the challenges you are facing. We hope that through all the ups and downs, the times of quiet and the times of chaos, you will find a kind of crazy beauty in your life with fresher and deeper connections with the people around you, a greater sense of intimacy with your family, and, for all of you, a fuller appreciation for the enormous gift of being alive.

With that said, let's get started.

CHAPTER 1

NAVIGATING YOUR FEELINGS

When your child has a chronic illness, you're on a journey. So, what should you pack? Your "suitcase" probably already contains medication or medical equipment, as well as knowledge of the special care regimens your child requires. It's likely heavy with lots of emotions, too. Let us offer you one more thing for your suitcase: confidence.

Think about what you have accomplished so far: You've learned to time and administer your child's home treatments. You know how to monitor your child's condition so that you can anticipate their medical needs and emergency situations. You've learned how various procedures and comfort measures benefit your child. With this knowledge you can help ease your own stress, even as you help your child tolerate and adjust to these new experiences. Be assured that most parents learn to manage this side of things, even routines that are highly technical and complicated, in the first 6 months.

Soon you will be an expert, not only on the upkeep requirements of your child's illness but also on his response to various interventions, when things seem to be working and when not, which symptoms are worsening and which are improving. As such, you become a valuable resource for your medical team, one who can intelligently evaluate their knowledge and skill. There was a time when you might have felt anxious about bringing your child home from the hospital, where the professional staff and equipment were monitoring his condition. But now that you've become more expert at providing care, you may experience anxiety when he is away from home, and in the hands of hospital staff. In short, you are already doing what some researchers have described as "parenting plus."

Parenting plus goes beyond just the medical aspects of your child's care. It includes everything you do to close the gaps for your child—to pave the way for his full, or as full as possible, participation in the outside world. It encompasses all the actions, behaviors, advocacy, education, and monitoring that parents do above and beyond either the requirements of the illness or that are typically required by your child's healthy peers.[1]

Despite all of the challenges, most families who have a child with chronic illness are able to handle it effectively. They are able to provide the medical care their child needs, balance the needs of all family members, and continue to enjoy the life they are given. In some cases, parents in families with an ill child have been found to spend more time playing with their child, in addition to the extra hours of care required, whereas parents in families with healthy children spend that extra time doing household chores.[2]

In this chapter we're going to share some facts about childhood chronic illness, to help you expand on what you already know about your own child's medical condition. Then we'll explore some of the feelings that might be cropping up for you. Finally, we'll share some findings from the science of positive psychology that may help you to feel hopeful, even as your emotions range all over the map. Our main purpose right now is to validate your feelings while also shoring up your confidence. This is challenging. But you've got this.

WHAT IS CHRONIC ILLNESS?

A "chronic illness" is a defined as a health problem that lasts 3 or more months; affects a child's normal activities; and requires frequent hospitalizations, home health care, and/or extensive medical care.[3] Children develop chronic illnesses as a result of genetic or environmental factors, such as a brain injury. There is typically no cure for the illness, but it can be managed by a variety of treatments. Chronic illnesses are referred to as being "in remission" when the symptoms and disease disappear and yet there remains the possibility that they will reappear. Although cancer is an illness that can sometimes be cured, we include it under the umbrella of chronic illnesses because cancer requires long-term treatment and it can greatly affect a child's well-being.

Chronic illness may also involve your child seeing a medical professional on a more frequent basis, taking medication in a variety of ways (for example, pills, intravenously), maintaining a specific diet, and using special medical equipment. Any of these may hinder your child's ability to attend school on a regular basis or to do their homework. They may also have to forego other activities, such as sports, band, dance, theater, or Scouts.

Metaphorically speaking, chronic illness is that one dark cloud in a clear and sunny sky. You keep your eye on it and proceed with caution. You feel as if you are always waiting for it to rain. Both child and parent, not to mention family and friends, feel like they are awaiting a crashing storm. This feeling has a name: "anticipatory anxiety." Anticipatory anxiety can be much more uncomfortable than the actual situation or condition you are anxious about.

At present, approximately 27% of U.S. children live with one or more chronic health conditions that affect their lives and activities[4] (see "The Unexpected Journey Begins," for a few other estimated numbers). Epidemiological studies show that in the United States alone, as many as 15 million to 18 million (one in four) children age 17 years or younger have a chronic illness.[5] Many studies suggest that chronic health problems appear to be on the rise and that some of these may be caused by obesity in children and teens. According to a 2010 study published in the *Journal of the American Medical Association*, chronic illnesses in children doubled between 1994 and 2006, from 12.8% to 26.6%, with low-income children and those who are members of racial or ethnic minority groups disproportionately affected.[6]

Catherine DeAngelis, a pediatrician and former editor of the *Journal of the American Medical Association*, noted that when children are diagnosed with a chronic medical condition they might endure 50 to 60 years of coping with and potentially suffering from that condition.[7] The flip side of this is that diseases that were once fatal are no longer an automatic death sentence. The chances of surviving a chronic illness are significantly better now than they were just 20 years ago! Advances in medicine are occurring every day, and early detection and diagnosis, and thus earlier treatment, are happening more frequently.

YOUR FEELINGS ARE ALL OVER THE MAP— AND THAT'S NORMAL

Feelings can be extremely overwhelming and complicated. Even within your own family, different people will express their emotions in a wide variety of ways. As a parent, you may find yourself trying to manage your own feelings along with those of your child, their siblings, your significant other, and others in your life.

There are also many levels of intensity when it comes to feelings. Our feelings lie on a spectrum and run the gamut of mild, to severe, to something in between. One day you may feel intense rage, and other days you may experience frustration and then return to intense rage again. This is also true for your child and family. The feelings we discuss are common, but know that there is no right or wrong way to feel. Some of the feelings we discuss may seem obvious. If you do not experience a feeling we discuss here, that doesn't mean anything is wrong with you. Everyone responds differently to life's challenges. Be kind to yourself: Feelings do not follow a predictable path.

The parents we work with in our practices report feeling tired all the time. Both physical and emotional fatigue can tax the body, our brain's ability to process information, and our patience in dealing with other people. When experiencing emotional fatigue, you are faced with difficult thoughts and feelings focused around your child's diagnosis and endeavoring to maintain a healthy balance. Whether the diagnosis is new or one you have been dealing with for many years, you need healthy coping mechanisms.

We must mention that gender, culture, ethnic background, and upbringing, among other influences, affect how people cope with and express their feelings. In relationships, we may be in touch with our feelings and express them freely; in the meantime, our partner may avoid dealing with feelings and instead turn to alcohol or drugs, immerse themselves in work, spend less time with the family, or even engage in extramarital relationships.

We have provided Worksheet 1.1, "Emotions and Strengths Inventory" to help you take inventory of your feelings and reflect on where they may be coming from.

Shock and Denial

We don't want to ever contemplate that bad things can happen to us, and we often push the thought of harm befalling our children to the back of our minds. When your child shows symptoms that warrant a medical diagnosis, the words of that diagnosis come as a

WORKSHEET 1.1. Emotions and Strengths Inventory

When it comes to feelings and coping, it may be helpful to ask yourself the following questions:

1. How have my partner and I (or other caregivers) reacted to and dealt with a crisis before? Reflecting on past experiences, specifically what worked and what didn't, can be extremely helpful in coping with a child's chronic illness.

2. How might our family background and our culture and religion inform the way I feel about my child's chronic illness? In what ways can my immediate family lean on our understandings and traditions around crises, illness, and health to help us right now?

3. What is the severity of the chronic illness? What skills do I need to learn right now to help my child? With chronic illnesses the future is always uncertain; however, different phases of a condition can often be managed by adjusting a routine you're already used to. Sometimes, just breaking down the practical actions you need to do into smaller units can help you manage feelings of sadness or overwhelm. Some illnesses may have a poorer prognosis—this may bring up intense feelings of sadness, or hopelessness; if this is the case, you should make a specific plan for getting the emotional support you need.

4. What are the dynamics of the parental unit, and how did each person handle family responsibilities before the diagnosis? Your family may have parents who share responsibilities, such as income earning and caregiving, or perhaps they divide them. You may be parenting solo. In the case of chronic illness, these roles and responsibilities may have to change, and be shared, and some people may be asked to step up to the plate in ways they never have before. Being aware of the possibilities of change in your family dynamic can help you cope.

Take a pause and reflect on these questions for as long as you need.

shock and engender feelings of denial and skepticism. You may find yourself completely unprepared for what you are hearing from the health care provider. You may feel frozen, as if time has stood still. You may feel faint and weak. You may also feel as if you are having an out-of-body experience—knowing that you are in the room but checking out from other bodily sensations, like your own weight in the chair. You may feel completely oblivious to the words and the people around you. You may also feel numb emotionally. These reactions are self-preserving and protect us from completely falling apart. The feeling of shock may also combine with other strong emotions, such as anger, denial, sadness, and guilt.

Feelings of shock may lead to feelings of denial. Denial is a common defense mechanism, whose function is to protect our psychological well-being. It keeps anxiety at bay and allows us to function. However, staying in a state of denial—for example, by not acknowledging your child's diagnosis—likely will impair your judgment and ability to care for your child, your family, and yourself. A parent of a child with a chronic illness cannot stay in denial for long and continue to function. If you or your significant other is experiencing denial for extended periods of time, and you are concerned, reach out for professional help.

Stress

For parents, stress often comes in the form of feeling pulled in multiple directions at once. You struggle sometimes, asking yourself almost endless questions: "How do I parent not only my child who is ill but the other children as well?" "How do I attend to my significant other?" "How do I care for my elderly parents?" "How do I nurture my friendships, my health, and myself?" "How do I make time for healthy dinners and adequate sleep?" "How do I find time to research doctors, medications, and treatments?"

Your child likely is experiencing stress as well, and the way you handle your stress sets an example for how your child learns to handle theirs.

With that in mind, it may be helpful to know that research on stress has shed light on the negative impact of stress on chronic illness. Research indicates that long-term stress can greatly damage not only the immune system but almost every system in the body.[8] The immune system destroys bacteria, viruses, and parasites. A damaged immune system impairs the body's ability to fight off infection and illness. Children with autoimmune diseases—for example, Crohn's disease, multiple sclerosis, Type 1 diabetes, ulcerative colitis, lupus, and scleroderma—need strong and healthy immune systems.

Your vulnerability to stress, and your child's, depend on several factors: genetics, coping styles, type of personality, and social support.[9] It is interesting to note that the correlation between stressful life events and psychiatric illness is stronger than the correlation between stressful events and physical illness.[10] Therefore, it's important to recognize when you and others in your family are feeling strain, and to reduce stress levels whenever possible, because it can have lasting effects on both the body and mind.

Anger

We have all experienced road rage, either on the giving end or the receiving end. A diagnosis of a chronic illness for your child often can induce strong feelings of anger that can spiral into rage. Often, it is the initial feeling of helplessness that leads to this reaction. Feeling powerless can cause you to direct your anger either inward, toward yourself, or outward, toward others.

Your life has changed, or it will change soon. Even small changes can make you feel stressed, and that may lead to feelings of anger too. Parents often ask, "Why my child?" "Why me?" or

"Why do I have to make major changes in my life while other parents don't have to?"

Anger may also be driven by fear. You are in uncharted territory and may realize you are getting angry at yourself, at medical professionals, at your significant other, at fate, at religion. You may be angry because at the time of your child's diagnosis you are uncertain about what you and your child are facing and are not aware of the resources available to you. It is difficult to see the bigger picture because everything is colliding into each other.

Sometimes the target of the anger is your child. This may be hard to believe, but it does happen. Parents feel the burden of a change in lifestyle, financial struggles, juggling other family and work responsibilities, marital issues, and fear of what might happen to their child.

> *After the diagnosis of our child, I found myself distancing myself from him. I know this wasn't right, but I was just so angry at the world and everyone. I worked really hard not to take it out on him. I spoke with a therapist, and it helped put things into perspective.*
> —Mother of a child with an immune disorder

Anger is often viewed as a negative emotion, but, in and of itself, it is not. What makes anger healthy or unhealthy, constructive or damaging, is how we express it. We encourage you to identify what you are experiencing emotionally and learn how to express those feelings appropriately. As noted above, anger often stems from feelings of frustration caused by not being able to help someone you love. Once you know this, your anger can give you the strength to learn what to do to help your child. We always have a choice about how we will express and deal with our feelings. Give yourself permission to feel anger, but be mindful of acting out toward others or yourself in destructive, unhealthy ways.

Fear

When faced with a perceived threat (in this case a chronic illness), we react. This reaction is commonly known as the "fight-or-flight response." This response protects us against threats and danger; it kicks in when we experience stress and fear. Adrenaline and other hormones released in the body give us the strength and courage to protect and defend others and ourselves. Fear, however, is not necessarily a maladaptive emotion; it can also be helpful. We go into fight mode when we perceive the threat as something we can defeat. Some examples of the fight response, as it relates to chronic illness, are the following:

- You gather knowledge about the illness.
- You speak with your child's pediatrician about referrals to specialists.
- You search online for information about the illness. You may locate national and local organizations that can give information, doctors who specialize in your area, and new research being conducted.
- You seek second opinions on diagnosis and treatment.
- You set up an appointment with a mental health professional to address concerns you or your child may have in regard to coping with the diagnosis and illness.
- You establish healthy routines for your child, such as to ensure proper nutrition and getting adequate sleep.
- You follow treatment recommendations from your physician; comply with medication and other supplements.

- You have the proper tests and procedures that will assist with diagnosis and treatment.

Conversely, in flight mode, we may perceive the threat to be too overwhelming and feel compelled to run from the threat. Similar to the fight response, the flight response also activates adrenaline and other stress hormones for survival. These are some examples of a flight response related to illness:

- not following the treatment team's recommendations in regard to medications, having medical tests done, and so on;
- deciding to leave your partner because the situation is too overwhelming;
- engaging in destructive habits or behaviors, such as alcohol or drug abuse; and
- avoiding home by becoming immersed in work and using it as an escape from the stress.

A third reaction to fear is to freeze. This is a disabling response to threat. When we freeze, we believe we cannot defeat (fight) or safely escape (flight) the threat. The freeze response can be paralyzing and is typically activated when we perceive a threat as dire.

In certain situations, freezing can be as adaptive as the fight-or-flight response. People often freeze in response to situations in which they feel totally helpless. You feel panic and terror, and your instinctive response is to freeze and numb yourself so you can psychologically and physically distance yourself from the present moment. This response can be adaptive in some cases because at that time it may be best to mentally block out what is happening; however, it is our hope that parents (and children) do not have a freeze response in reaction to a medical diagnosis. If you, your partner, or your child has this response, it may be appropriate to seek the help of a mental health professional.

When you receive a diagnosis of a chronic illness for your child, some of your fears may include

- fear of the unknown,
- fear that your child will not get better,
- fear of death,
- fear of loss of control,
- fear of interacting and trusting people with whom you have no prior relationship,
- fear of making the wrong decisions when it comes to medical care,
- fear of the future: What is going to happen to your child when they are 5, 12, and 22?
- fear of what will the treatments be like,
- fear of how your other children will be affected,
- fear of how your marriage will be affected,
- fear over money and what your insurance will cover, and
- fear of how you will balance this and other responsibilities.

Do any of these fears sound familiar to you? Take a moment and spend some time getting in touch with your thoughts and feelings that center on fear. What have you come up with? Are you engaged in a fight-or-flight response? Are you frozen? Take a moment and think about your partner. Are they in fight, flight, or freeze mode?

No one likes to be afraid. You may have never had to deal with a chronic illness, either your own or someone else's. Raising children in this world is no easy task. As a parent, you may have many sleepless nights, especially once you add a chronic illness to the mix. As much as fear can cause us to run away or become frozen, it can also serve a motivator to face whatever trials are in front of you. We encourage you to share your fears with your partners, your friends, your medical staff, and your community. You are not alone!

Your child may also feel fear about the unknown and living a life of uncertainty. In Chapter 4, we go into more detail about reassuring your child and different kinds of conversations to have with them at different ages.

Guilt

It's not unusual to feel guilty when your child has a chronic illness. Other people can take us on a guilt trip, or we can take the ride by ourselves; either way, it is dreadful. Guilt is a heavy, distasteful feeling that tends to linger in the center of your chest and be felt down to the pit of your stomach.

It's helpful to know that guilt usually comes from our thoughts rather than from actions we've taken or an act someone else has committed. Many parents believe that they somehow caused their child's illness, especially if there is no specific reason—medical, genetic, or other—for the chronic illness. Common guilt-inducing thoughts almost invariably involve "shoulds," "oughts," or "musts." Guilt does not help us move forward, and if you are not careful you will get stuck in its vicious cycle. Here are some questions and statements from parents that we've heard from time to time:

- "Did I do something wrong?"
- "Am I being punished?"
- "Did I do something to cause this?"
- "I should have taken better care of myself during my pregnancy."
- "Was there something I could have done to prevent this?"
- "My damn family genetics! I have such an unhealthy family!"
- "I'm an awful mother."

Parents often experience guilty feelings related to their other children, spouses, jobs, and friends. You may feel guilty because so much of your time, attention, energy, and finances are committed to the child who is ill. It is hard to find enough time and balance to attend to everyone's needs, including our own. You may feel you are a terrible parent, a neglectful partner, an absent friend, and a distracted worker. But know that being the parent of a chronically ill child is a full-time job on its own, and that, on top of the full-time job you likely already have, can consume your every thought, feeling, behavior, and decision.

> *I feel like I have so many balls in the air. They are more like eggs. I can't afford to drop one. All of them are so important.*
> —Father of a 12-year-old girl with cystic fibrosis

As with anger, when we feel guilty, we may project those feelings onto others. We can start blaming significant others, our parents, God or some other higher power, or even our child. This is part of the process of trying to understand your child's illness and find answers to what will help her feel better and resume a "normal" life. And, let's face it: It's easier to blame someone else. Doing so is very human. Blaming others, though, does not help foster healthy relationships; instead, it creates a wedge in those relationships.

Parents who have been leveled by their child's medical diagnosis need to work on coming together and work toward healing. Families who are committed to working through this challenge often make a conscious choice to see their child as separate from the illness; for example, they put the child first before the illness: "This is my child, Seth. He has hydrocephalus and may need to go to the hospital for a change to his shunt if he has a severe headache."

There is another aspect of guilt that many people find difficult to talk about: thoughts that arouse feelings of guilt. Parents have often reported they feel guilty when they have thoughts like the following ones:

- "I don't want to spend my time today in a doctor's office."
- "I wish my child wasn't sick so we can take that nice vacation."
- "I'm tired, and I don't want to spend the day fighting with my child about taking her medications."
- "I wish I could be like the other dads and spend my weekends golfing."
- "I'm tired of being tied down to this house."
- "I just don't want to have to deal with this today."
- "I wish my kid was like everyone else."

If sentiments like these have run through your mind from time to time, please be gentle to yourself. They are quite common, and you are not a horrible, selfish person. You likely feel resentful about, tired of, and fearful about your situation. Feelings of resentment toward a hurdle in one's life are completely human. Such feelings make you feel worse because they are being directed toward your innocent child, who did not ask to be in this situation in the first place. The child may also be suffering in some way, or living a limited life, which adds to the guilt you likely feel.

Beating yourself up about having these feelings does not make them go away. Acknowledge them. Talk to someone about them. It may be time to reevaluate things. You may be undergoing caregiver stress and burnout, which we discuss later. Pushing away these thoughts and feelings takes a lot of energy. When you feel overwhelmed, seek support from loved ones, other support systems, and professionals. Holding onto resentment can be like holding a hot coal in your hand: It hurts you and perhaps those around you.

Sadness

Sadness is different from feeling depressed. Feelings of depression arise when one has nothing left emotionally, whereas sadness is like when your car tires are low on air: You are still able to drive, but you must drive with caution. A specific situation, person, or event in one's life typically brings on sadness. Get in touch with a time when you were sad. Maybe it was an end of a relationship, or not getting a job or promotion you were expecting. Perhaps it was the death of a loved one, or when you found out your child was ill. When you are sad, you function well enough to get through the day. Things like sleep and appetite do not change drastically.

When you experience sadness, you might feel down for a day or two before bouncing back. Moreover, you are still able to enjoy things in life, like your favorite food, a hobby, a TV show, or your social life. Prolonged sadness can lead to depression. When you're sad, you typically do not experience the sense of worthlessness or the feelings of guilt that are often found in depressed people. If you are experiencing persistent feelings of sadness, reach out for help.

Depression

Although feelings of depression are common in parents of children who have a chronic medical condition, they should not be ignored. The term "depression" designates a diagnosed psychiatric condition, even though people often use the word to describe feelings of sadness. Clinical depression tends to be chronic in nature and is diagnosed by a medical professional or a licensed mental health professional. When you are depressed, you feel sad and hopeless about a variety of things. You may not experience joy or pleasure in anything; this is called "anhedonia." Feelings of depression have a longer duration than feelings of sadness, disrupting patterns of sleeping and eating and in some cases leading to thoughts of suicide. If you or others have thoughts of suicide, you need to reach out for help immediately by calling 911 or proceeding to your local emergency room. Never take thoughts or statements about suicide lightly.

Depending on the severity of depression, interventions such as psychotherapy or medication, or both, may be needed to alleviate symptoms. You or a loved one may be diagnosed with clinical depression if you are experiencing five or more symptoms during a 2-week period and at least one of the symptoms is either a depressed or irritable mood or a loss of interest or pleasure in daily activities.[11] This depressed mood must represent a significant change from a person's typical mood. Social, occupational, educational, or other important functioning must also be negatively affected by the change in mood before this diagnosis can be made. Perhaps you were diagnosed with depression before you received the news of your child's chronic illness. The stress of the diagnosis and the treatment that follows can exacerbate depression. When depression is impairing you or your ability to function and thoughts of suicide are present, we again urge you to seek help immediately.

People may say things like, "Of course you're depressed; your son was just diagnosed with cancer. Give yourself a break. Under the circumstances anyone would be depressed. Focus on getting your son well." Statements like these can make you feel angry and frustrated. Although people mean well, sometimes they think they are being compassionate and sensitive but instead come across as insensitive. Keep in mind, though, that despite how insensitive these statements may be, there is some truth to them. It is depressing that your child has a chronic illness. Your and your family's lives are going to change, and you may indeed feel things will never be the same. However, this should not imply that you must simply accept your feelings of depression and do nothing about them. Sometimes it is difficult to differentiate the effects of having a child with a chronic illness from the symptoms of a mood disorder such as depression. Parents may view the diagnosis of a chronic illness as the natural cause for the development of depression symptoms. If parents view such feelings as simply a reaction to their current situation, they may not seek the mental health help they need. People often place their mental concerns last when it comes to parenting a child with a chronic illness. If you are depressed, get help.

Grief

When we think about grief, death and dying usually come to mind. Grief is the feeling; grieving is the process. Grief does not apply only to literal instances of death and dying. When your child receives a diagnosis of a chronic illness, there is in fact a death: the death of a dream. No one gives birth to a child and dreams of them having a condition that threatens their health and well-being. No one wants to see their child suffer in any way. The discovery of a child's medical illness is often unexpected, and parents are not prepared. In addition, your child's illness may be unpredictable in nature, or you may simply feel uncertain about the future. It's not uncommon to grieve the loss of control you feel.

As with other feelings discussed in this chapter, your feelings of grief may change at various stages of your child's illness. For example, you may experience a new wave of grief, or grieve differently, when new medical issues or complications arise, or when your caregiving responsibilities change because your child is growing up and has different needs. The grieving process likely also includes a sense of loss of what you, your child, or your family's life used to be. You may be mourning the loss of time spent with your ill child (because of procedures, hospitalizations, etc.), the loss of time spent with your other children, and with your significant other and friends, as well as the loss of other personal dreams and goals. We discuss grief and the process of grieving again in Chapter 11, where we offer information about preparing for a child's passing. If you are struggling with grief, we advise you to read the section titled "Coming to the End of the Road" in Chapter 11 now.

HOW TO COPE WITH YOUR FEELINGS

Throughout this chapter we have been addressing some common emotions you and your family will likely experience after the diagnosis of a chronic medical illness and during the course of it in your child's life. Although there is no cookbook on feelings and chronic illness, and people are not all the same when it comes to experiencing, expressing, or coping with feelings, there are some tried-and-true ways of looking at your emotions that we'd like to share here.

First, ask yourself, "Am I dealing or dwelling?" Dealing with feelings is action oriented; dwelling is being stuck. Dwelling may look and feel like activity, but in reality it is like being on a treadmill or a gerbil wheel: It gets you nowhere. Dwelling may be a means of coping when you are trying to avoid something that is stressful, anxiety provoking, or threatening in some way, but ultimately it will not help you turn your feelings into actions that resolve your problems. Here are some ways of dealing:

- We discussed this earlier, but it's worth repeating: If you or anyone in your family has or has had thoughts of self-harm in the form of suicide or other self-injurious behaviors, you must call 911 or take that person to the nearest emergency room immediately. Do not ever take thoughts of suicide casually.

You and your family must be assessed for imminent danger to self. Safety must come first!

- Recognize there is nothing wrong about the feelings you are experiencing in regard to your child or your circumstances. Be gentle to yourself, and know that whatever you are feeling is both acceptable and typical of people in your situation. Allow yourself to feel these emotions rather than bottling them up or acting them out in unhelpful ways.
- One way you can allow yourself to feel difficult emotions, such as worry or anxiety, without letting them overwhelm you, is to dedicate a certain amount of time each day to them. Set a timer for 10 to 15 minutes. During this time speak your worries aloud, with or without a listener, or write out every last thing you're angry about—in short, go ahead and experience whatever feelings or thoughts you are having. When the time is up, stop. Routines like this help you keep strong feelings separate from the usual stream of thoughts and reactions, so you are free for doing what needs to be done the rest of the time.
- Seek support from others. Tell people what you need. People cannot read your mind. At times, people (although well-meaning) try to fix things and may say things that may annoy or anger you. Teach people to ask you, "How can I be there for you?" instead of giving advice and jumping in with solutions. People can be there for you in many ways: to listen, offer a hug, hold your hand, validate feelings, or take you out to get some emotional and physical space. Learning to understand your emotional needs and how others can help gives you the energy and strength to better adjust and engage in self-care and care for your family.
- Understand that you are beginning a journey that was completely unplanned and for which you had little or no time to prepare. No one likes forks in the road or speed bumps that

were not seen. Being on this journey includes finding a better understanding of the situation, of why you feel the way you do, and of what are you going to do about it.

- Avoid isolation. You may want to resist talking to anyone about what you are going through, to retreat into your room, crawl into bed, and cover your head. If you are engaging in avoidant or isolative behaviors, this may be a sign you are feeling depressed. If you or anyone in your family is displaying these behaviors, reach out for help. Remember, you are not alone.

- Strong emotions can hinder our decision making, judgment, and choices. Although alcohol, stress eating, or retail therapy may offer a temporary numbing effect, they can quickly compound problems you may already have with making smart decisions. Avoid these and other "numbing" types of self-medication. If you find yourself on this path, seek professional help.

- Surrender to the fact that you cannot control the universe. You are not a bad parent because your child got sick, because the medications or treatment did not work, because you are tired, or because you feel strong negative feelings. Sometimes bad things happen to good people. Watch what you say to yourself. Don't engage in negative self-talk.

- Understand that the people around you—partners, children, and extended family and friends—all have their own emotions. Be aware that not everyone will be in the same emotional space at the same time. Allow others to have their feelings, and do not try to talk them out of what they are feeling.

- You may absorb all the feelings of those around you. Like a wet sponge, you feel heavy and weighed down. Metaphorically speaking, we need to wring out our emotional sponge and own what is ours while letting go of whatever is not ours.

- It's normal to go into a kind of autopilot mode. You'll probably find yourself logging onto the internet and searching for information about your child's disease, medications, and doctors. Although this behavior is not inherently wrong, we encourage you to periodically stop, take a moment, and take an inventory of what you are feeling. In Chapter 2 we provide a worksheet to help you surf the internet in a mindful way.
- Seek professional help if you need it. Mental health professionals work with lots of people, not just those who are severely depressed, suicidal, or self-medicating with unhealthy substances.

Although the stigma of seeking mental health care is diminishing, the stereotype remains that if you need mental health help, you are weak, mentally ill, or have lost control. You fear being found out and worry that people will think less of you for seeking help. Try to reframe these thoughts. Look at seeking mental health care as *taking* control of your situation instead of *losing* control of it. Mental health professionals have specific training to help you, your child, and your family accept and manage a significant stressor such as chronic illness.

Even when things are going well with you and your family, it's beneficial to establish a relationship with a mental health clinician in the early stages of your child's diagnosis. It is always helpful to have an objective listener and problem-solver in your life. Establishing a relationship early on may help when new challenges arise during the course of the illness or during a different developmental stage in your child's life. Consider the teenage years as an example: Who couldn't benefit from talking to an expert on parenting during the tumultuous adolescent years? We will discuss mental health care, and how to find it, further in Chapter 3.

NEXT STEP: HOPE HELPS YOU COPE

Although healthy coping with strong feelings on a day-to-day basis is important, it can also be helpful to step back every so often and revisit your hopes and dreams. Doing this can bolster your ability to survive when you're in the thick of it.

What do you hope for your child? If this question results in answers that are too numerous to tackle all at once, take them a little at a time. If you wish, you can write your answers in the spaces provided:

- How do you see your child today—right now?

- How do you see your child in the future (you can think of "the future" as anything from 3 hours from now to 30 years from now)?

- In the future you envision, what is the same about your child? What is different?

- In that future, how is your child's world the same? How is it different?

You might think of hope as an emotion or mindset, but we like to think of it as a verb—an action. In the field of psychology, we also talk about hope as the ability to see a positive future. When you can envision a future, like we asked you to do just now, you develop a sense of agency, or the ability to take action to make the goals you envision come to life.[12]

Sometimes it's easy to see multiple or branching pathways toward achieving your goals and think that all you have to do is pick one and get started. More often, we take one tentative step along a possible pathway, stop and look around awhile, and then take another step into the swirling fog. Rarely do we know what the entire pathway looks like. But if you are reading this book right now, we're willing to bet that hope is something you already *have* and something you are already *doing*, whether you know it or not.

Science tells us that hope supports resilience in the face of unforeseen challenges. Also, having previous experience in working toward and achieving goals in life fuels our hope. People with higher hope tend to take on more difficult tasks. They are likely to think about goals not just as blissful "someday" situations but in more concrete terms, for example, "What challenges do my goals present?" "How likely am I to be successful at meeting my goal with what I'm doing now?" "How will I feel when I've achieved the goal?" "How, exactly, will my life be better?"[13]

We now return to your child: What would it look like for them to have their best possible life with their chronic illness? Take a moment and, if you wish, write or sketch out your ideas here.

The clearer your vision of your child thriving *with* their chronic illness is, the more likely you will be to take action to help them get there. People with higher hope tend to be less anxious and depressed; are more adaptable and able to cope when dealing with a child's chronic illness; and tend to set higher goals and attain them more often, even or especially in the face of obstacles and impediments.[14]

We recommend spending time each day thinking about your hopes, either in the big picture or the small one. Even just quickly reflecting "How do I hope this conversation with (or about) my child will turn out?" can help you in myriad ways. In practical terms, hope seems to bring with it

- better coping strategies,
- less avoidance,
- the ability to find more pathways out of "stuckness,"
- more effective thinking about the future,
- a better ability to find benefits buried in the challenges,
- higher investment in connecting with others, and
- the ability to develop more effective social support.[15]

That is all well and good, you may say, but how do I find hope when my child is in pain, or when her illness frightens her, or when she's frustrated that she can't do something other kids can do? There is no doubt that your child's diagnosis changes your understanding of what is possible and your resulting aspirations for your child. We all entertain hopes and dreams for our children, which we then have to accommodate to the people they actually are. This is especially true when our child has a chronic illness.

It may be difficult at first to imagine positive alternatives to your original vision for your child. In the immediate aftermath of the diagnosis, your mind may be filled with all the disappointments and impossibilities your child's condition presents—all the ways it trashes the hopes and dreams you had! It's okay to be angry and sad. Give yourself some time to feel those feelings.

Find Stories About What Is Possible

If you find yourself stuck, unable to imagine anything positive for your child's future, then start doing research. Support groups, in which you meet others who are dealing with the same or a similar situation, can be a potent source of alternate stories about what is possible. Books, magazine articles, and even movies can also be sources of stories about people who not only meet and survive challenging situations but are also able to thrive. In some of those stories, the "hero" has a big impact on our society. You don't have to envision your child or yourself as a hero, however; just find alternate stories about what is possible even with very challenging obstacles blocking one's path. Seeing beyond your child's illness might simply be imagining him finding love, companionship, and valuable work. This can be enough to generate hope and a vision for your child's future—even better, it can generate for both of you a present in which the path forward is more visible.

Focus on What Works for You and Your Family

As we discussed in "The Unexpected Journey Begins," chronic illnesses vary. Some are like a roller coaster ride, with many ups and downs, ranging from acute symptoms to remission to greater acuity. Some are terminal. Some remain pretty steady, with a greater degree of predictability and consistency of symptoms. They vary in terms of treatments, amount of time needed to manage the illness, number of specialists involved, overall health care costs, age when the child is diagnosed, number of family members affected, and other factors.

In our years of working with patients who have chronic illnesses, we have also learned that two children can share the same diagnosis, the same symptoms, the same treatments (medications, procedures, diets), and the course of the illness can be completely different. For example, certain children with inflammatory bowel diseases may require frequent hospitalizations for symptoms, while other children are never hospitalized. As you go along, finding your own stories and taking in those that we share in this book, you will find that some things apply to you but other things do not.

Try not close yourself off to other stories and experiences. Take what is helpful to you, and shelve or discard the rest. Stay on your path. In our work and personal experience, we have yet to encounter two journeys that are exactly alike.

CHAPTER 2

STAYING HEALTHY ON THE JOURNEY

If you have flown in an airplane, then you remember the safety instructions the flight attendants always give as you prepare to take off. They say that if there is a change in cabin pressure, oxygen masks will drop down from the panel above your head. The flight attendants, or the video on the plane, specifically note that adults must put their masks on first, before helping children or others in their care.

Why is this? Well, if you run out of oxygen, you will not be able to help anyone else with their oxygen mask. We emphasize this illustration because we believe it's vitally important to take care of yourself first so that you can take care of others. Your physical and mental stability are crucial to the physical and mental health of your child.

It's easy to make excuses about why we do not have the time to take care of ourselves. Parents often say that if they're practicing self-care, they're taking something away from their child or children. That belief could not be further from the truth! Your family needs you to take care of *you*. You are your children's role model— and when they are young, you are their world. If you are not taking care of yourself physically or emotionally, what does that say to your children and others around you? Children will learn self-care habits from watching you. Self-care habits include getting adequate sleep, exercising, organizing and prioritizing things, and expressing emotions in a healthy way, to name a few.

Excuses aside, you might be avoiding self-care because you believe you should not be struggling in the first place. If only you were a better, stronger, and more organized parent, you would not be struggling at all, right? Wrong. You might be looking at other parents' social media posts and basing your self-judgment on that, but comparisons are fruitless and not helpful. Everyone's situation is different. Plus, given how most of us filter our social media content or what we share with others in real-life interactions, any such comparison is likely false, anyway.

As parents and caregivers, we often place our needs last. But it doesn't have to be that way. In this chapter, we discuss ways you can incorporate self-care into your life so that you can feel less stressed and, we hope, avoid burnout. We also sketch out possible paths to self-care you can explore, such as mindfulness and spirituality. Along both of these pathways you may wish to pick up a single (metaphorical) rock or pine cone for a while, and see if it inspires you, then place it back on the path and try something else. We wrap up the chapter with some tips for incorporating humor and lightheartedness into your everyday rhythms. Even if you don't see yourself as a funny person or a jokester, we do believe it's possible to seek out daily laughs and eventually develop a lighter take on life. We also offer a few tips for staying sane when you search the internet. As we go through life, it is important that we maintain our physical and mental health. Self-care is *not* selfish; it's vital to you, your child and to your family.

BURNOUT AND COMPASSION FATIGUE

We have no doubt that you and your family have gone through many changes since your child's diagnosis. Your home environment may be "medicalized," with specialized equipment and routines to support your child, and family life may end up being organized around these medical regimens. Your child's daily care needs can be both relentless and exhausting. The uncertainty is stressful, as is the need to advocate for your child with medical providers and the medical system, including insurance companies (see Chapter 3 for tips on managing this). All of these changes contribute to the possibility of parental burnout, especially for the primary caregiver.

If your child has behavioral problems as part of, or a result of, their diagnosis (or if another child in your family develops behavior problems in response to all the change), your stress levels will increase. If you're unable to find appropriate child care providers, or other forms of respite care for yourself, up it goes another notch.[1] When you don't feel you have the resources to respond and effectively manage what your life demands of you, burnout often results.[2] Perfectionistic tendencies or high expectations of your own performance can be yet another risk factor. And the unrelenting tasks can lead to a kind of numbness and a sort of "giving up" attitude. If you find yourself distancing yourself from your ill child, feeling less compassion or even indifference toward him and his fate, this does not mean you are a bad parent! It is instead an urgently waving red flag signaling that you have exhausted your internal resources and may be experiencing burnout.

Burnout can affect your relationship with your partner and other children, as well as all the family dynamics we explore in Chapters 4, 5, and 6. Perhaps the biggest signs of impending burnout, however, are the effects on your body and health. Caregiver burnout results from too much long-term stress caused by taking care of another individual, and it leads to problems in many areas, including your physical and psychological health. Because this ongoing stress also affects the immune system, illness or inflammatory conditions may occur, and the body's sensitivity to medicines will be compromised.[3] Other health effects that may be signs of burnout include

- frequent illnesses, such as colds and the flu;
- chronic back pain;
- chronic fatigue syndrome;
- irritable bowel syndrome and other gastrointestinal complaints;
- migraines, psoriasis, and ulcers;
- elevated blood pressure;
- worsening of your own chronic illness, such as diabetes; and
- musculoskeletal disorders and the development of strain and pain in the back, shoulders, neck, and feet (e.g., when caring is physically demanding).

If you are in the habit of putting your own needs on the back burner, you might not notice your need for self-care until neglecting it begins to take a serious toll.

What Is Compassion Fatigue?

Another issue you may be dealing with is compassion fatigue: a state of emotional exhaustion that can make it hard for you to feel empathy for others, including your own child. In the past, the term "compassion fatigue," like "burnout," was associated with individuals who worked in the health care field who see others' suffering on a daily basis over many years. Because of technology, and round-the-clock news, all of us now can be bombarded daily with human suffering with the click of a mouse. Compassion fatigue no longer belongs only to certain professions.

Many of the symptoms of compassion fatigue are similar to the symptoms of caregiver stress and burnout. You likely are exposed to doctors' reports, laboratory results, your child's up-and-down progress, and seeing your child in pain. This can wear on you until you feel depleted not only physically but also emotionally. You may know other children and families, in the hospital or attending your support group, who are not doing well, and this too can contribute to compassion fatigue. As with caregiver stress and burnout, the best way to avoid falling into guilt, hopelessness, despair, or depression is to focus on your own self-care.

How Do I Deal With Burnout and Compassion Fatigue?

The first way of dealing with burnout and compassion fatigue is to recognize the signs. The American Medical Association created an 18-question assessment, the Caregiver Self-Assessment Questionnaire, to help determine the level of stress of caregivers helping chronically ill older adults. Although it was developed for older patients, we believe the questionnaire can be helpful for assessing your own level of stress in caring for your chronically ill child. The assessment, which can be accessed online at **https://www.healthinaging.org/ tools-and-tips/caregiver-self-assessment-questionnaire**, is intended to serve as a guide and can be used to communicate with health care providers. You can complete it online, or you can print it out. Instructions for scoring are easy to understand. If your score concerns you, speak with your doctor and consider speaking with a mental health professional as well.

As we stated at the beginning of this chapter, regardless of whether you "officially" have caregiver burnout or compassion fatigue, take good care of yourself by eating nutritious meals, getting regular physical activity, developing good sleep habits, and organizing your life so you can meet the many needs of your chronically ill child as well as your own. In addition, find social support—from family, friends, or an identified support group. These steps, which we lay out in more detail in Chapter 3, can be very effective in lowering your stress.

It is also important to have realistic expectations of your abilities, know how to set limits for yourself, get in touch with your instincts, and ask for help when you need it. These can all help you avoid unnecessary injury and energy depletion. Relaxation and other stress management techniques that we'll review later in this chapter are also useful in the management of ongoing stress.

So, what's your plan for taking care of yourself? Taking one action today to reduce your stress is good, but how will you build self-care into your routine? The word "PLAN" can be an acronym that serves as a reminder to not put things off for tomorrow or some later time.

P – Putting
L – Life
A – into Action
N – Now

There are several ways to keep your engine running well on the path to self-care. Mindfulness practices reduce both mental and physiological stress, and spirituality is especially helpful in maintaining perspective and finding meaning in your situation. Each of them adds to your toolkit for dealing with caregiver stress, burnout, and compassion fatigue. Also, humor relieves tension and lightens the weight of all you are dealing with. To be effective, all of the practices discussed in this chapter require a certain level of commitment. We know what you may be thinking, "Do I really need another commitment in my life?" Yes, you do! You need a commitment to self-care in your life. Mindfulness, spirituality, and even the tips about humor that we introduce here are not practices to which you should turn only when you are feeling bad or stressed; they are a way of being and living every day. There are no quick fixes in life. Change and healing take time.

EXPLORING MINDFULNESS PATHS

Mindfulness practices are a way to nurture not only your mind but also your whole being, and they are growing in popularity. More and more people, schools, businesses, hospitals, nursing homes, and other places of employment are teaching and using mindfulness practices to enhance well-being.

In our daily lives, we are in autopilot mode much of the time. Have you ever completed your morning drive to work or school, arriving at the location only to stop and think, "How did I get here?" Your mind has been elsewhere. It can be a pretty scary realization. When you have a child who is chronically ill, you may often find yourself on autopilot. You are running to appointments, picking up medications, calling insurance companies, and interacting with various professionals. In Chapter 1, we discussed searching the internet for information about your child's illness while in autopilot mode. Using the internet in this way can be the opposite of mindfulness. An alternative is to choose a more mindful strategy. See Worksheet 2.1, "Using the Internet Mindfully," at the end of this section, for details.

Mindfulness allows us to slow down and hit the brakes. We are so busy *doing* that we forget about *being*. Mindfulness encourages us to take a moment to notice our thoughts, feelings, bodily sensations, and surroundings. You bring your attention to what is occurring to you in the present moment. It is about noticing.

Research on the topic of mindfulness and its practices is growing. Researchers have concluded that studies in this area are still in their infancy, although good progress is being made.[4] Some of the benefits can include

- greater focus and attention,
- decreased anxiety and stress,
- enhanced health and general well-being,
- greater impulse control,
- greater ability to regulate emotions,
- increased self-awareness,
- increased empathy,
- reduced depression,
- better executive functioning skills (i.e., organization skills, planning), and
- better decision-making skills.

As you go through this list, you will see there are many benefits that relate directly to caregivers. Which items on the list are you struggling with? Which do you need help with? Which ones are you okay with? Which ones can your partner, or you child or children, improve on?

Let's do a quick self-assessment. Are you in the present, or are you thinking about something in the past or the future? What are you feeling? What does your body feel like? Is it cold? Warm? Tense? Relaxed? Whenever you find your thoughts wandering to the past or the future, try wiggling your toes. Do it now. When we wiggle our toes, it reminds us to be in the present. A study conducted by psychologists at Harvard University found that people spend 47% of their waking time thinking about something other than what they are engaged in at the moment. They found that pointless mind wandering causes people to be unhappy. They concluded that a wandering mind is an unhappy mind.[5]

Cultivating the practice of mindfulness takes time, patience, and practice. When you practice mindfulness, you are encouraged to keep an open, curious, accepting mind without judging yourself about what you are thinking, feeling, or experiencing. Focusing on the past is where depression, remorse, and regret reside. Placing our attention on the future is where anxiety lives. Mindfulness is being present to the here and now.

Mindfulness is not a religion or a cult, and it does not involve going into a trance. It is not a form of therapy; however, many therapists use it in their work. It helps with a variety of emotional and brain-related issues and problems. Almost everyone, including children, has the capacity to be mindful. Children—at least, when they are not overscheduled—tend to be more naturally mindful because they tend to live very much in the moment.

There are two types of mindfulness practice: formal and informal. Meditation and yoga are two formal practices of mindfulness because you set aside time each day to do them. Informal practices of mindfulness are shorter, ordinary exercises throughout your day that bring awareness of the present. Examples of informal practices can be mindful walking (paying attention to your feet hitting the ground, noticing how the muscles in your legs move and feel as you walk), mindful eating (smelling food; slowly chewing food; discerning different textures, tastes, and sensations), and mindful showering (How does each body part feel as you wash it with your hand? How do the water and washcloth feel on your body? Notice the temperature of the water on your skin). We promise that if you engage in one of these practices, you will walk more slowly and purposefully, you will enjoy your food and drinks more, and you will have an awesome shower. This will result in better self-care!

Meditation

Meditation is an exercise in quieting the mind and body. It is usually done while in a resting posture, either sitting or lying down. Often people report that they find it difficult to quiet their mind because thoughts keep coming in and out. This is completely normal and expected. It is often a misconception that when you meditate your mind should be completely clear. For most people, the knack of completely keeping thoughts from popping into our head is far beyond our abilities. Your mind has learned to be on the go. Being aware and acknowledging the busy-ness in your mind is being in the moment, which is the essence of mindfulness. The more we attempt to push out thoughts, the more they become prominent or increase in intensity. The teachings of mindfulness encourage us to accept and acknowledge thoughts, not to judge them, and not to get caught up in the stories of our thoughts. When your mind wanders during meditation, say to yourself, "thinking," "wandering." Think of your thoughts as bubbles floating away, or picture them on a conveyor belt passing you by. When you learn how to do this, you help the mind become calmer.

Think of your mind as a boat on turbulent waters. Like a boat, your mind is constantly moving and needs an anchor to keep it steady. Usually, the anchor is your breath, but it can also be a sound; a body sensation; or a "mantra," a specific word or phrase that you repeat silently in your mind, speak it out loud, or hear from a recorded device. Examples of mantra phrases are "I am calm," or "I am peaceful," or a mantra can be just a word, like "Peace," "Calm," "Breathe." Find a word or phrase that speaks to you. Mantras can be helpful in centering you and keeping your mind from wandering. The next time you are sitting in a waiting room and the doctor is running late, or you are feeling anxious and uncertain, close your eyes, takes some deep breaths, or repeat in your head a word or phrase. Try that now for a few minutes.

People have reported that when they meditate, they have certain reactions. They frequently report feeling sleepy. If you are sleepy during a meditation, just notice your feeling and acknowledge,

"I'm sleepy." Some people admit to feeling restless. As a culture, we often neglect to take the time to sit down and focus on our breathing. Our minds are in constant motion, and we are always on the go.

> *When I began meditating, I thought of the weirdest stuff and couldn't relax and just sit. I thought about work, appointments, paying bills. My legs were restless and I kept moving my shoulders.*
> —Dad, age 42, of a child with a chronic illness

Some people report doubting themselves as they practice meditating. They question whether they are doing it correctly or why they are doing this to begin with. Whenever we start something new, we all have feelings of doubt and self-consciousness. Our advice is: Give this practice time. Believe in yourself and understand that things don't change overnight.

There are several types of meditation practices. "Mindfulness meditation" helps you be in the present moment by focusing on the breath, a sound, or a bodily sensation. By focusing on the breath, you may begin to observe your thoughts, feelings, and bodily sensations and become more aware what is going on with your mind and body. Another meditation practice, "guided meditation," consists of listening to someone through a recording on an electronic device or in person. It can comprise words, music, or both. There are many apps available that offer guided meditations on myriad topics, such as reducing stress, improving sleep, and improving focus and concentration. Some guided meditations are more general in their content. Many evoke specific images, such as a calming scene or picturing yourself in a relaxed state or place. Another type of meditation is mantra meditation, which we mentioned earlier. If you are interested in mantra meditations, you may want to research transcendental meditation.

There is no one best way to meditate, and some practices may not appeal to you. Experiment with different types and see what works best for you. You can vary your meditation practice, doing a mantra meditation on some days and on others guided or mindfulness meditation. Have fun with it. Don't stress over meditating! If you are interested in learning how to mediate, we encourage you to look online for videos, books, and apps that can teach you ways to create a meditation practice. We list some apps in the Resources for Your Journey at the end of this book.

Yoga

Yoga is another formal practice of mindfulness. People practice yoga in gyms, private studios, community centers, and schools. It can be practiced alone or with a group. Yoga teaches us how to pause, take a breath, and notice how we feel in the moment. It enhances our well-being on a physical, mental, emotional and spiritual level and involves using breathing techniques, movement, and meditation. Yoga is often viewed as mindfulness in motion. It involves placing your body in variety of poses and using your breath and focused attention. Practicing yoga helps balance the nervous system; people report feeling more peaceful, focused, flexible, and stronger in mind and body. It can also help you stay fit. Practicing yoga several times a week will increase your endurance, and it is healthy for your lungs, blood vessels, and heart. Among other benefits, yoga can assist in coping with stress and other strong emotions, creating inner peace.

Researchers have explored what happens to your brain when you practice yoga. A study conducted at the University of Illinois found that 20 minutes of Hatha yoga improved people's ability to keep focus and to take in, retain and use new information significantly better than after 20 minutes of a moderate to vigorous aerobic workout.[6] Another study, conducted at Boston University, found that levels of gamma-aminobutyric acid (GABA) increase significantly during yoga. GABA is a chemical in your brain that is known to decrease anxiety and improve your mood.[7] It was further noted that practicing yoga increases levels of dopamine and serotonin in the brain. Dopamine and serotonin are chemicals that help a person feel more relaxed and prepared to handle stressful situations. Medical professionals often prescribe medications, such as antidepressants and anti-anxiety drugs, that influence these two chemicals in the brain.

As a caregiver, you may feel stressed often, and your stress levels may be elevated even when you aren't reacting to anything specific in the moment. The main stress hormone, cortisol, is connected to the fear center in the brain and shrinks the part of the brain that manages self-control. One study found that cortisol levels dropped in people who practice yoga on a regular basis.[8] Other aspects of yoga practice, such as the slow, steady breathing, can help reduce the amount of cortisol in your body.

There are many styles of yoga. Some styles are physically demanding, and others are more relaxing. We suggest trying out different styles and seeing what you enjoy and are comfortable with. We recommend you speak with your doctor before engaging in any practice of yoga. In yoga, you should never do anything that will injure yourself. You cannot afford to get hurt! If you are an experienced yogi, you may want to mix up styles (just like meditation practice) to keep things fresh and challenging. We encourage you to search online and speak to a credentialed yoga teacher about what type of style they teach and recommend on the basis of your goals and the level of demand you want on your body. We include some yoga apps in the Resources for Your Journey.

Mindfulness Based Stress Reduction

Jon Kabat-Zinn developed the Mindfulness Based Stress Reduction program at the University of Massachusetts Medical Center.[9] Commonly referred to as MBSR, it is a formal, 8-week, intensive program that is taught on a weekly basis and combines mindfulness meditation and yoga practice. The program has benefits for all individuals, but, interestingly, it was originally designed for patients with chronic medical disorders. It has been shown to help relieve anxiety, stress, depression, and chronic pain.

One study evaluated the MBSR program for caregivers of children with chronic conditions.[10] In the study, the caregivers, mostly mothers, participated in MBSR sessions. Before participating in the MBSR sessions, the caregivers reported very elevated stress levels and mood disturbances. The researchers found that after the caregivers participated in the 8-week MBSR program their scores on the mood and stress assessments decreased dramatically. They found an overall reduction in stress symptoms of 32% and a decrease in mood disturbance of 56%. They concluded that the MBSR program was effective in reducing stress symptoms and mood issues for caregivers. They did indicate that future research needed to apply more rigorous methodology and recommended applying MBSR to other groups of caregivers who are experiencing stress.

Another study on MBSR was conducted at Harvard University. The researchers compared the MRIs (magnetic resonance imaging scans) of people who meditated an average of 27 minutes a day with those of people who did not practice meditation, before and after their participation in the 8-week course in MBSR. The MRIs of the meditators showed a significant increase in gray matter in the hippocampus area, the area of the brain where learning and memory functions are located. The researchers also observed a decrease in gray matter in the amygdala, the area that modulates emotions and feelings such as anxiety and stress. People who did not meditate did not show any changes in the gray matter on their MRIs.[11]

MBSR programs are taught in hospitals, medical centers, private practices, and clinics, typically by physicians, nurses, psychologists, and social workers, as well as other health care professionals. Significant research has been emerging from major universities and medical centers that validates how effective this program is and indicates that it can actually change our brains and lives for the better. If you are interested in taking a course in MBSR, you can look online for places that offer the program by certified teachers, such as local hospitals in their patient education programs. Always make sure that the person doing the training has been certified as an MBSR trainer.

Are mindfulness practices a cure-all for everything? The answer is no. Don't go into meditation or yoga believing it's going to cure everything. If you do, you will be disappointed and frustrated, and you likely will abandon this type of self-care. The idea is to learn healthy ways to live with the stresses you experience and to reduce the amount of damage that stress does to your body and mind. The wonderful thing about mindfulness practices are the many choices to select from and the variety of ways to experiment. It is also about having fun while caring for yourself.

Using the Internet Mindfully

The internet is a powerful source of information, but it is also full of unsubstantiated claims, naked scare tactics, and just plain lies. The *Journal of the American Medical Association* reviewed 79 studies and concluded that online health information is frequently flawed, inaccurate, or biased. Many websites are funded by drug companies that don't reveal the source of their funds, and finance so-called "consumer groups" whose sole purpose is to create buyers for their products.[12] Surfer, beware! Remember, anyone can post anything they want, and in most cases there is no one else evaluating the information. You can also find horror stories galore, which will not be helpful!

Before you sit down to surf the internet, know your own limits. Some of us can sit in front of a screen for only an hour or so without feeling stressed and overloaded; others have more tolerance. Decide what the purpose of your session will be, and then give yourself a reasonable time frame. Set an alarm to tell you when you need to take a break. Also, remember compassion fatigue; if you start to notice you are feeling sad or pessimistic a lot more, stop reading sad or difficult stories. They can affect your outlook. (That goes for the news, too—there may be times it is best not to keep up with the latest in politics and other disasters!) Plan something uplifting, for even 5 minutes afterward, to help you shift, if you think you will need it. Review one of your gratitude lists!

Many people are also using alternative treatment approaches these days and taking various supplements. Rarely are these approaches evaluated with the type of large-scale studies we use for other medical information. What follows are some guidelines for getting the most accurate and appropriate information to address your situation, including two websites that can provide information on alternative procedures and the actual contents of dietary supplements. Be sure to discuss with your child's medical team any information you find, alternative strategies you want to try, and dietary supplements you are thinking of using.

In this worksheet we've provided two tables to help you stay focused and mindful when you search the internet. Feel free to make notes for yourself in the blank spaces.

Purpose of the search	
	Helpful internet sources
I want to get support.	Personal blogs in which people share their own stories.
	Message boards or community bulletin boards, where you can leave questions for others to respond to, and vice versa.
	Online forums, where you can engage in conversations in real time on a platform like Zoom. These may be led by experts, or by nonexperts.
	Cautions
	People can create phony personas.
	Some sites are meant to steer you to make purchases.
	Scammers can sell or leak your personal information.
	Other parents can be good sources of resources and support but may not have accurate medical information.
	Tips
	Start with your medical providers and the lists we provide in the Resources for Your Journey.
	Evaluate the quality of the website (see below).
I want specific information.	**Cautions**
	An accurate website may link to others that are not accurate.
	Be sure to check the privacy policy, and do not share personal information such as date of birth, Social Security number, or patient ID—especially if it isn't relevant.

(continues)

WORKSHEET 2.1. Using the Internet Mindfully (*Continued*)

How to Evaluate a Website: 1H/5W, or How, Why, Who, What, When, and Where

HOW does the website present itself?
- Is it easy to find what you're looking for?
- Is it hard to distinguish information from advertising?
- Is it well written, with correct grammar and spelling?

WHY does the webpage exist: What is its purpose?
- Commercial (i.e., to make money)
  - Are they selling space for other companies to place ads?
  - Note that .com websites as well as some .org and .net sites may be for profit.
- To educate
  - What is their agenda?
  - .edu refers to an educational institution. Make sure the content is from the institution itself and is not a student project.
  - .gov sites are U.S. government websites and should be accurate.
- To advocate a particular point of view
  - Do their values align with yours?

WHO publishes the website?
- Check "About Us" and "Contact Us." Are they individuals, an organization, or a company?
- Are the content provider's credentials relevant to the information? For example, people with a PhD can call themselves "Doctor," but they are not medical doctors (MDs).
- Who is paying for (or sponsoring) the content? Could that skew the information?
- Is there an independent group like an editorial board that reviews the content?
- Red flags
  - Hard to find who is actually providing the content
  - Lots of positive reviews and no negative ones

WORKSHEET 2.1. Using the Internet Mindfully (*Continued*)

WHAT information is on the website?
- Objective information that is not inflammatory or overly simplified.
- Explains medical terms, describes sources of information, supplies sources.
- Shares all treatment options, possible adverse outcomes, and side effects.
- Presents what is known and where more research is needed.
- Explains whether findings are from a case study (one person), a small group, or a large trial.
- Red flags
  - Conclusions are so broad or comprehensive that results seem unlikely.
  - If it sounds too good to be true—it probably is!

WHEN was the information uploaded?
- Remember that medical science is continually changing.
- Links broken? Information is probably old.
- Check dates of media appearances and coverage such as published articles.

WHERE is the information coming from?
- The two-letter code at the end of the URL is the country code (.ca is Canada, .au is Australia, .uk is Britain, .de is Germany, etc.).
- Research information from other countries may be accurate, but remember that each health care system is different.

Note. Two helpful websites for information on alternative treatments and dietary supplements are the National Center for Complementary and Integrative Health (https://nccih.nih.gov) and the Office of Dietary Supplements (https://ods.od.nih.gov).

EXPLORING SPIRITUAL PATHS

When your child has a chronic illness, you have to adjust not only your calendar but also your expectations and your outlook on life. The more uncertainty your child's illness presents, whether in its treatment or prognosis, the greater the impact on your ability to adjust to the situation will be.[13] So, where does the ability to "adjust" come from? It comes from the meaning you assign to your child's illness. Spirituality encompasses both belief systems and practices that help people make meaning, set expectations, and develop a positive outlook on life.

As human beings, we tend to make meaning out of our experiences. We may see difficult things that happen to us as lessons for us to learn something, or as the means by which we develop character. Some people feel they are being singled out for bad luck. But life events don't come with ready-made meanings; we have to create them. If you already have a particular way of seeing how and why things happen, you will interpret new things that happen through that lens. Life is unpredictable. When we can create meaning for ourselves, it can give us a sense of stability in an ever-changing world.

According to psychologist Roy Baumeister, meaning is made up of the following:

- finding a sense of purpose that connects us to our goals,
- the values that guide our actions based on what we think is beneficial or not,
- our sense of how capable we feel of acting on our values, and
- our ability to follow through given the circumstances.[14]

We find meaning in many different aspects of our lives: parenthood, family, work, religion, personal ventures. Having different sources of meaning protects us from the loss of meaning should one area fail us.

When thinking about what your child's illness means—whether in the philosophical sense of "Why did it happen?" or in the practical sense of "What now?"—it can be helpful to take a step back and look at your beliefs. Rather than looking at your beliefs from the perspective of whether or not they are true, we invite you to consider whether or not they are helpful and supportive of what you need in your present circumstances.

Beliefs About Events

Suffering invites us to explore deeper meanings, and it can shatter previous perspectives we had on life. It forces us to reset our beliefs and ideas. Suffering can cause a spiritual crisis, too, when our beliefs about God or other aspects of our faith are suddenly inadequate to deal with our difficulties. Sometimes our beliefs are just not broad enough to include the tragedies and challenges of life. The good news is that, with help and guidance, the struggles of dealing with your child's illness can leave you with a deeper understanding of your faith.

People commonly use three main strategies to deal with the need for meaning in the face of suffering. Going back to the bullet points above, one strategy is to look for purpose in the new situation, another is to find ways to rebuild your sense of mastery or control, and a third is to bolster your sense of self-worth. Let's say you hold your 6-year-old in your lap while she has blood drawn. It may seem a simple act that you'd do without thinking, but if you do it with a sense of dedication to your purpose (*to be there for my child always*), then you are making meaning. If you do it because you asked for it as an accommodation to the normal nursing protocol, then you're exercising a degree of control over the situation. If you hold your child with a sense of pride in being able to provide comfort for her, then you have enhanced your sense of self-worth.

Discovering the cause of your child's illness may be comforting, but there is also the danger of turning it into a judgment on you or your child. Negative beliefs—for example, that the illness is a result of some sin or transgression—can lead to self-blame, guilt, and even blaming the child. Belief systems that do this have been shown to increase psychological distress and lead to poor adjustment.[15] Remember that, because we are biological beings, random mistakes do occur in our lives. If your spiritual beliefs encourage the idea that someone did something wrong in order for your child to be afflicted, consider also that we live a universe where, sometimes, things just happen. Perhaps just by recognizing that chronic illness can happen to anyone, and not taking it as a personal assault, you can calm the waters enough to help you focus on what needs to be done.

Beliefs About God

When bad things happen, it's not unusual to wonder how they could happen in a universe where some god, a presumably benevolent being, is in charge. Many people experience anger or rage toward God for allowing the illness to affect their child. How can a loving, compassionate, and responsive god allow such suffering to exist?

Different faiths have different responses to this question. Christianity says we have free will, which allows people to choose whether or not to respond to God. Buddhism tells us that suffering is an inevitable part of human life. The fact that we have physical bodies does make us susceptible to the breakdown of those bodies, whatever our beliefs tell us about why. Whatever answers you find to the eternal question of why there is suffering in this world, the understanding of God that results can have both positive and negative effects on your psychological well-being.

We are not here to tell you what you should believe, or how you should view God, but we do want you to know what the research suggests, which is that seeing God as distant, harsh, or punitive can result in psychic distress. People who expect God to do everything may not have the impulse to take charge of their child's health the way they must. On the flip side, being able to view God as loving and compassionate can lead to higher levels of personal well-being. Seeing God as a partner in addressing the illness also results in better mental health and motivation.[16]

Self-Compassion

Compassion is and always has been a key religious and spiritual value. We are accustomed to thinking of that compassion being directed toward others: our families, our friends, and, in some faiths, even those we consider our enemies. It can be easy to forget that we need to include ourselves in any circle of compassion that we construct.

"Self-compassion," as defined by psychologist Kristin Neff, consists of three parts. First, you address errors and mistakes with kindness and understanding toward yourself, rather than judgment and self-criticism. Next, you recognize that making mistakes is part of the larger human experience of frailty. You don't entertain some idea of how uniquely bad you are, isolating yourself from others. Third and finally, you allow yourself to experience the painful feelings that often come with our mistakes rather than numbing yourself to them. Doing this helps us to pay attention to our mistakes and learn from them, without becoming overwhelmed.[17]

It can be hard to let go of the idea that self-criticism helps you do better next time, because in fact it often pulls people into a relentless cycle of rumination, shame, anger, and anxiety. Self-criticism shifts your focus away from the situation. Research shows that if you practice self-compassion instead, you form a more accurate picture of your abilities and performance, and you are more able to feel happiness and optimism.[18] Parents who practice self-compassion become more confident in their caregiving ability and less stressed by the parenting role. They are more able to accept their own short-comings as well as those of their children. They are more likely to show their children positive behaviors such as care, reassurance, guidance, and protection. As a result, children are less affected by whatever stress their parents are going through.[19] Self-compassion encourages you to take better care of yourself, reach out for support, and see your problems as solvable.

Most parents want to do their absolute best for their children and, as a parent of a child with a chronic illness, you want that too! But you might have to let go of the idea that you should perform at the height of your abilities at all times and in all situations. Even parents without this challenge tend to be too hard on themselves. It's okay—and in fact a good idea—to reprioritize your expectations.

> *Your child is not going to be the person you wanted her to be. You have to love the person that is there, and you have to teach them to have compassion for themselves. If you can't model what it is to have compassion for yourself, you need to ask for help. . . . There's no shame in asking for help, there's no shame in having a medical situation. If we don't do that, our kid is carrying our loss for us.*
>
> —Mother of a teen with epilepsy

Here is the reality: You will make mistakes. You will fail your child. When you are juggling so many things, you will invariably drop some from time to time. You will feel hopeless, angry, use-less, guilty, and ashamed. But remember: Beating up on yourself is not very helpful. It actually keeps you stuck in your shortcomings, caught up in guilt and shame and thus unable to see clearly what needs to be done. It increases your stress, makes burnout more likely, and interferes with your ability to be there for your child. Give yourself a break. You are only a human being.

Some religious traditions have specific rituals that help us deal with our mistakes. If you are seriously troubled by an error you have made, and find yourself unable to let go, seeking out a spiritual guide or leader can help you initiate a process that may ease your regret and reaffirm your spiritual commitments. Therapists can also help you learn to let go of errors and move on in a positive way. Just know that having compassion for yourself is not being "too easy" on yourself, or absolving you of responsibility. Instead it means coming to a place of acceptance of your humanness and being able to move on so you can be ready for the next challenge.

Gratitude

What can you be grateful for? This may seem like a bizarre question to someone whose child has a life-altering condition, but if you look closely, there are always things to be grateful for. You can start with treatments that are available; members of your medical team; and friends, neighbors, and family who have stepped up and been good listeners. There are still days of lovely weather and beautiful sunsets, moments of connection with your family, a perhaps rare but still attainable good night's sleep. What about your child and any siblings she may have? Did she smile today, or get excited about something? Have you witnessed her sibling doing something kind for her, or experiencing his own, even small, achievement?

Gratitude can be described "as a felt sense of wonder, thankfulness and appreciation for life,"[20] and it is considered a virtue in many spiritual and religious traditions. It often highlights our connection to others and can deepen personal meaning. In one study, participants described five major negative events in their lives. Those who were asked to also name what they were grateful for felt better about their lives as a whole and were more optimistic, even though they described just as many "negative" emotions as the group who didn't name what they were grateful for. In another study, participants who completed a 21-day gratitude journal had higher levels of psychological well-being and were more likely to have helped someone else than those who did not complete a journal.[21] Practicing gratitude before sleep may even enhance the quality of sleep you get!

Gratitude heightens your awareness of the small gifts in your difficulties. It can increase your well-being, strengthen your relationships, and support your desire to care for others. In this way it can feel like having more control. It may not come naturally, but it can be developed and taught to your children.

We often don't take in so-called "positive" experiences, especially when dealing with so many difficult ones. Pausing for a moment of gratitude, giving yourself 15 seconds or so to actually experience what you are grateful for in that moment, can be a brief respite from all that you are dealing with. As you notice more positive moments, the heavy load you feel may be lightened just a touch, enough to give you the strength to keep going one more day, do one more thing.

Starting a simple practice of remembering three things at the end of the day for which you are grateful can start to shift your everyday experience. It invites you to go to sleep remembering the moments that touched you, that reminded you of the beauty of life, and reassured you that you are not alone. Some people like to keep a gratitude journal to which they can refer when they are feeling particularly stressed. You are not living just to take care of your child; you are taking care of your child so that your family might live more fully and abundantly. Gratitude helps you experience that abundance now.

Prayer

Every religious tradition has some form of prayer, a way of connecting with the spiritual dimension of life. Prayers may ask for things for oneself or others, or they may express regret and ask pardon for mistakes; we may share gratitude for life's gifts or simply express awe and wonder at all that is. A moment of silence in the face of a beautiful sunset can be likened to a prayer; a child's smile, a much-needed hug, or a medical provider's pat of reassurance can all be seen as a form of prayer. Some traditions use physical movements for prayer; the practice of yoga can be seen from this perspective. Nearly all traditions have some form of prayer without words. In Buddhism, it is referred to as "mindfulness meditation" practice; Thomas Merton called it "contemplative prayer," and both Judaism and Islam have similar practices. This type of prayer is most associated with a personal sense of well-being and felt closeness to God.[22] Explore your own tradition for prayers that might speak to you in your most challenging moments; followers of one of the three Abrahamic faiths may also pray the Psalms, which contain every possible human emotion and circumstance.

If you are given to prayer or think that now might be a good time to start the practice, one prayer that has found a wide audience and may be helpful is the Serenity Prayer. It has been popularized by 12-step programs but was part of a longer prayer written by Reinhold Niebuhr, a 20th-century Christian theologian. It reads, in its original form:

> God, give us grace to accept with serenity
> the things that cannot be changed,
> Courage to change the things
> which should be changed,
> and the Wisdom to distinguish
> the one from the other.

If we turn the prayer on its head, it provides a path through challenging circumstances. We start with the wisdom of distinguishing the things we can control from the things we cannot. What in your situation do you actually have control over? You cannot control your or your child's feelings; you cannot control the course of their illness, though certainly you can influence it by applying recommended treatments (but even then, no treatment is certain). Thinking you can control what you cannot sends you in the wrong direction every time. You set off to pursue results you cannot achieve and that might even make things worse. It ends in frustration and burnout.

The Serenity Prayer asks you to start by sitting with that awareness, of all that you cannot control, and find some level of acceptance. Not that you will not do what you can do, not that you will sit idly by and just watch, but that on some level you have to accept what is beyond your control.

We want to offer just a word here about what "acceptance" means and does not mean when talking about your child's illness. It does not mean to condone illness, or to throw up our hands and say there is nothing to be done. It does not mean saying it is okay that your child is dealing with the illness, or that researchers shouldn't continue to experiment and find better treatments and potential cures. All it means is that you recognize its intrusion into your life: This illness is now part of the picture, and, other than taking the steps recommended for care and healing, you cannot change that. Allow yourself to sit with that reality.

It may seem surprising, but letting go of the idea that you can fix everything and being able to sit with feelings related to your lack of control can actually reduce the weight of your child's illness. It frees you from wild goose chases and helps you focus on what is in your control right in this moment. A parent whose teenager has epilepsy reflected on the tough work of acceptance. The parent had attended a support group meeting and was able to see, after interacting with another parent, the importance of acceptance:

> [The other parent] was not willing to accept the fact that her daughter's life was now different, she was going, "Suck it up and keep going kid," wasn't accepting or even having compassion for her daughter's situation, wasn't coming to terms with it. . . . We have to do our own work. We have to embrace the child that we have versus the child we dreamed we'd have . . . I get that you feel different, and it is not what you wanted but it's what we got. Being in denial does more damage than embracing. It's just what we have to do.

NEXT STEP: MAKE HUMOR PART OF YOUR EVERY DAY

There is an old, pithy saying, "Laughter is the best medicine." Anyone who laughs, smiles, or uses humor as a coping mechanism can attest to its healing and comforting power. You might think, "How can I laugh or smile when my child is sick?" There is nothing humorous about a child who has been diagnosed with a potentially life-long or life-threatening illness that may include pain, suffering, uncomfortable procedures, potential separations, and in some cases death.

Humor and laughter may be just the thing you need to cope with your child's having a chronic illness and the challenges you face. There will be times on this journey that you will cry, mourn, be angry, and feel other strong emotions. It is difficult for some to develop a sense of humor during difficult times in life. Some parents have shared that when they laugh and develop a sense of humor, they were better able to connect with others, take a different perspective, and balance priorities when things were overwhelming.

I found myself watching a lot of sitcoms when my son was sick. It gave me a much-needed break from all the things that were going on around me. Sometimes I felt guilty about laughing, but I needed a break from feeling overwhelmed, sad, and scared. I am eternally grateful for the cast of "Friends" for getting me through some rough patches.

—Mother of a child with an autoimmune disorder

There have been some noted positive effects and benefits of humor and laughter. Here are some benefits that should make you smile:

- Laughing increases the feel-good hormones known as "endorphins" in your brain. It produces feelings of euphoria similar to the narcotic drug heroin and actually increases pain tolerance.[23] When endorphins are released during laughter, pain tolerance increases. Laughter is a much safer treatment than the use of narcotics.
- Laughing also reduces the stress hormones cortisol, dopamine, adrenaline, and epinephrine.[24]
- Laughing can serve as a diversion from strong feelings of anger, guilt, stress, and anxiety. As we said earlier when discussing mindfulness, depression is living in the past. Anxiety is living in the future. Laughter keeps us in the present.
- Laughing is a free and accessible coping mechanism. Turn on your favorite funny show on your electronic device wherever you are.
- Laughing can allow a physical and emotional release from holding tension and other strong feelings inside. Some people

may scream or cry. Laughter may be a more enjoyable way to get the physical and emotional release you need.

- Laughter is believed to boost the immune system by promoting the release of white blood cells, which are critical to healthy immune functioning. When we have improved immune functioning, we heal faster and are less prone to illness, which frees up the energy to take care of others and ourselves.[25]
- Laughter has an anti-inflammatory effect that protects your heart and blood vessels from the harmful effects of cardiovascular disease. Laughter increases blood flow, thus keeping your blood vessels healthy, and it helps regulate and balance blood pressure. One way to take care of your heart is to have a good laugh.[26]
- Laughing helps our lung function. It provides more oxygen to the brain and the cells in the body by allowing us to have longer exhalations, and as a result it empties the lungs of residual air. Thus, when we laugh, we feel more energy, have more stamina, and are more productive.[27]
- Laughter has social benefits. Laughing together gives us a sense of togetherness and safety. It has a contagious effect. When one person laughs, others will join in even if they do not know what is funny. Laughter has a reciprocal effect: When we laugh with others, there are fewer confrontations and greater cooperation.[28]

Building Laughter Into Your Life

Here are some helpful tips on how you as a caregiver can incorporate laughter into your life:

- Use whatever media that works for you. Go to the movie theater or rent a movie on demand, watch live TV, pop in a

DVD, or watch programs online through various streaming services. Books and articles can also bring laughter. Even sending or looking at memes or social media posts can bring a chuckle.

- Go out with friends—maybe catch some live theater. Getting out changes your environment; you see and interact with different people. Laughter can be contagious, so you tend to laugh more with others. Plan get-togethers with friends to watch a movie or play a game. Depending on time and other commitments, make it a weekly date. Laughing together is good medicine.
- Laughing can serve as a great distraction and escape. You can't express feelings such as sadness, anger, and other strong feelings and laugh at the same time. Test it!
- Laughing changes our perspective. Humor and laughter can change our mindset, thereby making situations appear less threatening.[29]
- Be an actor. Your body cannot tell the difference between real and fake laughter. Sometimes from the fake laughter, you start to experience real laughter. Try it!

Take a Ride on Smile Street

The positive results of smiling are very similar to the effects of laughter. You may be thinking, "What do I have to smile about? My child has a chronic illness. He's in pain. We are all scared. Our lives have been turned upset down." We are empathic to the challenges you are facing and do not want to seem Pollyanna or insensitive about this. Although smiling is not going to cure your child or pay the bills, we do know that smiling can help with mood, stress, and other things that will allow you to take better care of yourself and your child.

Here are some benefits of smiling:

- Smiling can boost your mood and relax your brain and your body. As with laughter, when we smile, the feel-good chemicals in our brain (endorphins, serotonin, and dopamine) are released, and they can make us actually feel happier, rather than just looking like we are happy. When we smile, chemicals called "neuropeptides," which help with fighting off stress, are released. Smiling can also lower your heart rate and blood pressure.
- Smiling can be contagious, and it costs nothing but can offer so much. If someone smiles at you, it is likely that you cannot help but return the smile. We encourage you to test this out next time you are out!
- When we smile, we appear more attractive, friendly, approachable, and confident. Smiling conveys a sense of comfort. If medical staff are smiling as they come out of surgery or as they read test results, we are likely to feel relieved and less worried. A professional who does not smile can raise our anxiety and stress.

Should you fake a smile? According to research, it depends. A study published in *Psychological Science* found that faking a smile can be tiresome, but it can eventually result in a more positive outlook.[30] The researchers found that focusing on positive thoughts or reframing a difficult situation can help in improving feelings over time. An important finding was that smiling is not a cure for all kinds of stress, especially long-term stressors. Smiling was found to be more helpful for brief, acute stressors; for short periods of time; or as a solution to a passing negative mood. In coping with your child's illness, smiling may be helpful waiting on line at the pharmacy, and dealing with a snarky staff member, among others. Because your child's illness is long term, smiling may not make you feel better. Try it out. It may work for you.

Smiling Exercise

Let's do an experiment. Start out by making a half-smile. Now, make the half-smile into a full smile. Show all your teeth. Hold that smile for a bit. Notice what you are feeling. What thoughts come to your mind? How do you feel? Do you feel silly? If so, that is okay. Take notice of how this smile makes you feel. Hold it for awhile. When you are ready, you can stop smiling.

A note of caution here: If you or others you know are experiencing pain or depression at levels that interfere with your daily functioning, or if you have thoughts of harming yourself or others, we strongly recommend you seek the help of a medical professional. Moreover, if you are currently under the medical care of someone prescribing medications for pain, depression, heart issues, or blood pressure, we strongly recommend you follow the directions of your doctors and not discontinue using any prescribed medications for any of the conditions, problems, or diagnoses you or others may have. The suggestions we are providing for self-care are not to be used as substitutes or in place of what is recommended by your doctors and medical personnel.

CHAPTER 3

GETTING WHAT YOU NEED ON THE ROAD TO THE NEW NORMAL

At certain times on the parenting journey, regardless of whether our children are sick or well, we look for signs that point the way. Wouldn't it be great if we knew when various stages were about to start or end? If you saw a sign that said it would be exactly 20 miles until you arrive at a place called No More Napping For This Toddler, you'd know to make a stop for refreshments and then buckle up when getting back in the car! Entering the county of Teen Conquers Moodiness (coming up in 30 miles), you'd be able to stock up on practical and emotional "supplies" to support your teen as she develops coping skills in her life.

The road sign you're probably looking for now is one that points to the New Normal. Maybe you've found a life pattern that really works for your family. Everything is clicking along; family members are supporting your child's special medical needs while also doing well in their own school and work. You're sleeping at night again. Then, *bam!* Another change happens with your child's health—the medication stops working, she goes into a medical crisis—and all the pieces go flying. You feel like you've veered off the road and you're going the wrong way. Where is that mythical land of New Normal?

In Chapter 2 we talked about how self-care is not selfish; in fact, it's essential. Seeking stability for yourself and your family is also a vital part of your effort to support your child. This chapter is about taking self-care to the next level, when you advocate for your needs and those of your family. It's about making choices that affect the structural parts of your life—your job, your family's health insurance, your child care arrangements.

We believe that self-care and self-advocacy build on each other. The more you cultivate compassion and gratitude, and the more mindful you are about managing your stress levels, the more clearly you will see the gaps in your life that need to be filled as just that—gaps that need to be filled, not personal shortcomings and not reasons to blame God or the universe, health professionals, your genes, or your child himself for the illness. It is hard to look at the structures supporting our lives, like our homes and our finances, and try to reconfigure them when a child's health condition demands that we must. We want you to find the normal that works for your family and helps you feel more at ease on your journey.

Frank has a saying that he always teaches his patients: If you don't ask, you don't get. This is the heart of self-advocacy. As you take inventory of the areas in your life with the most gaps or potholes, ask yourself, "What is it that I need?" "How might others help me?" "How can I express my needs in the most effective way possible, while maintaining good relationships?" Doing so can be hard if you're not used to it. Persistence is key. Once you experience the satisfaction of speaking up on your own behalf, you will have more confidence.

The first topic we cover is finding psychological help and support for yourself or for your whole family. As we mentioned in Chapter 1, having an objective listener and problem solver in your life is always helpful. Establishing a relationship with a mental health provider early on may help when new challenges arise during the course of your child's illness and as different needs arise for your family, such as a change in child care or employment. Next, we discuss working with health insurance companies and your employer. We then offer some tips for finding good child care, whether for your ill child specifically or for them and their siblings. Finally, we offer an avenue for advocacy that you might not have thought about yet: having your child participate in studies or clinical trials.

"I DON'T HAVE TIME FOR ONE MORE APPOINTMENT!"

Even with the high prevalence of chronic illness in children and adolescents, very few parents and families receive psychological help. Unfortunately, there still is a stigma around receiving mental health care, despite its proven benefits. And it's natural to dismiss the psychological impact of the illness and accept emotional and relationship problems as "normal" or inevitable. "Of course my child is depressed, she has leukemia" or "It's understandable that our marriage isn't great right now. We haven't had time to focus on anything since Thomas got sick." It makes sense to sort out your child's medical needs first; however, your emotional needs and those of your family are important, too, so don't ignore them.

It's true that seeing a mental health professional is one more appointment in your already-busy schedule. "I just don't have the time!" is something we often hear from parents. And when your insurance policy lacks appropriate mental health coverage, or restricts the number of sessions it will cover, therapy can add to the growing stack of bills and eventually become too expensive. We know you have a busy week filled with many other things to do and places to be. Therapy does involve "time and dime," and most people cannot afford to waste either of those. However, it's a worthwhile—and at times, an essential—adjunct to medical treatment.

Parenting is tough work even in the best of times, and when a chronic illness enters the family system, parenting becomes even more arduous, stressful, and confusing. Helpful guidance from a mental health perspective can make all the difference. In addition to providing expertise, a therapist can help you tolerate difficult feelings—your own and others'—and help you deal with ambiguity. Therapists can also help you accept your own and others' limitations and shortcomings so you can move forward and be a better parent for your children. Getting psychological help can also assist with coping and thus with freeing up energy for self-care and other activities. If you struggle with depression, you should definitely receive treatment, because depression can weaken the immune system. That means you're more susceptible to colds and other illnesses that can sap the energy you need to care for your child, or possibly even put your child at higher risk of disease or complications to their condition.[1]

FINDING A THERAPIST

We recognize that different cultures have distinctive values when it comes to counseling and therapy. It is important, when seeking help, that the mental health professional be sensitive to your family's way of dealing with medical issues. Make sure, first of all, that the person you choose to work with

- has experience working with children and families with medical illnesses,
- has a good working knowledge of chronic medical illnesses or health psychology, and
- is willing to work and talk with a variety of other professionals.

Make sure, too, that they understand the following:

- what you call the chronic illness your child has (i.e., its name), and any special terminology for the medical treatments;
- how the chronic illness affects your child's health and ability to function;
- what you believe caused the illness, or if there is a particular cause for it;
- what problems the illness is causing for your child, you, or your family;
- what you fear most about your child's illness;
- what results you hope your child's treatment will have; and
- the type of help you want for yourself or your family.[2]

There are many different types of therapists. Any therapist, however, can have specialized training in the area that is most important to you. For example, marriage and family therapists (MFTs) are trained and licensed to work with couples. A psychologist (PhD or PsyD), licensed clinical social worker (LCSW), licensed professional counselor (LPC; note that "LPC" is used in 24 U.S. states, so your state may use a different designation, such as "LPCC"; you should make sure your provider's focus is mental health before consulting them), or licensed mental health counselor (LMHC) can also get special training to work with couples, although they each have slightly different training, focus, education, and licensure requirements.

The first differentiation between types of therapists is the educational requirement. LCSWs, LPCs, and MFTs all require a master's degree in psychology, counseling, marriage and family therapy, or social work; these usually involve a 2-year program. Psychologists, both PhD and PsyD recipients, have a doctoral degree that includes at least 4 years of school, a full year of internship training, and a dissertation, which is usually a lengthy research project. PsyD programs are newer, and they focus more on clinical work, whereas the traditional PhD programs remain research oriented. Psychiatrists represent the highest level of schooling; they are medical doctors who have completed years-long residencies in psychiatry. Most psychiatrists primarily focus on supplying medication for mental health disorders, though some still practice psychotherapy with their patients. Some states allow licensed psychologists to prescribe medication for mental disorders. Because of the lengthy and expensive schooling required, psychiatrists tend to be most expensive in terms of session costs, followed by psychologists and then by master's-level clinicians. All licensed therapists have had hours of supervised training (the number of hours varies from state to state) and some kind of written examination before they are formally licensed by the state where they practice.

All therapists are well equipped to handle such issues as anxiety and depression. Psychologists deal with the full range of mental disorders and life stresses and are qualified to administer psychological tests meant to assess such things as learning disabilities, IQ, personality, vocational interests, and, in the case of law enforcement officers and military personnel, fitness for duty. MFTs are trained in "systemic thinking," a perspective that sees the family as a system operating in ways you can't predict simply by knowing the individual participants. MFTs require training and therapy hours in which they work specifically with families and children. LCSWs also work with families and children, but they are specially trained in the social context of problems. Their expertise lies in connecting people with resources in the larger community. LPCs are trained to work with individual adults and have special training in career counseling.

Who is the best therapist for you? The answer to that depends on what is happening in the family. For example, if you and your partner keep having the same argument over and over, are having difficulty coming to an agreement on the overall course of action or how to parent your children, and these conflicts are causing distress and distance between you, then couples counseling may be in order. Any two adults can constitute a couple, for the purposes of counseling: Perhaps you are a single mom coparenting with one of the grandparents, or two siblings caring for your children together. Any group of more than two people is considered family counseling, regardless of the relationships involved.

As we'll note in Chapter 5, you may find resolution in as little as one session by getting help walking through a difficult conversation, but for many families more may be involved. Your child's illness and its effects are serious stresses on all your family relationships, and what were previously small, bridgeable differences may morph into greater problems because of this added stress.

When the issues at hand seem to involve the children as well, starting off with family therapy can get everyone on the same page. Even if it seems that one child in particular is acting out behaviorally, or experiencing serious anxiety or depressive symptoms, focusing on that child alone can send the message that she *is* the problem. Often, a child's reaction to a family situation, such as the illness of a sibling, expresses the upset, fear, and sadness that others in the family feel but perhaps don't have the time, energy, or permission to express. So, unless a child is specifically asking to see someone privately, start with a family session. That also gives the therapist a better picture of what is going on for everyone and helps them decide what approach would be most helpful to you. That approach can include additional family sessions, working with different pairs within the family, including not only the parents but also parent and child combinations, pairs or groups of siblings, and even extended family who may be involved, as well as with individual family members.

If, however, you find yourself overwhelmed by depression, anxiety, or other emotional states, especially if it leads to the fight, flight, or freeze response, or you are acting far outside the bounds of the partner and parent you want to be, individual therapy may be the best option. The general rule is that if the issue is seriously affecting your ability to function in more than one setting, such as home, and work or school, therapy is a good idea. Red flag issues in anyone, such as suicidality (which may include a child talking about death a lot), acute depression (which in children sometimes looks like excessive irritability), or severe anxiety that prevents usual functioning, or behavior that harms the self or others, need to be addressed promptly.

To find referrals to mental health professionals, start with your medical team, pediatricians, family and friends, and other parents you may have come to know who are dealing with a similar situation. Your medical team in particular, and other parents, may have already found therapists who are knowledgeable about and have expertise in helping families dealing with complications related to chronic medical illness and conditions. There also are many websites that can steer you to clinicians in your area. Local chapters of organizations focused on the disease that affects your child can be a resource, as can the many organizations, both local and national, that address some of the major childhood illnesses. Local and national organizations for the different types of therapists often have member listings on their websites, and there are numerous listing services (such as *Psychology Today*) that help therapists reach prospective clients. If you use such a website, be sure to look at its mission statement and values to discern any point of view on therapy it promotes, so you can determine whether it is compatible with what you are looking for. Don't neglect your insurance company's list of network providers! That is probably the fastest and easiest way to find someone who accepts your insurance, given that many clinicians in private practice don't take insurance.

We list some of these websites and resources in the Resources for Your Journey at the end of this book.

If your insurance plan doesn't cover therapy, and many don't, and your finances are too stretched to afford the out-of-pocket costs of therapy, do some research on counseling services in your area that specialize in lower fees or bill patients on a sliding scale. Many such organizations serve as training sites that help new, unlicensed therapists meet the training requirements and earn the clinical hours they need to become licensed. The clinicians providing services are supervised by licensed professionals in their field, and what they may lack in experience they often make up for in their enthusiasm and commitment to their patients.

In addition, many new online sources of therapeutic support are available. Some are email- and/or text based, and others are confidential online platforms that provide face-to-face contact. Some of these services would probably be effective for family sessions, but they could certainly work for adults and older children, providing support and expertise in a very cost-effective way.[3] Online video platforms can be more flexible, accommodating family or couple sessions as well as individual ones. Many providers in private practice also offer video conferencing options.[4] If you're considering online, email, or text-based therapy (also known as telehealth services) with a company or therapist that does not have a physical office, check to be sure the company is run by a licensed mental health professional. A 2017 article in the American Psychological Association's *Monitor on Psychology* noted that

> online therapy creates concerns over patient privacy, as well as legal and ethical issues [such as practicing outside the state in which one is licensed] for providers who contract to work for these companies, which may not share the same code of conduct and commitment to do no harm.[5]

Some clinicians may offer a first session at no cost, and most will be happy to provide at least a short conversation by phone, to give you a chance to ask some questions and get a sense of their style. In fact, we have reservations about clinicians who schedule an appointment without allowing you to speak briefly about your concerns and ask questions. In your initial conversation with a clinician, give them a short outline of your situation, and what you want the therapy to address, and then ask for some indication of how the therapist would approach it. Be sure to ask about the therapist's areas of specialization to make sure that they have the background for what you need. Some therapists, for instance, may specialize in the impact of medical issues on individuals and families; this would be very valuable background for your therapist to have. Don't assume that just because people hold a license that they are experts in the issues you are struggling with!

Many therapists take a "strengths-based" approach. This means different things to different therapists, but it can indicate a therapist who will approach the family and the individuals in it with a focus on their abilities rather than just the problems they are having. If ever you feel judged, criticized, or pathologized (that is, made to feel deficient or defective) by your therapist, discuss it with the therapist. If it continues, find someone else!

SUPPORT GROUPS

Support groups provide an opportunity for people of varying ages and backgrounds to offer one another encouragement and assistance in regard to a particular life circumstance. They are usually run by mental health or medical professionals, but they also may be run by laypeople who have been members for a considerable time, have dealt with the issue themselves, and then have received specialized training in running such a group. There are support groups for people dealing with the loss of a loved one; going through a divorce; struggling with various kinds of diagnoses, both medical and mental; or caring for someone with such a diagnosis, as well many other possibilities. Some groups may bring invited guests periodically, to provide expert information on either the illness or some aspect of its care. Some are intended for adults only, and others are for families, including extended family. And some support groups are child focused; the participants are children who have the health condition or their siblings. Many support groups are free; they are funded by donations or other sources.

Support groups offer many important benefits, especially the following:

- *They make your experience seem more "normal."* When you are sitting with people who truly understand what you are going through, you will start to realize "Oh, I am not going crazy; I am dealing with a crazy situation." Problems you may have been blaming yourself for, such as the difficulty of working with the medical system, become problems that are just part of the situation, not something that you in particular are doing wrong. You get to see that other people have times when they feel overwhelmed, think they are unable to continue, and believe they are failing everyone involved, and you can see clearly in those others this isn't true. This realization will help you take yourself off the hook, so to speak, and realize that these feelings are entirely normal. There is nothing more comforting than sharing your experience with a group of people who really get it.
- *You get exposure to different stages of the process.* Most support groups are ongoing, so some people in the group might be on Months 3–6 after their child's diagnosis, or even years down the road. Hearing others' stories can foster hope in your

family's ability to survive and even thrive in the face of this challenge. The support offered by these groups can help you see a way forward through the thicket of your current crisis and provide an opportunity to be mentored by people with more experience. Simply knowing that others are somehow managing this journey can help you feel more confident.

- *Other members offer good tips and advice.* A support group consists of ready-made experts who have the experience to provide specific tips and advice. People couch their suggestions in their own experience, which makes it more accessible and useful. Friends who are unfamiliar of the nuances of your experience tend to offer abstract advice, or tidbits from something they read or heard about. Support group members are on the inside track, and they can save you a lot of trial and error during your search for information, often offering connections to resources you might not even have thought of looking for. With their help, sometimes you can start anticipating future needs and reduce the pressure of continually having to deal with the unexpected.

- *Support groups also give you an opportunity, as time goes on, to offer your understanding, support, and useful advice to others.* Many people consider this the most helpful aspect of all. It gives meaning to your suffering, provides a sense of being part of a mutually supportive community, and enhances your sense of your own capability when what is going on may have left you feeling hopelessly incompetent. Getting to know people who are struggling even more than you have awakens a sense of compassion toward them, just as you received compassion from the longer term members of the group. Many spiritual paths speak of service as the way out of our own suffering, and a support group gives you that opportunity. It allows you to see and acknowledge your own strengths and abilities and the progress you have made toward managing a situation that at first felt impossible.

Support groups may be the single most helpful activity for everyone involved. Finding them is similar to the process of finding a therapist—make use of your medical team, other parents whose children have medical conditions, and the other resources we mentioned earlier.

WORKING WITH YOUR INSURANCE COMPANY

If you are among the most fortunate Americans, your health insurance is probably supplied by your employer. Public programs, such as Medicaid and the Children's Health Insurance Program (CHIP), offer various state plans for people in lower income brackets. Before the Patient Protection and Affordable Care Act (ACA),[6] people whose employer didn't cover their plan, and whose income was too high to qualify for public plans, were out of luck. They either bought expensive individual coverage on the open market or went without it. Since the passage of the ACA, however, people can now buy insurance coverage at group rates in state and federal marketplaces. You cannot be rejected or charged ridiculously high premiums for having a preexisting condition, and with the coverage come generous subsidies if you meet the income requirements. Although the ACA has helped many families obtain health coverage, it has also increased the complexity of the insurance market. You may need to explore numerous plans and options before you find the right one, and the stress of needing to sign up during designated periods can be intense.

Many insurance plans are not geared toward addressing the kinds of medical issues you are facing. Even with good insurance plans, you may have problems accessing knowledgeable pediatric and other specialists, getting authorizations for services (and a sufficient number of sessions), and being able to make timely appointments. You will likely be on your own as you coordinate care among different service providers. Many services, such as physical therapy, speech therapy, and in particular, home health services, which provide much-needed respite care, may not be covered.

In addition, there are a bewildering number of public and community resources stemming from various legislative mandates, which also offer needed services but are hard to navigate on your own. Title V of the Social Security Act[7] mandates maternal and child care services; the Individuals With Disabilities Education Improvement Act (IDEA)[8] requires early intervention and special education services; and the Supplemental Security Income (SSI) provisions of the Social Security Act[9] provide income-support benefits. There also are state services funded through such agencies as Departments of Mental Health and the Offices for People With Developmental Disabilities, as well as public insurance programs, such as the aforementioned Medicaid, which have also been greatly expanded under the ACA. You can find the websites for this alphabet soup of programs in the Resources for Your Journey at the end of the book.

One perhaps lesser known change the ACA made to the health insurance landscape is the "Concurrent Care for Children" provision, which requires state Medicaid programs to pay for both curative and palliative care services for children under age 21 who qualify.[10] In light of this provision, many private plans also now cover what is known as *pediatric palliative care*, *comfort care*, or *supportive care*. This type of care can begin as early as a child's diagnosis and is intended to work alongside any treatments that target the illness itself, or manage symptoms. We provide more details about this in Chapter 10.

Most parents with a child with special health care needs (CSHCN, the term used by public plans to cover a range of conditions, including chronic medical illness), even those fortunate enough to have private insurance, receive services from at least one or more of these community service organizations, in addition to their primary (and sometimes secondary) insurance.[11] For help navigating multiple services and providers, we recommend first checking what your health insurer can do for you. For example, some plans and programs will provide a case manager for your child's care, who can help you coordinate among caregivers and access community resources. In some situations, case managers may change so frequently that they aren't very helpful, but when case management is consistent over time parents find it a very useful resource. Although a good case manager won't relieve you entirely of the burden of coordinating the care of your child, they are knowledgeable about all the care required by your child's illness, as well as what community resources are available. They can help you find these resources and meet deadlines for applications.

We need to make a distinction between CSHCN and children whose chronic illness qualifies as a disability. In a helpful pamphlet from the Social Security website titled "Benefits for Children with Disabilities," *disability* is defined as having "a medical condition, or a combination of conditions, that result in 'marked and severe functional limitations'," meaning that the child has serious limitations on the activities, in particular those of daily life, in which they are able to engage as a result of their condition. Applying for disability benefits is a complicated and demanding process, but it could be well worth it. If your child's condition qualifies as a disability, you will be able to access more services through public programs (for example, CHIP and Medicaid) with fewer income restrictions than if the condition does not qualify.[12]

When looking for the right insurance plan, it pays to read the fine print of the benefits that will be provided. Parents of children who have a condition similar to your child's can be good resources when researching plans that cover the necessary treatment. You can also call the billing offices of providers you have been using to find out which insurance plans they accept. Most insurance companies also have representatives available by phone who can answer your questions, and often they provide booklets that list the providers who accept their various plans and the medications they will reimburse. Get all your information and questions together, and have this conversation before making your final commitment.

When communicating with your insurance company, whether it is a private corporation or a public program, approach them with confidence. You are a valued customer! If you are, or your company is, paying premiums for your coverage, remember that retaining you as a consumer is their plan. They want your business. With public programs, keep in mind that you are entitled to the benefits designated by the federal or state legislature that has mandated them. Still, dealing with insurance companies on the phone can be very frustrating. Keeping your cool and being unfailingly polite will get you farther than venting. The person on the phone is probably not responsible for the problems you're having, and you don't want to get a reputation as a "difficult" consumer. Learn to be assertive with strength, clarity, calm, and persistence.

Before making a call to your insurance provider, be clear about why you are making the call, what you want to learn or make happen, and what you want to say. Know your benefits, and what is covered and what is not, as well as your rights as an insurance consumer. Consult your records to be clear about anything that may be related to your conversation, which could include bills you have received and payments you have made; tests, procedures, and treatments your child has received, as well as the results; recommendations from your treatment team; and other documentation that will support your request. This could include information from reputable sources and published medical articles addressing the treatment options for the particular illness your child has. Remember to be clear and concise, provide only the most relevant information, and be ready to answer any questions the contact person may ask to facilitate her understanding of what is needed. Some of the information you might need to have at hand includes

- the name of the person who holds the policy, as well as their relationship to the patient, your child;
- your child's birth date; and
- identifying data, such as the policy number, case number, individual identification number, invoice number, and so on.

In order to have a productive conversation with both health care providers and insurance companies, you need to have all your information in one place, so you can reference it easily during the call if need be. Even if you have all the files you need on your computer, it may be difficult to access and refer to them quickly while you are on the phone. Perhaps a combination of hard copies and electronic files that you can open before the call will work for you. We recommend getting a spiral-bound notebook, the kind commonly found in drugstores and grocery stores, in which you can take notes on every conversation that you have. This provides a written record that you can refer to when you are following up. Many such notebooks include pockets where you can store loose papers, such as

- letters from the insurance company or program and from providers or any other people or programs involved in your child's care;
- bills and records of payments;
- tests and procedure results; and
- authorizations for procedures, treatments, and prescriptions.

It can be helpful to keep a small paper calendar as well, to help you track all the appointments and procedures as well as deadlines for filing paperwork and prescription renewals. Even if you prefer to keep a calendar on your phone, having it with all your other papers can make it easy to refer to. In the Resources for Your Journey we list many apps that can help with your calendar and organization.

During conversations with your insurance carrier, take notes in the spiral notebook. Be sure to include the following:

- date and time of the conversation;
- first and last name of person you are talking to, with their job title and phone extension number;
- notes regarding the substance of the conversation, including specific steps that are agreed upon—ask questions and repeat what you believe has been agreed to before writing it down;
- dates for any follow-up conversations to take place in writing or by phone, and who will start that conversation; and
- a direct number where this person can be reached, if available, in case you wish to clarify or confirm what has been agreed on.

After you hang up, follow up with either a letter or an email outlining the substance of the conversation, what has been agreed on, and any timeline involved, for you and for them.

If you are not getting the response you hope for, ask to speak to a supervisor, or whoever is directly above the person you are talking to. If they say that a particular test or service cannot be authorized, then ask to speak to a person who does have that authority. Persistence is effective, as long as you maintain your cool and don't take things personally.

If you have a case manager, know that they should be able to help you find other resources if the insurance people don't provide them. A case manager also should help you effectively navigate the insurance landscape. Don't take "No" for an answer! Think of yourself as an educator, explaining to the insurance program what children like yours actually need for effective treatment. Even health insurance providers can change coverage rules when they have more information. Your persistence could pave the way for better treatment for other children like yours and make the path easier for the parents who follow you.

Some pharmaceutical companies will offer coupons for reduced prices at pharmacies, or even, in some cases, provide the medication for free, so if there are medications your child needs but your insurance plan won't cover, or if the copay is beyond your means, reach out. You can contact the company that manufactures the medication, either by phone or online, to determine whether such coupons or waivers are available, and whether you qualify. We list some of these websites in the Resources for Your Journey.

WORKING WITH YOUR EMPLOYER

One of the biggest decisions you will have to make is whether or not to tell your employer that your child has a chronic medical illness. If you do share this information with your employer, then you also have to decide when and how to do it. Depending on your workplace and the kind of benefits your employer offers, you will either be in a situation that supports what you need, or you will find yourself threatened with the loss of your job. Even if you aren't the primary caregiver, you may find yourself having difficulty keeping up at work, and you may prefer to turn down promotions and extra projects in order to be more available to your family. Many workplaces lack flexibility, which can lead to parents sacrificing more career-focused work for pickup jobs with lower pay.[13]

If you are in a low-paying job, especially one in which your work schedule changes frequently, your choices may be even more difficult. You may have to transition from full- to part-time work or even stop working altogether. If it's an option, you might consider going from the private sector to a public sector position, where pay is often lower but job security and stability are higher.

Your first step is to find out if your workplace has a family leave policy. Remember, you don't have to take your time off all at once; if you are the one taking your child to the doctor's office, and you can arrange to always have your appointment on the same day, you will need to take off only one day at a time, or even half a day, if the appointments are predictable. Check with the human resources department about how to manage your leave on an ongoing basis.

Are you able to work from home one or more days a week? Can you set your own hours, so that if you need to come in late one day, you can stay late another day? More and more workplaces are starting to offer their employees options like these. If your workplace offers this kind of flexibility, and you feel confident about your boss's support, explaining to them what is going on, and what your child's ongoing needs look like, can lead to a conversation about how to work together so that everyone gets what they need.

If you suspect, however, that your workplace is liable to start setting up obstacles in response to learning about your situation, possibly as a way to move you out of your position, it may be best to keep silent. If you have to turn down promising work opportunities, however, the time may come when you will be forced to share what is going on at home. Turn to your union representative for advice, if you have a union job. Members of professional associations may have similar avenues for this kind of support. If you feel your employer will actually discriminate against you for taking care of your child, consider what is involved with filing an Equal Employment Opportunity Commission (EEOC) claim in the event that this does happen. Resolving a workplace discrimination claim in your favor can be a huge win for your family and possibly for others—however, pursuing it can also be a huge drain on your energy, so make sure that any action you take keeps in mind your own health and your family's best interests.

If you do shift work, you may already find it impossible to plan your life more than a week in advance. Companies that use shift workers have developed complex algorithms to maximize the company's efficiency and minimize their costs. But what's good for them can wreak havoc for you. It may be impossible to set up doctor's appointments or find regular child care with the limited amount of advance notice that comes with shift work.[14] If this is your reality, you can buffer yourself by developing a network of coworkers who can cover your shifts from time to time, and friends and family members who can jump in at the last minute with child care help.

BE PERSISTENT AND INSISTENT

It is an unfortunate reality that people who live in an economically challenged community are also more likely to have a child with a chronic illness. Low-income neighborhoods are more likely to be adjacent to toxic waste sites or to present other environmental risks. You may have difficulty getting adequate health care as well. Out-of-pocket expenses can make your family's finances even more shaky. SSI can help offset the impact of these added costs, and Medicaid may be able to absorb costs better for your family than for those with private health insurance.[15]

You may also face multiple challenges. If you use public transportation, you probably will have to find a friend or neighbor with a car to take your child home if she gets sick at school, or the school nurse might not release her. Also, if you use a low-fee clinic, in addition to having to sit for many hours waiting to be seen, you may have to see a different doctor each time you go. You may not even get a primary doctor assigned to your case! As a result, you won't be able to develop a strong relationship with your child's doctor, and will have to explain the same things visit after visit. The overall picture of your child's condition and progress, or lack thereof, may be missed. You may not get the referrals to specialists that you child needs and that are given automatically in more affluent settings. This is all the more reason to learn to be persistent and insistent.

Another obstacle you might be facing in all this is the lack of what is called "social" and "cultural" capital. "Social capital" refers to the resources in your social networks, including any groups you belong to, such as your church, mosque, or synagogue, or the parent–teacher association at your child's school. It includes your friends and neighbors as well as extended family and friends of friends. We tend to segregate ourselves economically in this country, with people of like incomes living in the same neighborhoods. Better paid medical professionals are thus more likely to live in affluent neighborhoods. Having medical personnel in your social network helps you feel more comfortable with other medical personnel you are dealing with. You can also use these contacts as resources for information about the medical field and how our system works. If you live in a less affluent community you may not have opportunities to create friendships with people who are doctors, for example.

"Cultural" capital refers to an individual's alignment with the dominant cultural norms where they live. It can also be defined as "the degree of mastery one has over cultural practices which a given society recognizes as legitimate."[16] Because attributes such as white skin, English as a first language, U.S. citizenship, higher levels of education, and generally conforming to so-called "American" culture are considered standard by some people, many people of color, immigrants, and those with less education get the short end of the stick. People in the so-called "majority" culture may feel more comfortable speaking up, and they may be listened to more seriously when they do.

The solution to cases of both limited social capital and limited cultural capital is the same: Work through the friends and family in your network to find people who can lend their own knowledge and capital to help your family. For example, think about who in your network is involved in the health care system. This could include the school nurse. Sources could also be a distant cousin, or a friend of a friend who works in a hospital or other health care setting. Talk with the people you know and try to identify people you could connect with who might be able to share their knowledge with you and help you understand better how to work the system for your child. Finding someone like this to consult with can help you get better results.

If English is not your first language, know that health care clinics and hospitals should provide an interpreter so that you and your health care providers can fully understand each other. You may have to insist that one be provided. Children who are more adapted to U.S. culture and speak better English than their parents can help raise the cultural capital of the family by serving as an interpreter. This can be difficult for the child, however, because it puts them in a position of responsibility they may not feel ready for. In addition, professionals may not take children as seriously as they do adults. A native English speaker in your network who would be willing to accompany you to a particularly important appointment can be helpful, and they might be in a better position to lobby for something you have not been able to make happen, such as a referral to a specialist.[17]

There is no doubt the issues we have discussed can be significant challenges. We hope that by openly talking about them you will be better prepared to ferret out additional support within your networks so you can more effectively work with medical providers to get the best possible care for your child. Every child deserves the best of what our system has to offer.

FINDING CHILD CARE AND RESPITE CARE

You might be having a hard time finding appropriate care for your child and any other children you have. You may need this care to cover times when you are working or just to get some occasional relief from the relentless tasks that accompany being the parent of a child with a chronic illness. If the illness requires complex or very diligent care, trusting someone else to do as good a job as you do can be difficult. Child care in general is difficult to find, and it is doubly hard to find people who are willing, capable, and knowledgeable enough to provide the care your child needs. This is especially true if she needs help with tasks of daily life, but even if the condition is less demanding, such as asthma, but still involves the possibility of an emergency, care can be quite challenging.[18] Accessible and more cost-effective community child care centers may not be willing to accept children with special medical needs.[19]

If you are reading this section, you may have already exhausted nearby family members and friends who might be able and willing to help with child care. Other parents of children with chronic illness, even if the illness is not the same as the one your child has, are often the next-best resources. Health care providers, any therapists you're working with, or even the child's school or teachers may be able to provide resources or referrals. Home care nurses have often been a bridge for families trying to address their ill child's needs outside of a medical setting.[20] Remember, too, that some of the public programs we have discussed provide, at no cost, respite care with appropriate caregivers, and these costs may be covered if you are working with a "comfort" or "supportive" care team (see Chapter 10). If you are using one of these programs, be sure to determine what, exactly, is covered.

There are numerous online resources where you can list your specific needs, even in terms of required medical capacities, as a filter to find appropriate child care. We list several of these in the Resources for Your Journey at the end of the book. The American Autism Association has published a pamphlet, available on their website, that describes all these important steps and considerations. Although a discussion of autism itself is beyond the scope of this book, children with autism need caregivers who have particular skills, so the advice given in the pamphlet applies equally well to children with chronic medical illnesses.[21]

Before beginning your search for child care, list all the specific requirements that are necessary for you to feel comfortable leaving your child in someone else's care. For example, although being able to give CPR to a child appropriately would be beneficial for any family, your child's illness may make that a requirement. Once you are clear about the skills you deem necessary, not just for the appropriate care of your child but also to give you the confidence to leave your child without undue worry (are you ever completely free of worry when your child has a chronic illness?), you can begin your search for the right caregiver.

Before engaging someone, thoroughly check their references; perhaps do a background check—some online resources do this as part of the service they provide—and make sure that person has whatever certificates or qualifications you have decided are important. Then interview them; in person is best, but an online interview may end up being more convenient and keeps the process moving. Be sure to ask them about their experience working with children who have chronic illnesses. What kinds of medical procedures that you need done have they actually performed for other children? What additional training might they need? If your child is sensitive to strangers, especially in regard to their medical needs, find out how available the person is for the times you need someone, and how consistent they can be. Invite them into your home, where you can supervise them as they practice any pertinent procedures until you feel satisfied that they are entirely capable. Depending on the situation, you may have to pay them for their time, but the investment will be well worth the peace of mind you will have when you are away from home.[22]

All parents need to leave appropriate contact information when leaving their children with other caregivers, but in your case this is absolutely crucial. If you are not going to be available, be sure to have someone knowledgeable to back you up who can be accessed in your absence, particularly if you are going to be gone overnight or will be out of the immediate area. You will want to include on your list symptoms and indications that require a call to the doctor or a visit to the emergency room. Even though you will have already told them these things, do write them down so they have all your instructions available to refer to. Include a detailed description of the information you have already given them about your child's care, such as medication schedules and means of administering, and where to find the medication and any other equipment necessary, as well as step-by-step instructions for any medical procedures required. Consider also giving caregivers a notarized letter that grants your permission to seek medical care for your child if needed. As with any family, you want to be clear about behavioral limits for all your children, and how you expect them to be handled, as well as the usual bedtime routines.

We cannot stress too strongly the importance of taking time off, both as respite care if you are the primary caregiver and to provide intimate time, if you are part of a couple, to preserve the strength of your connection. In addition to the benefits for the parents, leaving your child with someone else is also a way to help develop the independence he may need in the future. It is easy for parents of a child with chronic illness to begin to believe that they are the only ones who can really care for him, but this belief is a disservice to the child. Learning that he can trust people other than his parents to help him, and gradually learning to take ownership of his condition as his age and maturity increase, he can begin to help the helper. This process can foster a sense of agency in the face of an illness that can leave him feeling at the mercy of life's twists and turns, especially if his condition means he will need some sort of care or help throughout his life. That sense of empowerment can support better emotional adjustment and mental health outcomes.

NEXT STEP: CONSIDER PARTICIPATING IN CLINICAL RESEARCH

Sometimes insurance companies will not provide reimbursement for a promising treatment because it is still considered experimental or unproven. If there are drug or treatment trials in process, and your child fits the criteria, you may be able to participate in one, with the hope of receiving the treatment they are researching. You may also be invited to join a study, because researchers often contact health care providers looking for likely subjects. It is important to be clear about the kinds of studies that exist with regard to the treatment of diseases, as well as how they are conducted and what that means about the likelihood of your child getting a direct health benefit from participation.

There are two basic kinds of studies:

1. Observational studies, which simply observe the course of the disease and its response to existing treatments and medications. This may include administering various minor laboratory procedures, such as blood tests.
2. Intervention studies, which are intended to determine the effectiveness of some new treatment or medication.

The best intervention studies include what is called a "control"— that is, in addition to the group getting the intervention, there is a group of people who do not get the new treatment or drug. The purpose is to determine whether the effects of the drug or treatment exceed the so-called "placebo effect." A placebo is either a substance that has no effects on human physiology, such as a sugar pill, or a meaningless or irrelevant treatment, such as talking with someone about the weather. Such is the power of the human mind that even the *suggestion* that a treatment or medication might be helpful can lead to improvements for some people! In order to show that the chosen intervention exceeds the placebo effect, these studies include a group of people who are not receiving the treatment but think they are. Researchers achieve this by what is called a "double-blind" technique, in which neither the researchers, nor those administering the intervention, nor the study subjects know which category they belong to. If the results from the control group equal or even exceed the effects of the intervention being studied, the researchers will conclude that the placebo effect is active and that the proposed intervention is not actually effective.

These are important distinctions to make, because the possibility of a new, effective treatment can be especially appealing to you if you have been frustrated by the treatments or medications currently available. However, there are some important things to understand about participating in intervention research:

- The purpose of the research is *not* to treat your child. It is to determine how well the proposed intervention works, or if it works at all.
- There is no guarantee that your child will get any health benefit stemming directly from the intervention being studied. There are situations in which research studies have been interrupted when it becomes clear that the intervention is so effective—or so dangerous—that to continue the research would be unethical, and the intervention is either offered to all subjects or ended.

Be clear and honest with your child about what results will likely be. Younger children are more prone to conclude that they will receive some direct benefit, even with observational studies, than older children. "Therapeutic optimism"—the hope for personal benefit beyond what study participation is actually likely to achieve—can lead to disappointment, regret, or resentment, for both adults and children.[23]

If you are asked, or wish to join, either an observational study or an intervention study, you and your child will need to sign an informed consent form, which should describe to you what is required of you and your child in order to participate and what the potential benefits and risks are. Ask questions so you are clear about the kind of study it is and exactly what it requires of you both. The following are some collateral, or indirect, benefits from participating in research studies:

- They advance scientific knowledge and may lead to better interventions and treatment down the road.
- They give you a sense that you are contributing to a process that may help other parents and children and may improve everyone's understanding of the disease process.
- Even observational studies, in which no intervention is actually being tested, may result in enhanced understanding and monitoring of your child's condition, because of the regular meetings with health care providers and various tests that may be part of the study's protocol and provided at no cost to you.

If you are interested in finding a clinical trial, speak to your health care provider. You can also find websites that provide this information, such as **clinicaltrials.gov**, WebMD (**https://www.webmd.com**), and **https://www.cancer.gov/about-cancer/treatment/clinical-trials/search/trial-guide**.

CHAPTER 4

COMMUNICATING WITH YOUR CHILD: IT'S A TWO-WAY STREET

Over the course of the previous three chapters we've offered tips for loving and accepting yourself—your strengths, your limitations—both as an individual and as a parent. In this chapter we show you how to share that love and acceptance with your child who has a chronic illness. All children need love and acceptance, maybe even more so when they have a special health condition. Seventeen-year-old Max, one of Frank's patients, illustrated this need vividly:

> Because of my ostomy, I am unable to do certain sports in school. The pain medication for my condition makes me feel horrible. I hate that my week is filled with appointment after appointment. I have no time for myself. I hate to be reminded every day that I have a disease and that I'm different. I hate this bag that I have to wear. Although it helps me, I hate when I look in the mirror after I shower. It's a constant reminder to me.

Loving a child who feels like Max does requires being honest. It's true that we are our children's guardians and protectors. As parents, we see our role as making the pain and hurt go away. As much as we want to do this, we know that it's unrealistic. That's why in this chapter we want to give you some ways to talk openly with your child about their medical diagnosis. We offer tips for helping your child manage their emotions, in ways appropriate for their age and developmental stage. We also include information about how to set limits and behavior expectations for your child.

When we create structure and consistency for our children around interacting with others and managing emotions, we buffer them (at least a little bit) from the unpredictability of their illness. We give them things they can control when so much is out of their control. Even if your child has survived life-threatening episodes, you can still give them a sense of safety and security. By modeling clear, predictable, consistent behaviors, you help make their world seem a bit less scary. We are a sounding board for our children. However, despite their situation, your child shouldn't be allowed to be verbally or physically aggressive toward you or others. It is okay to be angry, but there need to be limits regarding the use of inappropriate language, name calling, aggressiveness toward anyone in the house or outside of the home, or destruction of property.

BREAKING THE NEWS TO YOUR CHILD ABOUT THEIR ILLNESS

You may dread talking with your child about their medical diagnosis and all that it may encompass. Procedures are uncomfortable, needles hurt, and medications can taste horrible. Our job as parents isn't to take the pain away or prevent it from ever happening; instead, it's to be available to our children and provide emotional support as well as an open door for communication. We need to help our children navigate through the thoughts, words, and emotions that occur when we disclose to them that they have a chronic illness.

Sharing the news is hard because you may also be feeling strong emotions, such as anger, confusion, hurt, and loss. Children sense our feelings through the tone of our voice and our body language. You can be proactive about how you show your own feelings by learning as much as you can about the diagnosis and by practicing the tips for self-care that we shared in Chapter 2.

As children grow, they will take more and more responsibility for their own health information and play a greater role in their own care. When we teach our children about their health, we are empowering them to learn how to advocate for themselves and engage in self-care that will keep them safe and healthy when you are not around.

How Much Do I Tell My Child About What Is Happening to Them?

We advise you, as parents, to be as open and honest as possible with your child and talk in a way they can understand. If they think their illness is a taboo topic, they will not have words for discussing it when they are responsible for managing the condition themselves. We encourage you to give your child the words they need to educate them, calm any anxiety, enable them to get help if needed, and advocate for themselves.

Provide information in simple language. Younger children may understand things better with pictures. Some organizations have created materials for young children, such as comic books or coloring books, that are illustrated in a way your child will readily understand. When you read books with your child, you can explore and discuss what the characters are thinking and feeling in the story as well as recognize and label facial expressions. There are also picture books and YouTube videos related to certain conditions that can help you discuss things with your child and help them identify, express, and cope with their feelings. Some of these are listed in the Resources for Your Journey at the end of this book.

Typically, children have the following sorts of questions:

- "Will it hurt?"
- "How does the medicine taste?"
- "Will I miss school?"
- "Will I not be able to play with friends?"
- "Will I be able to participate in my favorite activity?"
- "How long will this test take?"
- "How long will I be sick?"
- "Why am I taking this medication/having this test?"

Can you think of other questions your child may ask you?

Older children may have concerns about the side effects of medications, treatments, and procedures as well as how their illness may affect their social life. You know your child best and understand how they handle things that are difficult to hear and understand.

Be Open, and Don't Lie to Your Child

Children are more perceptive than we give them credit for. Just as we know when our children are lying to us, they know when we are not telling the whole truth. Lying to children will lead to mistrust and create anxiety, which can spill over into other parts of life beyond their illness and treatment. Answer your child's questions honestly and directly.

Don't avoid talking about the illness with your child and family. You don't want them to hear things from someone else. Ignoring their illness can create fear and anxiety. They may interpret your silence or lack of desire to discuss what is going on as a signal that something is much worse, that there is something to be afraid of.

That said, it's also a good idea to *not* give your child more information if they are not asking for it. Giving smaller amounts of information at a time allows your child to absorb what you are telling them. They may not be emotionally ready to know everything about their illness all at once. Think about when you heard the news—it was hard enough for you as an adult to integrate all that was being told to you! Your child's growing mind may not be ready to absorb all of the information.

Pay attention to your child's nonverbal behavior, which may speak louder than words. Watch facial expressions and body language such as turning away, crossing of arms, changes in skin color. If you are unsure of what to say, how to present it, or how much to say, consult your health care provider or a mental health specialist. These professionals can give you information on how to explain the illness in a way your child will understand and how to deal with the possible emotional and behavioral fallout. One intervention is *play therapy*, a technique used by some mental health clinicians. Through various play activities children are provided the opportunity to explore their feelings and thoughts about what is going on in their lives. *Medical play*, in which children use medical props and choose their role in imagined scenarios, is especially useful. It helps them become familiar with the medical aspects of their experience and provides the opportunity to explore what it's like to be the doctor, the nurse, or the parent. In caring for their "patient" they may reveal fears and worries as well as misconceptions about their illness. In Chapter 7 we explore in more detail different types of professionals who work with children with special health needs, and we provide some tips for how to get your questions answered.

MANAGING THE BOOSTER SEATS: TALKING WITH YOUR PRESCHOOL-AGE CHILD

Young children understand the concept of being sick; however, they may not understand the cause and nature of the illness. Their fear of being hurt and separated from their loved ones is strong during this period of development.[1] Make sure they know, above all else, that you or another trusted family member will be by their side whenever possible.

Children at this age may make the association that they did something to cause them to be ill.[2] Make sure your child understands that they did nothing to cause their illness. They are too young to understand the long-term progression of their illness, or how far away next month or next week's appointment is. Their timeline is short, so stay in the immediate present as much as possible.

Preschool-age children are beginning to develop a sense of themselves as separate from others. In cultures that place a high value on individuality, experts will say that your child wants independence. This is why you may see your child begin to refuse medications and treatments. When possible, give them choices, but don't do this unless there really *is* a choice. For example, don't ask, "Do you want to take your medication now?" Most likely the answer will be an emphatic "No!" However, you might be flexible in scheduling doctor's appointments and certain tests and procedures, for example, "Do you want to have your blood test before or after your game?" or "Do you want the pill or the liquid first?" Real choices help you avoid power struggles and build trust and security with your child.

Never deny or minimize your child's feelings or give them the impression that what they are feeling is "wrong," "irrational," "silly," or "sissy-like." Don't make statements like "There is no reason to be that upset about this" or "You are making a bigger deal about this than there really needs to be." When we respond this way, we are being judgmental and rejecting what our child is feeling. Dismissing feelings will inevitably create a wall between you and your child.

Denying or minimizing your child's feelings may be an indication that you are having difficulty dealing with your child's feelings.

We need to communicate respect and openness to what our child is experiencing even if we believe their reactions are over the top or frivolous.

Help Them Find Ways to Participate in the Medical Regimen

Because small children cannot manage their own regimens, whether medical procedures or simple day-to-day routines, you will naturally be doing all these things for them. In the same way, however, that you are teaching them to do things themselves, like putting on clothes, look for ways to involve them and empower them in regard to the medical procedures that are necessary for their daily life. This can be as simple as giving your child the job of playing with a toy or singing a song as a distraction, looking into your eyes and breathing with you as part of a relaxation effort, or focusing on a video. Emphasize how helpful it is when he "does his job." At this age, most children are still focused on their parents and immediate family and truly desire to please you. Expressing pride in his ability not only invites his cooperation in the future but also emphasizes the areas where he does have some control, which can be empowering in the face of so much that he does not control.

Have Appropriate Expectations

Even though your child has some limitations because of her medical condition, she can still be expected to develop the skills appropriate for her age and participate in household chores, adapted to her particular situation. If there are tasks she truly cannot perform, that you might normally expect a child of her age to do, either adapt the task so she can perform it or substitute a task more suited to her capabilities. Having expectations for your child's behavior helps her develop the social and emotional competence she needs to feel accepted in the world outside the family. Remember that because she was diagnosed very early in life, she is probably much more accepting of it than you are, or than an older child would be. It is all she has ever known, and so it is more likely to be knit into her self-image and identity in a way that is much harder for older people to accomplish.

We tend to be familiar with the challenges we have had and see them as more doable than challenges we see other people face. Have respect for your child's ability to adapt, and know that she can excel despite whatever limitations her illness imposes.

The danger lurking here is developing an overly protective attitude toward your child. Feeling protective of a young child makes sense, and in fact you are still at the stage of doing many things for him. If you act like you don't think he is capable, however, there is a good chance that he will see himself in the same way—as incapable of doing what his peers can do. This will make it hard for him to learn to care for himself, develop a sense of competence, and have good relationships with peers.

Regressions and Tantrums

If your family is going through changes, such as the birth of a new sibling, a new daily routine, a new babysitter, a family member's illness or death, moving to a new home, or conflict in the home, your child may regress (act younger or return to "baby" behaviors). This can actually be a way for a child to get their emotional needs met at times when they feel overwhelmed. An example of a regression at this age relates to potty training. Your child may have been potty trained and doing very well. Chronic illness and all that may accompany it (tests, procedures, separations) may cause the child to have bowel and bladder accidents or begin again at square one. Regressions can also be emotional and take the form of angry outbursts or refusing to talk.[3]

Little children have big emotions. They can be plunged into despair one minute and laughing and joyful 10 minutes later. Babies have only one way to let you know something is wrong—crying, but just because your child is now a talkative 3- or 4-year-old doesn't mean they know how to express their feelings to get what they want or need. If you notice how being stirred up emotionally can short-circuit your clear thinking, think of how much that is the case for a preschooler, who does not yet have the language to communicate with you what they are experiencing.

All of this doesn't mean that tantrums are okay! Just remember that a tantrum may be the only way the child, at that moment, can deal with the emotional storms that have taken hold. He needs help developing the language that will eventually enable him to simply say that he is upset or angry or afraid. You can help first by articulating what you see, or what you imagine, he is feeling, for example, "You're upset that you can't do this. I bet you're thinking it's pretty unfair, huh?" or "Boy, I can see that you really want that candy bar, but you know we have dinner waiting at home."

The general guideline is never give in to a tantrum, because the child then learns it is a way to get what she wants. And she will use it, again and again. In fact, giving in only occasionally can be the worst strategy because irregular reinforcement is the most difficult kind to stop. Think about slot machines: They are set up to operate on a schedule of irregular reinforcement. Every once in awhile you win, which encourages you to continue playing.

Develop a strategy of dealing with tantrums that includes empathy for the feelings she is having—"I'm sorry you're so upset," or "I can see it is really hard for you not to get what you want"—with a firm boundary that says, "This is not the way to get what you want." Instead, say something like, "I understand you're upset, and I am sorry this is hard for you, but this is not appropriate behavior for the grocery store, so you need to pull yourself together or we will have to leave."

Young children also may react aggressively to their illness by biting, throwing toys and other objects, and hitting others.[4] Empathize with their feelings, but be consistent with setting limits to and boundaries around acting-out behaviors. Don't be afraid to implement consequences for behavior. We talk more about setting boundaries and consequences for misbehaviors in the next section. All children require structure and security, especially when illness leads to frequent disruptions in their routines.

TEACHING THEM TO BUCKLE UP: TALKING WITH YOUR SCHOOL-AGE CHILD

School-age children are opening up to the world. They are engaged in learning, and friends are becoming more important.

> At first I was hurt my daughter wanted to spend more time her friends than with me. I felt hurt because of everything I do for her regarding her care. After speaking with a friend, I realized my daughter wasn't being mean or disrespectful. She was being a kid and doing what other kids do. I had to check myself. I made this about me, and that wasn't fair to my daughter. In the beginning I placed some guilt on my daughter, which I apologized for. My feelings of hurt were real. I was happy that she felt happy to do friend things.
> —Mother of an 11-year-old girl with a chronic illness

As your child's brain and thinking skills increase, so too does their understanding of their illness and what is happening to them. Like preschoolers, however, they may make false connections, such as believing that they are sick because they were not nice to their siblings, they are not a good person, or they are not a good student. When you talk to your child about this, teach them to value themselves as a human being and stop blaming themselves. Help them understand that their condition is not their fault.

When you do give your child information about their medical situation, explain things in a concrete way. Children at this age are still very black-and-white thinkers. They may take things quite literally. Hearing someone say they need to "take some blood" may have them wonder if they will have enough blood left! Answer the questions they ask of you, but do not get overly detailed and technical.

Because the importance of friends and activities is mounting at this age, your child may feel anger and resentment at having to miss time and experiences with friends at school, sports, sleepovers, and other related activities. Be careful not to be too overprotective of your child by limiting their participation in such activities. We want to support their confidence and the development of healthy social relationships. As a parent, it may be difficult to let go, but peer interaction and activities are important for your child's emotional growth and development. If you have specific concerns about germs, not getting enough rest, or exposure to other dangers, it's a good idea to reach out to other parents, your community, or your health provider for advice.

Let Feelings Be a Part of the Daily Routine

It may be helpful to set up a daily time each day to talk. Cars are great places to have conversations, provided the discussion does not get heated. When in a car, you have a captive audience. If things do start to get heated, pull the car over, have everyone cool down, and leave the conversation for another time. Safety comes first.

Find a quiet, private space, away from any interruptions from others or electronic devices, to talk with your child. This conveys respect and the importance of sharing thoughts and feelings. You can open the conversation by saying, "Is there anything you want to share with me or need me to know?" or ask if they've been saving any topics to ask or talk about. For a young child who has difficulty expressing feelings, a fun activity is to create an actual "feelings box" where they can place their feelings and thoughts at night or any time of the day. Get a shoebox, some arts and crafts supplies, and old magazines. In the box, words can be written out on paper, or pictures can be either drawn or cut out from magazines. Having a feelings box may allow the child to unload what is weighing on their mind and place it somewhere to be discussed at another time when they are ready to share. Sometimes having a child write feelings down or find or create images of those feelings helps them articulate what is going on for them. Pick a special one-on-one time of the day to go through the box and discuss the contents. You could even refer to your "daily talk" routine as the time when you "open up the box" to see what needs to be "unpacked."

Help your child identify triggers to their feelings and behaviors. Triggers can be body related (side effects of medication, being tired, being hungry or "hangry," not feeling well), social (being rejected by a peer or a crush, not being invited to a party, seeing something unsettling on social media), or cognitive, that is, thoughts (thinking about how unfair it is to have this illness, thoughts of the future with the illness, thoughts about school).

For older school-age children, you can suggest keeping a feelings journal. When we journal, it helps us see our feelings and problems in more concrete ways and makes problem solving easier. Writing frees us from filters, judgments, and defenses that can hold us back when we speak. It helps get what is going on in our heads onto paper. Journaling can make children feel less burdened when they have too many thoughts and feelings running through their minds. Teens and adults can journal, too!

Foster Friendships and Fun

For a parent with a chronically ill child, driving and time management become more complicated during the elementary school years. Now add in doctor appointments, tests, procedures, various therapies, tutoring, and so on, and it's clear you have a lot to juggle. Your child may feel isolated and different from her peers because of her chronic illness and all the extra commitments involved. It is really important for parents to foster friendships during these years.

We also need to include fun. Life is difficult for a child with a chronic illness. They may interact with many adults in the course of their days and spend little time with friends. Letting your child get together with friends once or twice a week can help balance medical care and other obligations. Doing fun things with friends eases stress and makes it easier for your child to feel "normal" in a not-so-normal situation. If you can organize play dates around common interests that are also adapted to your child's needs (especially at home, where you have more control), you can help her emphasize what she has in common with friends and cast her chronic illness into the background.

Research has demonstrated that children with chronic illnesses may not show or develop certain skills or competencies because of reasons such as hospital stays, parental overprotection, and other factors. In an analysis of 954 studies that looked at the academic, physical, and social functioning of children and adolescents with chronic physical illnesses, researchers found that children with visible illnesses showed below-average impairment in social functioning. This is interesting because you might think children with visible illnesses would be *more* subject to social rejection and bullying. The researchers also found that children with nonvisible illnesses, such as kidney or liver disease, showed more impairment in social functioning despite the fact that their illness was not able to be seen.[5]

This means that some kids—even, and especially, those with invisible illnesses—may need help in the "social functioning" or "friend-making" department. If the play date approach doesn't work for your child, another approach is to help him develop special skills that his peers can enjoy and admire. Is he interested in coding; does he enjoy singing or art? Is he good at making his friends laugh? When the friends clue into and enjoy whatever his special talent is, they forget about the ways his chronic illness sets him apart and see him with different eyes. And through that process of fitting in, he also experiences himself as part of "normal" life.[6]

Play continues to be an excellent means by which children at this age express themselves. It can create a sense of control in an uncontrollable situation. It also provides predictability, which is often absent during the course of an illness. Play also provides a healthy diversion from not feeling well, doctor visits, uncomfortable procedures, and being in the hospital.

If your child's condition prevents her from playing a sport, perhaps there is another role that will let her contribute to the success of the team. Coaches in extracurricular sports are often volunteers and need help with organizational tasks, keeping score, tracking statistics, and so on. Playing a supporting role will help her develop skills that are recognized by her peers as useful and important, even though they are not the physical skills required by the sport. Through all these approaches, you are developing the whole child, seeing her beyond—and helping her see herself beyond—the limitations of her chronic illness.

Help Your Child Feel Safe

When children of this age are diagnosed, they may be hesitant to ask questions, or they may pretend to know something when they do not. They are starting to develop more awareness of their illness, the treatments, the consequences of their illness, its treatments, the consequences of both, and to understand the concept of death. Ask your child on a regular basis what they understand, and have them relay their understanding back to you. Reassurance can go a long way, and it can take different forms. Don't we all like to be told we have someone on our side? Don't we all appreciate kind, gentle, and comforting words when life is difficult? Your child probably does, too.

Develop and Communicate Behavioral Expectations

At this age, although you are still probably doing many of the main medical maintenance tasks, keeping track of schedules, and conversing with your medical team, look for ways your child can participate in her own self-management. Organization can be challenging. Behavior charts are a great way to keep things organized and keep children accountable for their chores or behaviors. That can include things like brushing teeth, putting clothes out for school the night before, making the bed, setting the table for dinner, or any of a number of tasks and behaviors you want to encourage. This may also include aspects of her medical care that are appropriate for her to manage. She could help you plan menus and chose nutritious, healthy snacks, or she could enter her blood pressure into a medical log. Behavior charts can also include items such as using appropriate words when expressing thoughts and feelings, keeping one's hands to oneself, and such. We encourage you to search online for various behavior charts and find ones that fit your family's and child's needs.

You can customize them and even decorate them with clip art of superheroes and other kid-friendly images.

Think through what tasks are appropriate for both your child's age and medical condition. Does he have mobility issues? If so, assign things that can be done in one place, like folding the laundry. If he is usually too tired in the evening because of his illness, plan a task he can do early in the day, perhaps before school, or on a weekend. Children this age love rewards; even simple things like stickers can be an encouragement. Special time with you is a good reward, too.

Having boundaries around misbehavior is also important; set up rules with clear consequences, and then let the consequences do the job for you. If there is a time set for turning off the TV or video games, be clear about what will happen if your child does not comply. Will there be a warning? A worsening consequence for the number of warnings needed to get them to shut it off? Set consequences, such as a day without their game for one warning, 3 days without for two warnings, and a week without them for three. This is only an example, and it might not be the right schedule for your household.

The main point is that if the rules are made clear ahead of time, he cannot complain that things are unfair, because he had the information he needed to make a good decision. But by all means be sympathetic with his dilemma. Let him know you understand how difficult it is, then remind him that he is ultimately in charge of what happens and that next time he can make a different choice! When he owns his choices, he will take more responsibility for his behavior and avoid blaming you and others.

What does all this have to do with children who have a chronic illness? First of all, they are likely to have a lot of limits as a result of their condition; they may have to undergo uncomfortable procedures, watch what they eat, take medication on a schedule, and endure many interventions that interrupt their day and make their life more difficult. It can be tempting to make the rest of their life that much easier. If you do, however, you will do them no favors! Although the time when they will leave the family home lies in the future, now is when they must develop their sense of competence in the world. If you give them an easy pass through these important, formative tasks, they will be unequipped when the time comes to handle what life brings.

Remember that school is essentially your child's "job," so encouraging her to keep up with her assignments will ensure she stays on track both academically and socially. Of course, if your child is having an acute episode, accommodations may need to be made, but expecting children to keep up with their peers in terms of finishing their homework, handing it in on time, and studying for tests encourages them to make the effort even when it is difficult. Your child is likely to take her cues from you as to what she is capable of, so if your expectations are too low she will assume that she does not have the ability to keep up. Unless her illness affects her cognitive abilities, there is no reason to automatically expect that she cannot satisfactorily complete the requirements of school, given some flexibility depending on her symptoms and their severity.

DRIVING LESSONS: CONVERSATIONS WITH YOUR TEEN

As children mature, their understanding of medical issues grows more nuanced and sophisticated. Your teen may have had their illness for some time now, or they may have just been diagnosed. This is a good time to clarify any misunderstandings they may have developed about their illness and offer more detailed explanations. Invite your teen to describe what they understand about their condition. You can share the information you have, encourage them to ask questions of their health care providers, and suggest they do research on their own. School-based information, or that obtained from illness-focused camps, can also be very helpful. Input from many different sources will increase your child's understanding of the process of the illness and help them recognize their symptoms better. It can also help them see the illness as simply a fact of their existence, thus lowering their anxiety and strengthening their ability to self-manage.[7]

Adolescence is a time when the child's identity develops and they begin to separate from family. Teens will often be concerned about how their illness affects their social relationships (friendships, dating) and their school and extracurricular activities. During this stage of development teens want to be more involved in their care and be part of the decision-making process regarding treatments and medications; however, they can feel ambivalent about taking on the responsibilities for their disease management. The challenge for you at this stage is to begin the process of shifting your role from manager of the illness to a coach for your child in the face of this ambivalence. Over the long term, adolescents who experience themselves as competent to handle their lives have better health behaviors, adhere more closely to their medical routines, and more effectively manage their disease overall.[8] In this section we emphasize tips for you to support your teenager in monitoring and managing their chronic illness.

Your Teen Still Needs You

The journey of adolescence is quite a trip. Your child may act like they do not need you, but deep down they do. They also think they know it all and see you as a dinosaur. You may often be told, "You just don't understand!" Sometimes they're right—you really don't understand what's going on. But know that this kind of statement also has a function: It keeps you, the parent, at a distance so your teen is in a better position to win the power struggle of independence.

Regardless of the fact that your teenager may act like a little adult, they are not adults—yet. They are still children, and they still need you. An adolescent with a chronic illness may be more prone to rebellious acting out.[9] They may engage in self-destructive choices, and if they do it's possible they're driven by the attitude of, "Who cares anyway? I have a chronic health condition. Might as well live it up now." This is a very dangerous mindset for your teen to possess. When you hear or see your adolescent engage in that "I don't care" attitude, meet those statements with love, empathy, and understanding. This is the time to listen to your teen, not lecture them.

Because of brain changes in adolescence, a process that goes well into the 20s, teens are able to understand abstract concepts, and they begin to see themselves, for the first time, as other people may be seeing them. This is the source of your teen's extreme self-consciousness and obsession with how they look![10] Along with this they may develop a story about themselves as utterly different and unique, as they have so many first-time-ever experiences. They may feel that no one has ever felt the way they do or could ever fully understand them. David Elkind refers to this as a "personal fable," and the extreme self-consciousness, that sense that everyone is always looking at them, as the "imaginary audience." Unfortunately, along with this uniqueness comes a sense of invulnerability that may lead them to take risks because "it can't happen to me."[11]

As a result of all this physical and emotional turmoil, teenagers may, regardless of their illness, experiment with alcohol, vaping, and other substances. They may use substances to self-medicate, based on advice from peers or misinformation they find online. They may also use other behaviors to numb or deny their feelings: overeating, engaging in risky sexual behavior, or self-harm. Seek help to address these harmful behaviors.

If your child is "medicating" in this way, it may also be because they do not know what to do with what they are feeling and thinking.

They have nowhere to park these powerful emotions, thoughts, images, and bodily sensations. For example, your older child may actually *want* to make you angry, because they want you to feel like they do. The goal here is to recognize this and not fall into responding in a way that is hurtful or damaging to the relationship. Our advice is to drop the metaphorical tennis racquet and get off the court. A person cannot play tennis by themselves. When your child wants to engage in unhealthy communication with you, tell them that it's a good time to take a break and revisit the topic later. Let them know you are not avoiding a conversation but simply need to break so that the conflict does not escalate.

At times when your children have the "I don't care" attitude it brings up strong feelings in you, such as anger and frustration. These emotions can be a cover for our fear and sadness. Be mindful not to respond in a dismissive way by saying things like "Oh, you don't mean that" or "Get over it. Just deal." Do not make it about you, either. Statements like "You think this has been easy on me?" "You're not the only one running around for appointments," and "This is hard on everyone" create a huge communication barrier and dump a whole bucket of guilt on your teen. Your issues with your child's illness should not be placed onto your child. Speak with another adult or a professional about your fears, frustrations, and anger.

Appearance and Fitting In

Because appearance and fitting in are so critical to teenagers, it is important that they know the potential side effects of medications and treatments and how they may affect their appearance and other physical qualities. Talking with and listening to your teenager in an open and honest way will go very far to establish trust, consistency in following treatment and self-care routines, and reduce acting out at home or at school.

Side effects that occur from some medications and treatments include hair loss, acne, weight gain or loss, or feeling tired all the time. These physical changes may greatly affect a teen's self-confidence and self-esteem. Self-image may be hampered by changes in physical appearance. Girls may not develop breasts or get their first period until late. Boys may lose weight and feel "scrawny" compared with their peers. Boys have often reported to us that when they are thin, they often are overlooked in being selected for sports. Chronic illness makes adolescents feel alone and isolated.

> *I hated taking oral steroids for my asthma! I gained a bunch of weight, and people made comments and stared at me. I hated going to school or anywhere in public.*
>
> —16-year-old girl with asthma

Medications aside, sometimes the condition itself leads to delayed puberty, growth, and sexual development.[12] One study noted that many chronic illnesses can cause delayed puberty because of recurrent infections, immunodeficiency, gastrointestinal disease, renal (kidney) disturbances, respiratory illnesses, chronic anemia (iron-poor blood), endocrine (glandular) disease, eating disorders, and other issues.[13] Although they may have an intellectual understanding of their developmental delays, your teen's emotional understanding may not have caught up just yet. Be sensitive to and empathic with your teenager. Trying to talk about sexual development with them may elicit a response such as "Ewww, Mom. This is private! I don't want to talk about it!" Respect their privacy, and give them space.

Sometimes children do not feel comfortable talking to their parents about certain topics. If you find your child is shutting you out, or you have concerns about safety and other issues, we advise reaching out to a mental health professional to help you and your family navigate communication and trust issues. A family doctor, with your permission, can also be someone your teen can talk to about their sexuality and their illness. Your teen may also have someone in the community they can talk with, like a coach, a teacher, or a religious leader. Involve these individuals in your life. The most important thing is that your child is talking to someone.

As the research mentioned earlier in this chapter tells us, invisible conditions may cause more social problems for kids than visible ones. Some examples of invisible illness are multiple sclerosis, lupus, inflammatory bowel disease (Crohn's disease and ulcerative colitis), asthma, diabetes, and Lyme disease. These invisible illnesses lead to confusion because people do not understand fully what is happening to a person and make erroneous judgments because they do not easily see that the person is ill.[14]

> I always hated to have to explain to people at school why certain days I had to leave early or were gone for extended periods of time due to my treatments. I started getting the nickname "Part-Time Peter." I hated that.
> —17-year-old boy with rheumatoid arthritis

A teen with an invisible illness may choose to hide her condition, not wanting to be singled out or ostracized for something that makes her "different." The result may be a lack of closeness in her friendships as she hides something vital and profound about herself from others. With a visible illness, she at least knows that her friends know and like her even though she has an illness. With an invisible illness, she may live in constant dread of someone finding out and exposing her and worry about how that could affect her close relationships. A visible illness, therefore, may be easier for an adolescent to accept as part of her identity.[15]

Support groups that focus on specific chronic illnesses may be particularly helpful in reducing feelings of isolation. Adolescents sometimes respond better to feedback and advice given by peers rather than by adults. It may also be helpful to get your teen involved in walks for their foundations, join chat rooms, and go to specialized camps. Know, though, that not every adolescent feels comfortable talking in front of others in a group setting. Also, be aware that a 6- or 8-week program may not be sufficient; it often takes ongoing contact in these situations for the teen to build strong and influential relationships.[16]

> *My mother made me go to this group. I hated it. I don't want to listen to other people talk about their illness. I don't care. I have my own problems. I don't want to hear their horror stories. I have my own.*
> —15-year-old boy with diabetes
>
> *I really enjoy going to group. I learn a lot and realize I'm not the only one feeling scared. Sometimes it is hard to talk, but I'm glad I go. I made some friends. We text each other a lot, and it's nice to know someone my age understands.*
> —13-year-old girl with ulcerative colitis

Being in Control

It might be hard for your teen to learn that it is okay to ask and even depend on others for help. For example, Frank has had adolescent patients with *dystonia*, a movement disorder in which one's muscles contract involuntarily. The muscles can move in a repetitive or twisting movement. Writer's cramp is a type of dystonia that happens during fine motor activities, such as writing, or playing a musical instrument. This affects the hand and/or the forearm muscles. One of Frank's patients had a scribe at school—another student who would take notes for him during class and do other assignments with him. The boy with dystonia didn't mind the help, except when he got teased for being lazy (he was not lazy).

One way your teenager can feel a sense of control is by being able to "control the message" about their illness—that is, by being the one to educate others about their illness. Many conditions, especially the invisible ones, are difficult for people to understand. When children educate others about their illnesses it can be quite an empowering experience. It allows the child to dispel any myths or misconceptions about their illness to their peers and others. They can explain how their illness influences their daily and school functioning. It can build empathy in their friends and others in their communities. When they get tired of explaining, over and over again, help them make up business cards that give a short sentence explaining their illness. An example might be, "I have Crohn's disease, which affects my gastrointestinal tract. As a result, I have to use the restroom more often, and may need to move quickly. If I run off, this is probably why."

Some of our teenage patients do not want to share with others what is going on with them regarding their chronic illness. This is their choice, and it gives them a measure of control over an uncontrollable circumstance. Respect their decision not to disclose to others. This is their body, their life, and their illness. It may be helpful to discuss how they would like their illness referred to, both in conversations with family and with others outside the family. Perhaps there are particular words your child would prefer to use.[17] Your teen may also want to restrict discussions outside the family, or even with some members inside the family, limiting what information is communicated and to whom. Do help them figure out if they have a friend they can trust with this information; even one peer relationship in which they can really be themselves can support their healthy relational development.

From a developmental perspective, adolescents want to have control. As a result of this desire for control, teens often think they know everything, and you don't know anything! Just at the time when adolescents are seeking more independence from their parents and wanting to spend more time with their friends, the illness may require a level of dependence on parents that directly works against this. Adolescents often resent having to check in, and that resentment is only increased if they have to note both their whereabouts and their blood levels or other routine illness-related information. Pick your battles carefully, and give your teen some options whenever possible. Depending on the illness, and the advice of your health care providers, it might be feasible to give your teen an occasional break from treatments. We say this with caution, and we strongly suggest that you always check with your medical team first. Perhaps your teen can have some breaks between medications, appointments, tests, and other procedures. Is there flexibility in his treatment schedule that will allow your adolescent to attend important school functions (prom, special sporting events) or activities with a friend?

Teaching Your Teen to Manage the Illness and Self-Advocate

As children grow and mature, we expect more of them in terms of their own self-care and participation in the household. This is equally important, perhaps even more so, for children with a chronic illness because they will eventually have to include the tasks of managing their illness on top of the usual tasks of adulthood. You may even be looking forward to shifting some of your responsibilities to them, but proceed with caution. What aspects of management are they ready to take on? Putting together a list of all the tasks, or perhaps those tasks you think may be within reach for your particular adolescent, can start a conversation about what they feel ready for, or confident about doing, and which tasks feel too scary or overwhelming. Again, sometimes these shifts need to happen over several conversations, so both parents and children start to get used to the idea.

At a minimum, your adolescent should know what their diagnosis is and what their medications are. They should keep names and dosages in their minds, phones, and wallets. In case of an emergency when you are not able to be reached, your child and other adults close to them should have access to that information. Many apps available on smartphones can store health information for quick access. Discuss with your teenager who should have this information, and work out a plan for emergencies before any emergency occurs.

If you child worries he will not be able to follow through effectively with his medical tasks, be sure to tell him what he is already doing well. Let him know that you are there for him to fall back on. As long as he is living at home with you, he has a safety net, so it's better to hand over as much responsibility as possible during the time he is still at home—that way, if he fails, you are there to catch him.[18]

As you move step by step through this process, go at a pace that both you and your child are comfortable with, according to her maturity, sense of responsibility, emotional stability, and capacity for self-care. Maintain some flexibility with your child's compliance with her medical regimen.[19] As your adolescent begins to take on some of these important tasks, she will undoubtedly make mistakes or fail to follow through as thoroughly as you think she should. Expect some level of failure as normal; think of it as an opportunity for her to learn directly some of the consequences of not following the guidelines. As always, avoid judgment when she makes a mistake, to keep the road of communication open.

Include your adolescent in conversations with health care providers. Encourage him to ask questions in those meetings, and encourage the providers to address him directly by keeping your eyes toward him, rather than looking at the provider. If they are in the habit of talking primarily to you, this will help them shift their focus. By the time your adolescent graduates high school, he may even be meeting with his primary health care providers by himself, which will help facilitate the eventual transition to adult care. Adult care providers may not be comfortable with having parents involved in these meetings because of privacy concerns and the belief that parents lose the right to information about their child's care once that child is an adult, which in this country is age 18. Open conversations with your adolescent about how he would like your continued involvement in his health care helps him take charge at a pace that feels right.[20]

Studies have shown that many parents and adolescents find the transition to adult care unsatisfactory. They feel unprepared and often abandoned by the pediatric medical system, which is warmer and more personal than the adult system. Trusted relationships are ended, and adult providers are often unskilled and lack knowledge about illnesses that begin in childhood, including their effects and proper management. The adult system can seem indifferent by comparison, and there is often much less coordination between caregivers. It can feel like falling off a cliff and landing in a new and unknown world.[21] A thorough explanation of the transition to adult care is beyond the scope of this book, but adolescence can be a fruitful time to begin to prepare both parents and children for this important transition.

NEXT STEP: YOU CAN'T ALWAYS FIX IT, BUT YOU CAN BE PRESENT

As a parent of a child with a chronic illness, it's important above all that you be *present*. We noted earlier that we can't always take our child's pain away, as much as we want to. Sometimes our job is simply to be there. In this section we've chosen to underline this point by providing a few additional examples of how to be available to your child and communicate openly with them:

- Hold space for your child to be a child (a preschooler, fun-loving 9-year-old, or a "typical" moody teen). In other words, practice empathy; accept your child's truth. In practical terms, this can mean that you simply try to maintain your child's normal schedule as much as possible given the interruption of procedures, appointments, and such. For an older child or teen this may mean that you transport them to and from social meetings or school events (as well as their medical appointments). Assure them that you feel the extra effort is worthwhile, that their activities and interests are meaningful and important.
- Be present during procedures and hospitalizations as much as you can, providing soothing words and holding your child or holding her hand when possible. Provide safety and security in the form of stuffed animals or a favorite blanket, or other portable items that can travel with your young child outside the home.
- Help your child express himself when he feels overwhelmed. Art, puppets, or other toys may be a powerful avenue for helping young children express their feelings.[22]

- Ask your child open-ended questions. These are the five Ws: Who? When? Why? What? Where? and How? (It's really 5 Ws with an H.)
  - Some school-age and younger children may have some difficulty with these types of questions because having to fill in details feels overwhelming and they don't have the words to respond.
  - Sometimes children and teens feel like the five Ws are an interrogation. After all, children with a chronic illness get asked questions all the time: "How are you feeling?" "How does it feel when I press your stomach there?" "What's bothering you?" Try to ask non–health-related questions as often as you can.

> *I hated going to the doctors. First the nurse would ask me a ton of questions. Then the doctor would come in ask me the same questions. At one point I felt like screaming, "Read the damn chart!"*
> —16-year-old girl with a chronic illness

- Closed-ended questions—the ones responded to with "yes" or "no" replies—may be more helpful when you are trying to gather information. Sometimes we do not need detailed information but just need to get right to the point: "Did you take your medication today?" "Did you have trouble breathing when you ran on the playground today?" "Did you tell the lunch server to give you the sugar-free dessert?"
- When you are communicating with your child, make sure that you provide them your full attention, and give them the respect

and time to answer you. Sometimes when children take too long to respond, others want to jump in and answer for them. This may occur at medical appointments when the professionals are speaking to the child or adolescent and you jump in to make sure the information is accurate, or you are feeling anxious and talk over and answer for your child. Remember, if your child learns to speak up, they will learn to advocate for their needs and own their illness.

- If your child forgets something, you can always gently remind her to tell the doctor. You could say something like, "Julia, remember you were telling me about the rash you developed?" When you do this, you place the child a bit more in the control position without having lost or given up parental control.

Sometimes children with chronic illnesses do not wish to talk about their concerns or share their feelings with others about what is happening to them. Your child might fear upsetting you. Perhaps talking about the illness gets them upset and angry. Instead of talking about their feelings, your child may act out their feelings on others and on themselves. You may notice an increase in tantrums, fighting with you and siblings, sleeplessness, nightmares, tearfulness, and explosive behavior in and out of the home. Make sure that you do the following:

- Teach younger children "feeling" words.
- Teach children that there are gradient elements of emotion. Anger, for example, can range from mild irritation and frustration to full-blown rage.
- If your child seems angry often, understand that the anger may actually serve an important developmental need; for example, one of Frank's patients (a 13-year-old with leukemia) commented, "Anger is the only thing that makes me feel strong."

We want to encourage healthy ways of expressing feelings. When you're feeling guilty over your child being ill it's tempting to want to turn the other away when your child misbehaves. But remember that modeling and having clear behavior expectations actually helps your child develop independence and feel safe and secure.

A nonjudgmental approach is vital to preserving honesty. If your child or teen fears punishment or criticism when she makes a mistake, she may hide her failures instead of being open about them. Teach your child that mistakes are part of the process of learning something new, rather than a deviation from what is usual.

CHAPTER 5

YOUR COPILOTS: OTHER PARENTS AND PARENT FIGURES IN YOUR CHILD'S LIFE

By now you are learning how to meet the needs of your child with a chronic illness, while taking care of yourself in the process. You're spending hours on email, phone calls, and meetings with others. You are finding ways of communicating honestly and appropriately with your kids, and you may have had to make some hard decisions about jobs and finances. You're developing your emotional coping skills more than most parents ever have to, just to keep yourself on an even keel. Every day, you are doing more as a parent than you ever thought would be necessary. You are doing an amazing job! Still, we're guessing you could probably use more help from your partner or another copilot in your family circle.

Families come in all configurations. What does "family" mean to you? Who do you count on; what other adults in your life support you in raising your child? Think of your spouse or your ex, your in-laws, your aunt, or a close friend who is known to your child as "basically family": How well are your copilots doing at supporting you, and how well are you supporting them?

You have likely noticed how important and helpful it is when your medical team works together to coordinate the care your child needs. You may also have noticed the havoc that can result when they aren't doing that! Being able to coordinate your child's care with the other adults in their family life is at least as important, if not more so. In the coming chapters we'll address school and medical teams, as well as your broader circles of family and friends. Here, though, we are talking about the other adults you live with or depend on multiple times per week to support you. We believe that any steps you can take toward kindling warmth and trust with the copilots on your journey will be well worth the effort. Strengthening these relationships, in addition to giving you practical and emotional support you can rely on, provides a stronger foundation for the family as a whole.

Have you ever seen a terrarium? Soil and plants are put into a covered glass or plastic container, which supports ideal conditions for the plants to grow, capturing the sun's warmth and maintaining ideal moisture levels. You and your adult partners are like that: providing a nurturing environment in which your children can feel safe, secure, and well provided for.

Supporting your child alongside a copilot hinges on two things: awareness of your emotions and good communication. So, in this chapter we're going to cover those two topics in detail and offer ideas for different parenting scenarios: when you're a solo parent and need to recruit copilots, when you're living with your copilot or swapping responsibilities back and forth frequently, or when you and your copilot are not in a relationship. We wrap up the chapter with some tips and worksheets to help you manage your emotions and improve your communication skills.

STAYING CALM AT THE WHEEL

In Chapter 1 we discussed the emotions that are likely coming up for you. Which ones seem to arise most regularly? What kinds of situations most typically set them off?

You might feel stress because of the logistics involved in taking care of your child: dealing with doctors and tests, administering medication and other interventions, possibly even scheduling out-of-town hospital visits. Needing to be present for your child may affect your work and increase the financial toll of the illness. Often, when we get upset or overwhelmed, we tend to take it out on people nearby, blaming them for things that aren't their fault. Even when someone does make a mistake, jumping all over them because we are feeling so stressed doesn't help. Lashing out is just one of the ways our own feelings can get in the way of having a good copilot partnership.

Identifying Your Feelings

Remember in Chapter 1 when we discussed the fight, flight, or freeze responses and all the chemicals that get released? Those chemicals cause us to feel all kinds of different physical sensations in our bodies, which we then label as various emotions. What do you notice about yourself when you get very upset? You might feel a knot in your stomach, tension in your arms and legs. You might find yourself pacing, shouting, or getting a glass of water. That is the moment to stop and take stock. Ask yourself, "What's going on for me right now?"

Along with physical sensations, you may be having stressful thoughts, like "This is never going to work," "She never does anything right," or "He is always forgetting." "Never" and "always" are clues that you're not really seeing the whole picture. None of us, frankly, is unfailingly consistent! So, in the moment when those stressful thoughts are bubbling up, you are missing the times when the person you are thinking about didn't forget or when they did do something right. These thoughts are part of the vicious cycle that keeps our emotions pumped up, triggering more of the fight, flight, or freeze response, the release of more stress hormones and neurochemicals, which prompt more thoughts, and so on and so forth. So, as a first step toward staying calm, try to disconnect the thoughts from the sensations and just focus on what you are feeling in your body.

We have included a little cheat sheet (Worksheet 5.1, "Identifying My Feelings")[1] to help you notice and sit with what you are feeling. If you do this regularly, you will begin to see patterns. This is where calming practices also come in handy, so that you can reduce the arousal you are feeling. Practicing mindfulness meditation (discussed in Chapter 2), engaging in a short burst of intense physical activity, or breathing long, slow, deep breaths can all help. Afterward, reflect on those feelings. Do they seem familiar? Often, feelings we had as a child are restimulated in stressful adult situations, and we see what is happening through the lens of that early experience instead of through our more mature, experienced eyes. If that is the case for you, remind yourself that you are an adult, with strengths and resources that were not available to you as a child.

WORKSHEET 5.1. Identifying My Feelings	
Ask yourself:	**Symptoms**
What am I feeling in my body?	• Rapid heartbeat • Tears or tearfulness • Knots in my stomach • Clenching my jaw • Throat constricted • Feeling heat or a red flush on my chest
What behaviors am I doing as a result?	• Pacing • Getting a drink of water • Raising my voice

WORKSHEET 5.1. Identifying My Feelings (*Continued*)

Ask yourself:	Symptoms
What emotions can I name? (Write down words for the feelings themselves, not the situation)	• Mad or frustrated • Sad • Glad • Afraid or worried • Helpless, hopeless, or powerless
What thoughts are going through my mind?	• How are we going to manage? • I can't take any more! • What is going to happen to us? • I can't do this—what is wrong with me?
Am I **H**ungry–**A**ngry–**L**onely–**T**ired?	HALT and address this condition

Calm Your Racing Mind

Techniques
- If you feel the need to vent verbally before settling down, sit and write automatically, without thinking, whatever is in your head for 15 minutes, with no censor. Then destroy the paper so your partner never finds it.
- Do 5 to 10 minutes of a high-energy activity, like running in place or jumping jacks.
- Find one part of your body that isn't affected by anxious feelings—often, it is the feet—and focus your attention there to ground yourself.
- Put a weighted blanket on your lap or your feet. A 10-lb burlap bag of rice, or anything similar, works well.

Reflect on Your Experience

- Are these feelings familiar?
- What are the current situations that tend to set them off?
- What memories are they connected to, especially from childhood? These emotions were the best way you had then to take care of yourself. Have compassion for that little child.
- What is different for me now than it was then?

Sharing Your Feelings

Let's say your partner or your child's grandparent has to back out of their usual job of meeting your child at the bus one afternoon. You want to explode. But you know that blowing up at them won't help; they're already torn between your child and another pressing issue. You may not want to share your feelings for fear of ruining a delicate balance of goodwill. Or you may want to protect your loved one from the intensity of your emotions. The problem is, we communicate our feelings whether we choose to or not. Chances are that person is picking up on something, and not knowing what that "something" is causes her more stress than hearing about it directly. In addition, you are left holding a lot of emotions inside, without an outlet for them. Sharing your feelings in an appropriate—that is, calm—way with your copilot helps both of you reduce stress and provide mutual support.

One challenge happens when you are both having very different feelings. One person may be more frightened or sad, the other angry; these differences can lead to questions or doubts about the other, such as "How can you not feel the way I am feeling?" Sometimes people read meaning into these differences, jumping to wrong conclusions like "You don't love our child the way I do, or you would feel the way I feel!" Recognize that all emotional reactions are just that, emotions we cannot control.

We all have our own unique patterns in the way we feel and express emotions. Ask yourself, "What happens to me when I feel helpless or out of control?" A sick child sets off strong reactions for parents. We want to protect our children from pain and suffering, and you have been presented with a situation in which his suffering is unavoidable.

Trust that other parent figures in your child's life love your child as much as you do, but perhaps they express that love, and experience emotional reactions as a result of that love, in ways that differ from yours. Try to listen to others' feelings, and validate them, even if they are different from your own. Understanding and supporting one another despite these differences helps you form a strong foundation for the rest of the family. Using Worksheet 5.1 ("Identifying My Feelings") is a good way to start the conversation. Share what you each feel and what you have learned about the origins of those feelings. In this way, you and your copilot can develop a better understanding of each other and greater sensitivity to one another's tender spots.

Shared feelings are better managed feelings, as many parents and couples could attest.

> It did cause a strain with us. I retreated into my man cave. I was feeling this depression and fear, and I thought if I shared that with [my wife] I would add to her burden. We went to couples therapy, and there we were able to have some of these conversations, and when I did share, she knew she was not alone. We realized that if we're going to get through this we have to recognize we're on the same team and not against each other.

Feelings don't need to be fixed. Listening and doing your best to understand are often all that are required to lower stress.

Communicating

Maintaining your car involves changing out the oil and the brake, power steering, and other fluids from time to time, so they don't get clogged with dirt and to ensure all the interlocking parts keep moving together smoothly. People aren't cars, of course, but the analogy may help you see how important it is to make sure your daily communication remains clear and as free of "gunk" as possible. The decisions that have to be made, and the research and contingency planning that have to be done, can be quite overwhelming. Unexpected events can occur that need an immediate response. So, to stay calm at the wheel when parenting alongside other adults, it pays to work on clear and effective communication. Being able to talk through all the possibilities and their potential effects on your family is vital to making decisions you can feel good about. So often it is not possible to know exactly what the outcome will be; respecting your copilot's input will enable you to explore possibilities together.

Relationship expert John Gottman observed both live and videotaped couple interactions and coded elements of each interaction as positive or negative. Gottman noticed a pattern of four particular types of negative responses that may predict trouble for a relationship when people overuse them. He labeled them "the Four Horsemen of the Apocalypse":

1. *Criticism*—attacking the personality or character of the partner
2. *Contempt*—showing a lack of respect for the partner when you are emotionally wound up
3. *Defensiveness*—attacking or discrediting the partner's observations or point of view
4. *Stonewalling*—removing oneself from the conflict and refusing to engage further[2]

Gottman's relationship research was mainly focused on married couples, but we feel his advice is helpful for any adult who wants to maintain close emotional connections with one or more other adults around coparenting a child with special needs.

Most of us fall into the Four Horsemen responses at one time or another; the key seems to be whether or not we counterbalance them with other, more positive responses. Gottman found through his research that partners who communicate effectively use a ratio of at least five positive responses to each negative one. The following are some examples of positive types of responses:

- validating the other person's feelings or perspective, even when you don't agree with them (for example, "I see that you're upset about this" or "I can understand why that might make you angry")
- using humor to release the tension (for example, impersonating a character using a hat or glasses, or saying something silly, like "I studied that in nincompoop school!")
- expressions of affection or endearment (for example, using pet names like "Sweetheart," saying "I love you")
- active listening, which encourages the other person to continue telling you what they want to say (for example, simple words like "Yeah" or "Uh-huh," or asking leading questions that invite elaboration, like "What was that like for you?")
- expressing empathy for their feelings (for example, "I am so sorry you had to deal with that")
- expressing the sense that you are working the situation out together (for example, "You know I couldn't do this without you")

Examples of negative interactions include

- blaming the other person;
- attacking, especially starting sentences with phrases like "You always . . ." or "You never . . .";
- trying to read the other person's mind or judge what their behaviors mean (for example, saying "You didn't [do a certain action], so you just don't care about . . .");
- judging their feelings (for example, by saying, "You have no reason to feel that way"); and
- defending yourself against attacks by trying to establish proof.

Maintaining a Meaningful Connection

There are some simple and easy ways to keep the connection with your copilot alive and vital despite all the stress, whatever your relationship might be—and they don't require vacationing together in Tahiti! Paying attention to a few important strategies that help you focus on supporting your relationship can not only strengthen the relationship but also create small islands of emotional support for both of you when you need it most. The best part is they won't cost you a thing, except some time and attention.

CATCH YOUR COPILOT BEING HELPFUL

Remember that ratio of five positive interactions to balance one negative interaction? Do you tend to notice only your copilot's failures? Look for ways in which they are helping. They may be small things, but taking note of them can help you rebalance your view. When you notice how they contribute to the household or to making life smoother in general, make a point of letting them know. Tell them what you appreciate specifically. This can be as simple as saying, "I noticed you put gas in the car; I appreciate that," or "It was really helpful that you were able to pick up the prescription refill today—thanks!" This simple appreciation practice can help you set up a virtuous cycle, whereby your appreciation leads to their appreciation, back to yours, and on and on. Everyone likes to be appreciated!

By the way, this works really well with your kids, too!

THE "THREE *T*S": TOUCH, TALK, AND TIME TOGETHER

Everyone has different ways of enjoying a relationship, but the "Three *T*s"—touch, talk, and time together—usually work for most people.[3] "Touch" refers to physical touch and affection, from hugs all the way through sexual engagement, if that is part of your relationship. Sometimes just taking a moment to share eye contact, or touch a shoulder, can communicate support. Human touch is also known to calm the central nervous system, reducing arousal and soothing anxiety, so the additional value of this practice can be to relieve your mutual stress. Some families like to pile up on the couch together, which makes sure everyone is part of giving and getting the physical affection.

The second of the Three *T*s, "talk" refers to sharing your feelings with one another, including your stresses and the good and bad of your day. It can mean remembering what you most enjoy together, happy memories you share, as well as your hopes and plans. What we are *not* talking about here are conversations focused on your issues, specific points of disagreement, logistics, or decisions that have to be made. Those are important conversations, but here we are pointing to talk that builds connection and mutual support, that reminds you of the best parts of your relationship—the kind of talk that strengthens the positive connection you have that has been challenged.

The third T, "time together," can mean as little as 15 to 20 minutes once to a few times a week doing something you both enjoy. It can be as simple as listening to music together, watching a favorite TV show, or taking a walk. Spending time with someone is one of the most important ways we show a person that they are important to us.

Enjoy High-Energy Fun

Some families like to laugh until their sides ache; others enjoy a high-energy game of Charades or Monopoly. Families make music together, sing together, dance together. All these are examples of high-energy fun.[4] What gets you really up and excited? What do you like to do with the other adults copiloting with you? This should be something the whole family can enjoy. Pretend-wrestling with kids and tickling sessions are great—just make sure to check that it is fun for everyone involved, especially your littlest ones.

WHEN YOU'RE DRIVING ALONE

Sole parenting doesn't always mean "driving alone." Whether you are a solo parent by choice or circumstance, if you have a strong social support network you may be able to count one or more adults in your close circle as copilots. On the flip side, if you're in a part-nered relationship but you feel solely responsible for your child's medical needs, the lack of a copilot can really hurt. Although single parents are more likely to struggle financially, in a marriage where one partner becomes the primary caregiver of the child with a health condition, the stress has been shown to lead to mental health issues such as anxiety, depression, and feelings of hopelessness. If this describes your situation, we recommend finding a mental health pro-vider to talk to. Likewise, if you often have thoughts about your child being vulnerable, and it makes you feel paralyzed or so anxious that you can't cope, we encourage you to reach out for professional help.

If you're parenting by yourself, you may feel socially isolated and exhausted more often than not, especially if you are struggling financially or experiencing discrimination at work. Your support network might not include another adult who is willing or capable of being a coparent with you. You are carrying the burden of your own worries, and your child's special care needs, while also trying to ensure the survival of your family unit. That's a lot! The good news, though, is that, despite these challenges, most solo-parent families do quite well, and you may even find your family has better cohe-sion, higher levels of trust, and more frequent communication than other families.[5]

All the things we have said about self-care go double for you. Your survival, and that of your family, relies on your ability to keep going. If you find yourself getting triggered, give yourself a time-out. Even taking 5 minutes to sit in your kitchen, look at a tree outside the window, and just breathe can help you calm down. Your kids will totally get it! Teach them to understand when you need a break; it will help them learn about the give-and-take of relationships and educate them about our human need for self-care. Transparency is really key, so help your kids understand that these short breaks help you continue the job of making sure they are all well taken care of.

Take advantage of any resources you can find that can give you even a short period of respite from the challenges you are dealing with. If you are working with a comfort care team (see Chapter 10 for more information), some of the resources may be free. Reach out to your networks, too, even if you have to piece something together with several different people or communities. The coordination may be tricky, but using some of the shareable calendars that we cite in the Resources for Your Journey may be helpful. Asking for help may be difficult when you are so used to doing everything yourself, but we encourage you to reach out wherever you can. You may be surprised at who is willing to step in!

SHARING THE WHEEL: WHEN YOU ARE IN A COMMITTED RELATIONSHIP

Your relationship as a couple forms the foundation for the family. Your ability to work together as partners and manage all of the various tasks and stressors that are hitting the family now that your child has been diagnosed with a chronic illness has a big impact on how well the family adjusts to a "new normal." Although there is no doubt that having a child with a chronic illness increases stress on partners, most couples do very well.[6]

When you and your partner use less effective communication and have insufficient time together, you may have more conflict, or you may just feel less satisfied in the relationship.[7] Research has shown that, on an individual level, partners may experience higher levels of depression,[8] worry and anxiety,[9] and even symptoms of posttraumatic stress.[10] Take heart, though: If these issues are affecting your life with your partner, it does not necessarily mean you are headed for a divorce. Because your child's health condition raises basic issues of life and death, you and your partner may have to refocus on what's most important in life. For some couples, this might mean lowering their expectations of each other. This can actually be one way to lower your stress. Another, more active way of refocusing is to directly address the relationship issues that surround caring for your chronically ill child. Remember, the goal is to be as supportive of one another as possible.

Who Does What?

Couples have different ways of divvying up all the things that need to be done in the household. Some families split up the tasks, with one partner earning the money and the other caring for the home and children, but in many families both partners have outside jobs. These couples may share the additional tasks, or there may be a tendency for one person—in a heterosexual partnership, often the woman—to handle all the home- and child-related tasks. Gay and lesbian couples have a tendency to share responsibilities more equally,[11] but they too may choose what can be called "specialization." The problem doesn't seem to be how the couple divides up or shares the tasks but instead how each partner feels about what they are expected to do.

If you generally already share household- and child-related needs with your partner, you probably have a process in place but will need to figure out how to split up the additional tasks required by your child's chronic illness. If you have chosen an income earner/

home manager way of organizing your tasks, be careful that the additional requirements of your child's care do not overwhelm the person in charge of the household. You may have to be more flexible in your approach. In either case, this could be a good time to sit down and talk through all of the responsibilities you both are managing, to see what each of you is really comfortable with, and discuss how to incorporate the additional tasks, fitting them with each person's schedule and abilities, regardless of how you have done things in the past.

For some families, the added tasks required by their child's illness are so demanding that the most sensible option is for one partner to focus exclusively on those tasks, even if they need to stop outside work or downshift from full time to part time. If you decide this is the best choice for your family, keep in mind that you and your partner may find yourself living in two different worlds. One of you will spend her days with adults, pursuing adult tasks, seeing actual progress, and perhaps also finding intellectual and social stimulation at work. The other will be immersed in a world of children, including tasks that are never fully completed because they must be repeated over and over, and seeing and talking with few adults. For some, this may be a dream come true: They thrive being at home with children all day, even with the added tasks. For others, it can be, at times, a living nightmare, and they crave adult conversation and engagement (outside of dealing with doctors and insurance, that is).

When you and your partner reconnect in the evening, you may have very different needs. At the end of the day, ask yourself, "What do I need to do so that I can be available for whatever it is my partner needs?" For instance, do you need to take your rant about a workplace situation to a friend rather than rehashing it with your partner? Can you spend 30 minutes walking alone to offload the emotional challenges of the day so you can be more available to your partner? Couples who live in different daytime worlds encounter many areas where they can come into conflict, and the demands of caring for an ill child may increase this.

The other danger with specialization is that the working partner may use distancing as a coping mechanism. Do you or your partner seem to spend more and more time immersed in work? Do work responsibilities intrude on home time, for example, in the form of important phone calls or emails that must be addressed in the evening? Does it seem like you, or they, are never fully present when at home? As we have mentioned, having a child with an illness can be very distressing for parents, and distancing is a way to keep those difficult emotions at bay. Unfortunately, this can lead to emotional disconnection from your partner, leaving them overwhelmed with the burden of all that needs to be done, and it can negatively affect your children as well. Again, if this feels like a pattern in your relationship, it could be helpful to get some couples therapy.

Couples who specialize also need to be careful of overstepping boundaries. If your partner is handling the day-to-day needs of an ill child, don't correct, oversee, or offer advice unless that is specifically requested. We all have a tendency to try to fix the "problem"—to tell our partner what to do if they are struggling. If our partners are stressed, we get stressed, and so we try to solve their problem and make it go away. What most of us actually need, though, is just someone to listen and understand our feelings.

With a child who is ill, whose condition may change day to day, whose future holds uncertainty, and whose life may even be threatened, these interpersonal issues are magnified. It can take a lot of discipline to simply listen to your partner and say things like "Sounds like that really stressed you out," "I'm sorry you had to go through that," and "Is there anything I can do right now to help you feel better?" The surprise is, when you are able to sit back and let your partner share their feelings, you will probably feel a sense of relief that you don't actually need to fix anything. Your partner can handle what needs to be handled and will ask for help if they need it.

Making Decisions

There may be times when decisions have to be made in the moment and one or the other of you might not be available. Be sure to have "What if . . .?" conversations about potential complications or interventions before the need arises. As much as possible, try to agree on some guidelines about how specific issues may need to be handled; then, if one of you is unavailable, the other can proceed based on that common ground. The unavailable party must agree to accept that decision without criticism or second-guessing. Maybe you would have advocated for a different choice, but keep in mind that you weren't there. Sometimes, making any decision is more important than making the absolute "right" decision. As your child grows older, you will need to have more such conversations and adjust your ground rules, but each of you has to be empowered to make decisions in emergencies as best you can without fearing backlash from the other partner.

Sustaining a Connection

Too often, time together falls to the bottom of the to-do list, even without the added challenges of having a child with a chronic illness. Remember, taking care of your relationship is like self-care for the family. Enlivening your connection will do a lot to counteract the stress that sometimes overwhelms you.

Remember the Three *T*s!

Earlier, we discussed Three *T*s as being applicable to any copilot in your life, but we want to emphasize them here when it comes to building a long-lasting relationship with your spouse or partner. Touch? Don't be afraid to close the door and let the kids know that their parents are having private time! This will teach them how to prioritize their own relationship as adults. Talk, and time together? Even after living with someone for years, there are still new things to discover. Look for those things.

CAPTURE YOUR UNIQUE WAYS OF REVIVING THE SPARK

Every couple is on a unique journey and can find in their history particular touchstones that remind them what they mean to each other. What are your touchstones? Perhaps they are photos that bring you back to a particularly happy time or to a place you visited. What helps each of you feel connected? Pet names? Private jokes? Get creative! Remembering why you fell in love can bring back some of those feelings as antidotes to the stress you face.

TAKING TURNS AT THE WHEEL: WHEN YOU'RE SEPARATED OR DIVORCED

When you're separated or divorced, coparenting can be tricky at the best of times. With two residences, finances are often strained, and your usual family routines are disrupted. Your physical and/or mental health may suffer as well. If your ex-partner is far away from you geographically, engaging them in coparenting can be difficult.

In addition to all this, conflict and poor communication skills can make it harder to coordinate your child's complex medical regimen and stay consistent with medication schedules. Despite these obstacles, though, most people who coparent with their ex are successful in providing the care their child needs.

If you and your ex had poor communication before divorcing, this probably won't change on its own. For some couples, conflict is often worst in the first year after the separation, and tensions tend to ease over the long term. Others may be able to put their differences aside during a crisis—such as the period following a diagnosis or an acute episode—but over time they tend to return to previous ways of interacting.[12]

To lessen relationship conflicts and make copiloting with an ex easier, focus first on supporting your child. Reestablish household routines that include the medical regimen required by the child's illness, including scheduling regular mealtimes, addressing school needs and homework, establishing healthy bedtime routines, and planning recreational activities for the whole family. Siblings can help create structure in this way, too, since they are also longing for normalcy and routine. Work with your ex to make sure your two routines, which don't have to be exactly the same, are at least compatible.

Coparenting Patterns

When thinking about copiloting successfully with an ex, it can help to look at some common patterns that postdivorce relationships take and see where yours falls. If you are cooperating well, like the majority of coparents, you are able work together effectively to manage your child's chronic illness. In what we call "parallel coparenting," including about 25% of ex-couples, you may have some strong disagreements, but you are able to put your own conflicts and feelings aside, assume a businesslike approach, and thus effectively work together as well as the cooperative coparents. Congratulations! You are doing well making sure your child has the care they need.

If you fall into the other 25%, those involved in conflictual coparenting, what we call "conflictual coparents," you may have difficulty interacting with your ex without conflict and disagreement about parenting practices. As a result, it may be difficult to provide a positive emotional and social environment for your child.[13] Perhaps your partner, often the father in a heterosexual couple, has lessened his involvement in your child's life. You may feel a sense of relief and increased control at being able to make decisions on your own—or you may feel overwhelmed at being alone with all the responsibility of not only making the decisions but also of providing the care for your child.[14]

Effective communication seems to be the key to a good collaborative parenting relationship between ex-partners, especially when caring for a child with chronic illness. If you and your ex have shared custody, your children may be moving back and forth between two homes. Both you and your ex need to be clear on the requirements of the medical regimen, including administering medications in the right dose and at the correct intervals, knowing how to perform whatever procedures are required in the home, and being alert to symptoms to watch for that might indicate a worsening of the condition or a potential crisis. Regular phone calls, emails, and texts can keep both of you on the same page and aware of what happens when your child is not at your home. When decisions need to be made, if you have joint legal custody, you need to have a process of talking things through, forming a plan, and following that plan through together.

A lack of trust is one of the prime elements that can sabotage good communication and collaborative postdivorce relationships. Whether the circumstances of the separation involved betrayal, abandonment, or manipulation, trusting your ex to follow through with things that need to be done, or even to have the same understanding of the child's chronic illness, may be difficult or even impossible. This can be especially true if new romantic partners are participating in the child's care, making you or your ex uncomfortable.

When parents see the child's illness and its severity differently, they may not be equally on board with the necessary care. In our practice we have found that some fathers in heterosexual relationships see the illness as less severe than mothers and may even be in a state of denial about its existence. One adult we interviewed, whose juvenile arthritis was diagnosed at age 14, described her situation as a child:

> My father had a very difficult time accepting that his daughter was sick, especially due to the nature of the disease: You can feel lousy in the a.m., take a shower, in the middle of the day you feel better, and by the evening you seize up again. It created a distance between my father and myself. He falsely believed that I was making some of this stuff up.

The father in this story may have been influenced by a masculine notion of "toughness," and perhaps saw the mother as "coddling" their child, but he may also have had legitimate concerns about overmedication and overtreatment. If this is a concern for you or your ex, you need to address it openly. If you don't, home treatments may end up being inconsistent, negatively affecting your child's physical well-being, especially if you and your ex are not communicating about changes that have been made in home routines.

Getting Support From Neutral Others

If there is someone in your families whom both you and your ex trust and respect, that person can be an effective intermediary for coming to agreements and keeping everyone informed. Grandparents, nannies, or other people seen as neutral by both of you can serve in this role. If you know someone whom you and your conflictual ex-partner can agree on, do your best not to contaminate the relationship by sharing your negative opinions or frustrations about your ex.

Setting up alternating meetings with trusted health care providers can provide both partners with equal access to the medical team, including any new partners, and keep conflict out of the consultation room. Perhaps two providers on the same team could work together and meet separately with your two families, giving each of you a private, personal relationship.

Seek out your own support: allies, friends, or other family members who can listen to all your frustrations and complaints. They can give you the encouragement you need to show up ready to work with your ex, no matter how problematic the relationship. They can also provide another perspective on your child's condition and on your interactions with the treatment team. Be aware, though, that if such a person gives you unhelpful advice or piles on about your ex, they can torpedo a decent working relationship. Your child will be the one to suffer.

Although you might think of couples therapy as a step couples take to "save" a marriage, know that working with a professional to reduce conflict and differences in how they handle the child's illness can be helpful to separated or divorced couples as well. Couples therapy can help each of you learn to focus on your child's best interests, agree on certain issues, and let go of other areas where you cannot agree. This will lead to better health outcomes for your child and a more positive emotional environment for everyone.[15]

Some couples find themselves entrenched in unavoidable conflict and wind up calling in competing experts, leading to an escalation of conflict and, sometimes, legal action. You may not be able to prevent an ex from doing this but, beyond defending yourself, try to not to go the same route. The results are never good for the children, especially the one who is chronically ill, and conflict escalations only deplete emotional, psychological, social, and financial resources. Even if you have decided you must call an expert or consult an attorney to gain final decision-making power because of the danger you believe your ex's behavior represents, know that you will be sacrificing the opportunity at some point to form a more collaborative relationship.

NEXT STEP: GET THAT ENGINE RUNNING MORE SMOOTHLY

When parenting a child with chronic illness, it's important that you and any coparents work together the best you can. One skill that will help you get your coparenting "engine" running smoothly is being able to have a difficult conversation. Nothing can derail a useful conversation better than a surge of emotion. Have you had an experience with your copilot in which you started off talking through some logistics, such as who will do what, and suddenly found you were having an argument? How did you get *there*? Probably, one or the other of you—or both—reacted to either something the other person said, something they understood as implied criticism, or something about the situation as a whole. Once that process gets going, most of us jump into attack-and-defend mode, and all chances of getting something done are gone with the wind!

In the movie *Thanks For Sharing*, Tim Robbins's character speaks about emotions. "Emotions are like children," he says. "You can't let them drive, but you can't lock them in the trunk either."[16] If we don't know what we are feeling and ignore the sensations that are arising, we are more liable to be taken over when we least expect it. In that case, emotions end up having more power than they should.

Emotions have less power over us when

- we know they are happening,
- we experience them in our body, and
- we make a choice about what we want to do.

If you and your copilot are family members with a long history, there are undoubtedly land mines galore in your relationship that either one of you can inadvertently set off. If you are intimate partners, the very power of your bond can make you much more sensitive to each other's comments. The key is to recognize when somebody has been set off emotionally and to then end the conversation. If you continue beyond that point, you won't get anything done, and you likely will damage the goodwill you need to work well together.

The first step in having a difficult conversation is to identify the feelings each of you are having, as we note in the "Identifying My Feelings" worksheet. The next step is to prevent or stop an emotional escalation from taking over your conversation. There are two ways of doing this, which we share in Worksheet 5.2, "Two Ways to Handle a Difficult Conversation." Both ask you to be familiar with your own emotional triggers, the thoughts and feelings that come up, and the behaviors that you notice. One option is to slow the conversation down and is built on mindful talking and listening (which we describe in more detail in Chapter 9). The other option requires you to create a plan for taking a time-out from the conversation and resume it afterward. This starts with deciding on a word or phrase that you both agree either party can use when they experience an emotional escalation. You both must agree to end the conversation promptly, and take time by yourselves for 20 to 60 minutes. Settle on the amount of time you need, and commit to coming back together at the end of that interval to have the alternative conversation we describe.

We often notice another person's escalation more easily than our own, but be careful about pointing it out. It can make matters worse! That said, if you begin to compare notes on Worksheet 5.1 ("Identifying My Feelings"), you might find ways to collaborate with

your copilot in noticing and addressing these emotional escalations. Just be very careful to be respectful and use language to
which the other person can respond positively even when they are
emotionally charged.

If you and your partner agree that your conversations are getting out of hand, and you want to get some perspective on it, pull out
your phone and audio- or video-record one conversation while it is
happening. Unless you want to keep it for yourself as a reminder of
how *you* act, delete it afterward. The idea is to listen to *yourself* and
try to imagine what it is like for the other party to hear you. Listen
to what you say as well as how you say it. Sometimes you will each
see clear patterns in your conversations that you can build some
guidelines and expectations around. Even if you don't have time to
record a conversation and listen or watch it again, you can still tune
in to details about your conversations, such as the following:

- Do you interrupt each other a lot? Slowing the conversation
  will help.
- Is there a lot of name calling? Agree on some boundaries
  around language.
- Do fights always happen at night, or after a glass of wine?
  Have conversations earlier in the day, when you are both
  rested and before consuming alcohol.

If you find you still are not able to have the conversation you
need to have with your coparent without it degenerating into a fight,
it may be time to look for a therapist who specializes in working
with couples

Be sure the person you contact has specific training working
with "couples" rather than with individuals only. You don't need to
sign up for long-term therapy. As we discussed in Chapter 3, when

you call someone, be clear about your situation and what you are looking for. Perhaps coming in and having that one conversation you need to have will be enough. Just knowing there is someone to call if you need them can be a potent stress reliever.

A Special Note About Violence

If there has ever been violence in your relationship, added stress may increase the possibility that it will happen again. If you ever have concerns that you and your children may not be safe, be aware that there are many shelters and hotlines that can give you help and advice for how to stay safe or leave the relationship if you need to. Call the National Domestic Violence Hotline for more information and help if you need it: 1-800-799-7223.

WORKSHEET 5.2. **Two Ways to Handle a Difficult Conversation**

Slow the conversation down. It may help to skip ahead to Chapter 9 and review the sections on mindful listening and talking. Decide who speaks first. Keep going until you both have said what you need to say.

Speaker	Listener
State briefly what you are trying to say.	• Listen attentively. • Encourage your partner to say more until you get it. • Repeat what you understand. • "Is that right?"
Correct, restate, or elaborate until the Listener gets it.	Repeat until you get a "yes."

WORKSHEET 5.2. Two Ways to Handle a Difficult Conversation (*Continued*)

Become the Listener	Become the Speaker
• Listen attentively. • Encourage your partner to say more until you get it. • Repeat what you understand. • "Is that right?"	State briefly what you are trying to say.
Repeat until you get a "yes."	Correct, restate, or elaborate until the Listener gets it.

Take a time out. Agree on a word or phrase that you both will recognize as calling for an immediate end to the conversation. When you find yourself caught in an escalating conversation/fight, one of you should use the agreed-on word, to stop and take a time-out for 20 to 60 minutes. Make a plan to meet again after the time-out.

Step	Technique suggestions
Calm yourself down by taking steps that will slow your heart rate and alleviate other physical sensations of stress.	• Use the "4–4–4–4" method, also known as "4-squared breathing." Breathe in as you count to 4. Hold for 4 counts. Breathe out as you count to 4. Repeat for 4 minutes. • 5 to 10 minutes of your mindfulness practice, if you have one • 5 to 10 minutes of vigorous exercise • Any other technique that helps you calm down physically

(continues)

WORKSHEET 5.2. Two Ways to Handle a Difficult Conversation (*Continued*)

Step	Technique suggestions
Think calming thoughts	• "We can get through this." • "Deep down I know we care a lot for each other and our child." • "We're both under a lot of stress." • "We both want what's best for the family."
Come together for a short conversation	• Share your feelings, especially the more vulnerable ones. • Speak from an "I" perspective, and don't talk about the other person (no statements such as "I feel that YOU . . .," because what follows is not a feeling but a thought, and it isn't about you). • Make a plan to talk about the issue and address what you will each do to contribute to a calmer conversation.

CHAPTER 6

GETTING EVERYONE ON BOARD: SIBLINGS AND OTHER FAMILY MEMBERS

Your family is not simply a collection of individuals, operating independently though living together; instead, it is more like a biological system, in which the whole is more than the sum of its parts. When something happens to one member of your family, it affects all the other members individually, *and* it affects the relationships that help your family function. As with a pebble tossed into a pond, the ripple effects of a chronic illness diagnosis expand outward. So far, we've looked at your parent–child relationships and your relationship with your partner or other copilots. In this chapter, we'll look at how to manage relationships between siblings when one of them has a chronic illness, and we'll address the ways grandparents and stepparents (that is, those who aren't already in coparenting roles) can feed positivity into the family system.

Your family is going through a lot right now. No one can control the course of your child's illness, so you are probably experiencing a whole range of feelings as you come to terms with that reality. Changes in routine, noticing how their parents' attention is diverted to dealing with the illness, and sensing their parents' financial and emotional stress can put kids at risk for behavioral problems or for poor academic achievement. You may have noticed increased conflict and squabbling and a sense of having to work extra hard to maintain family cohesion and communication since the diagnosis. It's not just your imagination—it takes energy to keep your family's emotional connection strong.

In practical terms, your days are likely disrupted because of the medical-related errands and research tasks that now fill your time, meaning you have to reorganize on all fronts. Siblings might be feeling upset or left out if their activities and social time have been affected. In addition to this day-to-day change, your children's deeper ideas and beliefs about safety, normalcy, and what it's like to live as a family are upended. Siblings, grandparents, stepparents, and other members of your family system may also be wondering what it all means. On some level we all grapple with existential issues of disability and mortality.[1]

What is remarkable, however, is that the vast majority of families with a child who has a chronic illness manage to do well, meeting their child's medical needs as well as the needs of other family members. They are able to adapt their routines and find a new sense of normal in the face of all the added stressors. They find support where they can, from health care professionals, family and friends, and other families facing similar situations. They are able to maintain good communication among all members of the family and move through crises without sacrificing their family's well-being. There can even be positive effects, as the family becomes more deeply connected to their strengths, broadens their horizons, develops a new perspective on what is truly important, and finds deeper connections to community groups and their own religious traditions.[2]

In addition to these positives, you will probably increase your patience, compassion, and altruism. This can strengthen your family relationships and help you open up to your community in ways you might not have envisioned before: You may develop positive relationships with school personnel, professionals, and other community members. You will also develop stronger coping skills and strategies to deal with stress and gain a sense of empowerment from your ability to effectively communicate with medical and other professionals and to advocate for your family's needs.[3] If you approach your family relationships with intention, then everyone can benefit from and learn these skills as well.

BRINGING SIBLINGS ON BOARD

If you grew up with one or more siblings, you know how they helped make you the person you are now. Psychologists have identified many ways sibling relationships affect children's emotional development. Siblings experiment with competition and cooperation, develop feelings of empathy and protectiveness, and learn to negotiate the terms of a relationship. When one of the siblings has a chronic illness, the others may sense that certain types of conflict and companionship with their sibling are now (or always have been) out of bounds.[4] Having the different kind of sibling relationship that comes when one of them has a chronic illness can seem limiting or unfair, but there are also ways the illness can lead to a stronger sibling relationships.[5] The most important thing for your well children is that they are heard and understood, even though they may not volunteer information about what is going on with them.

Children who are older than their ill sibling seem to cope better with the diagnosis and the resulting changes than younger siblings.[6] Younger children may be affected more deeply because older siblings often play a bigger role in the younger ones' lives, as they often look up to their older siblings as a role model and guide.

When it comes to informing your children about their sibling's diagnosis, or telling them about how family life may be different going forward, many of the same strategies we have outlined for your ill child will also work for their sibling(s). Child life or other developmental specialists can be particularly helpful providing useful tips, appropriate play materials, videos, and other strategies for helping your well child understand and participate meaningfully in the family project of caring for the ill child. Without information that makes sense to her, younger children in particular are liable to fill in the blanks with misunderstandings and misinterpretations. In addition, therapeutic play and various expressive arts therapies can provide a way for your child to explore whatever she is feeling with regard to her ill sibling, regardless of her age.

Your child's emotional reactions to a sibling's illness may not make sense to you at first. Let's walk through some of the most common feelings in some detail so you are better equipped to antic-ipate, hear, understand, and validate their feelings and reactions. Just keep in mind that, despite some troubling responses, the vast majority of siblings do quite well, and many will develop a stronger relationship with their ill sibling than they might have otherwise.[7]

Fear

In the same way that you and your ill child first experience fear about the illness and its diagnosis, the well sibling also finds herself facing many new fears and anxieties. Some of the questions she may worry about start with issues of the ill sibling's health:

- "Will my sibling die?"
- "Will his illness get worse?"
- "If he has to go to the hospital, will something bad happen to him there?"

If the well child has some understanding of the treatment or moni-toring required by the illness, she may worry about these areas:

- "Will he monitor himself properly so he doesn't get sicker?"
- "What if he doesn't notice signs that mean he's getting worse?"
- "What if something happens and I am not there to help?"

She may also worry about her own health, and that of her parents:

- "Will I catch this illness myself?"
- "What if my parents got sick? Then what would happen?"

If a sibling is worrying about her own health, she may be quite persistent in wanting to have a doctor check out these symptoms. This can lead to chronic self-monitoring.

If she is old enough to participate in caring for her ill sibling, she may have additional concerns:

- "Am I able to do what I need to do to keep my sibling well?"
- "What happens if I make a mistake?"
- "What if I hurt him when we are playing together?"
- "Am I doing enough to help my parents?"

Depending on her developmental level, her sense of her own power is likely overblown. She may genuinely fear upsetting the family's delicate balance and bringing about a greater disaster than is already happening. She may be afraid that if she asks for too much from her parents, she may burden them, adding to their stress and perhaps triggering an angry response. She may also worry that this will take important attention away from her ill sibling and lead to a worsening of his condition, perhaps even resulting in death. In addition, she may be worrying about the future: What will happen when her parents are no longer able to care for her sibling? Will she have a child with the same illness?[8]

As you did with your ill child, the first thing to do is to let her know that her feelings are completely understandable. Be sure to invite her to describe all her fears, so you can correct any misunderstandings she has. This can help her develop a more accurate understanding of the illness, suited to her age level. If she expresses concerns about you, and the stress you are under, let her know that you appreciate her concern but that although the stress is difficult, you are handling it.

This may be an opportunity to invite her to participate in her sibling's care. Assign age-appropriate jobs she can do that contribute. This will help ease her worries and give her something she can do to help the family. Perhaps she can be in charge of something simple but helpful, such as getting a glass of water for her sibling's medication dose.

Jealousy and Resentment

It may seem counterintuitive that your well child may be jealous of someone who has an illness. What is there to be jealous of? You see your ill child suffering with pain and discomfort, perhaps being stigmatized by friends or classmates, and dealing with all the disruptions in their life, and you are filled with compassion for them. How could anyone be jealous of this?

For children, attention is the most important currency. Small children who don't get enough, or the right kind, of attention may experience developmental delays, so it is not surprising that they want attention and don't always care how they get it. When you are so busy attending to all the additional tasks your ill child requires, you can't give your other children as much attention as you would like. They notice this, and they often become jealous and resentful as a result.

What do we mean by all this? Let's say you give your ill child a special treat for their patience during a medical test. They may get a pass on expected chores or homework, for example. You may even excuse them for breaking a family rule more readily than you'd excuse one of their siblings. Children are particularly tuned in to "fairness," and the well sibling is likely to feel that this special treatment is terribly unfair, leading to resentment of what you expect of him. Furthermore, if a well sibling is not part of the caregiving activities— even if your motive is to protect him—he may feel left out of something important, leading to jealousy.[9,10]

Teenagers in particular will likely be resentful of extra responsibilities they must take on. Even if your teen continues with the same caretaking responsibilities he's had for years, he may feel conflicted about it and resentful about his position in the family.[11] He may want more independence from the family, just at the time when your expectations of him are going up because he is older and more mature. Adolescents are already dealing with emotional and hormonal changes, so even if things are stable with their ill sibling their own development and changing needs may make them moody and overreactive. Your teen may also be angry about his family's suffering and the injustice of having to deal with some random illness. Feelings of anger and resentment can sometimes lead to rebellious behavior.[12]

These kinds of behaviors may be especially triggering to you as the parent; it may feel as if your teen is deliberately trying to make things worse! The changes in his behavior may come as a surprise, especially if before he had been willing and cooperative. Keep in mind that adolescence, in U.S. culture at least, is a time of self-assertion, and expressing anger may be the only way he knows to say that he feels overburdened by the expectations around his sibling's illness. In fact, it may be more concerning if there is no anger or conflict when he reaches adolescence. If he is having these feelings and not expressing them, he may become depressed.

Being able to validate and support these feelings without condoning inappropriate behavior is the tricky balance you need to aim for. Be aware, though, that your relationship with your child may be too volatile for you to be the one in whom they confide. That doesn't mean you have done anything wrong—it just means you have, probably through no fault of your own, become the focal point of your teen's anger and frustration. If that seems to be the case, help them find someone they can talk to, whether that is another family member, participants in a support group they attend, a teacher, a coach, a religious leader, or some other trusted adult. Someone they already know on their sibling's medical team may also be a good choice. A therapist can also be helpful, but remember not to frame therapy as being about the teen sibling and "their problem." Instead, talk about therapy as working on your relationship as parent and child, and try going with them. Later, if they decide they would prefer it, they can continue therapy on their own.

Embarrassment

Well siblings may become more self-conscious and embarrassed around their ill sibling, especially if the illness results in different behaviors, changes in appearance, and the need to be in and out of school, or there are other, especially socially unacceptable, noticeable side effects, such as smells.[13] Your well child may cope with this by distancing himself from his ill sibling, particularly at school or when out with friends. He may even join in with others teasing her, even if he refrains from such behavior at home. Find a way to talk this through, and validate and support his feelings while making him aware of how hurtful such behavior is. Perhaps some compromises are available, such as giving him appropriate distance without disconnecting from his sibling.

Sadness and Depression

Research indicates that well siblings often report their belief that in families where the mother is the primary caregiver for the ill child, she is the unhappiest member of the family and they are the second unhappiest. They may struggle with continual feelings of sadness and emotional distress over their ill sibling, as well as the sadness of seeing their mother so sad, tired, and anxious.[14] Depression may also be an issue (see Chapter 1 for details about how to tell sadness and depression apart). The challenge is that, depending on their age, they may be adept at hiding what is going on with them so as not to burden you or their ill sibling. Hiding these unhappy feelings can lead to isolation and withdrawal, problems with peer relationships outside the family and even academic difficulties. Also, be aware that in children, depression is often characterized by irritability. Anger can also be a cover for depression. You should check in periodically with your well children, to see how they are doing. Creating times for the family to enjoy activities together reminds everyone that life isn't just about the illness. Also, as we have said before, if you see signs of serious depression, or any indication of self-harm, including talking excessively about death, please seek professional help.

Pressure and Responsibility

Perhaps you have noticed that the well siblings in your family, in particular, those older than the ill child, are stepping up in a dramatic way. They may take on more adult responsibilities both at home and in caring for their sibling. They may demonstrate a high level of ability in doing such tasks and may even become protective of their sibling. In a study of siblings of children with diabetes, the well siblings reported executing such tasks as helping their sibling with insulin injections, monitoring blood sugar and diet, and monitoring their sibling's energy level as a way of anticipating potentially dangerous drops in blood glucose levels.[15] You may welcome the help they offer, and it may be necessary for your family to cover all the bases. You may praise them and express pride in their ability to perform at such a high level, which encourages them to keep doing it.[16] Although this can be very helpful for family bonding, it can also result in siblings feeling like they are under pressure to perform, or to keep performing.

In addition to this kind of pressure, a well sibling may feel compelled to achieve in ways that the ill sibling perhaps no longer can. They may work hard to excel academically or through sports, as compensation. Or they may feel pressure to be the "good" child—that is, the "easy" child—and not share their own concerns or worries or express what they need.[17] By doing so well, however, they also become easy to ignore. They look like they handle everything effortlessly, the proverbial nonsqueaky wheel, hoping to lighten their parents' burden. This may set them up for greater difficulties down the road.[18] Again, be sure to check in regularly with how they truly feel about the responsibilities they have taken on, so you can anticipate when they might need a break. Reminding them about the importance of their own self-care, as you model yours, can help them find the balance they need.

Guilt

Of all the so-called "negative" feelings that well children experience in reaction to the diagnosis of a sibling, guilt seems to be the most universal. The situation provides endless opportunities for guilt! First, a child may feel "survivor guilt." The simple fact that he doesn't have the illness can invite guilt.[19] He can feel guilty about developing skills, or academic or sports-related success, perhaps outshining his ill sibling.[20] All of the other "negative" feelings can encourage guilt too. He is liable to feel guilty if

- he feels angry at his ill sibling for any reason;
- he feels resentment of the attention they receive;
- he has an aggressive thought like "I wish they'd just go away somewhere";

- he feels a longing for more attention;
- he feels embarrassed because of their symptoms, appearance, or behavior; or
- he feels jealous of them for any reason, because of special privileges and attention they may get, or for things that have nothing to do with their illness.

Guilt is so sneaky it can show up even in the most ordinary of interactions with her sibling. She may feel guilty if they are mean to her, and just learns to take it. If she feels competitive, she may feel guilty that she is hurting them in some way. If she and the sibling have a conflict, she may feel guilty no matter what happens. Some children feel so guilty about their angry feelings toward an ill sibling that they can't even talk about them without becoming anxious and tearful.[21]

Guilt can show up in your relationship to her also. She can see how hard this is for you and feels guilty for many reasons: that she isn't doing more to help, or any time she wants something from you, whether time, attention, or emotional support. If she gets some positive attention, she feels guilty! She may feel guilty about doing things away from home or playing with her own friends instead of her sibling. She is inadvertently buying into the idea that her ill sibling's needs are more important than her own.[22]

The real problem arises, though, when guilt traps a child into an escalating vicious cycle. She feels guilty and then tries to make up for her "bad" thoughts or "bad" feelings by working harder to help and be perfect. When she feels resentful about how difficult this is, she feels guilty again, and so works harder. She is in a no-win situation! And if she does express some of these feelings, and they are not understood and validated, the cycle gets reinforced.

Even if that doesn't happen, children are often very aware of their parents' struggles, and they naturally don't want to make things worse for you. A child may feel his only option is silence and withdrawal, which can lead to isolation, not only from friends and other people outside the family but also within the family itself. His attempts to live up to a level of perfection that is not within his power may paradoxically instill a stronger sense of responsibility, a feeling that his ill sibling's fate rests in his hands.[23]

Remember that young children, in particular, often entertain a kind of magical thinking that makes them think they are much more powerful than they actually are. They may believe they somehow caused their sibling's illness, or that something they said or did, or thought, caused a medical problem to arise. If a child shoves her ill brother, and several days later he has a health problem, she may genuinely believe that her behavior caused his problem. Clarifying these misunderstandings to your children, using medical play or other interventions, is especially important in order to relieve the guilt and anxiety that can result. Again, checking in regularly with your well children will help alert you to whether any of these unhelpful emotional cycles are happening. You can then validate the feelings that guilt says are wrong and help her find the balance she needs to be a good sibling and child and to take care of herself as well.

Positive Responses

So far we have focused on so-called "negative" feelings, but the good news is that some siblings will respond positively to your child's diagnosis. As they see him dealing with difficult situations, at home and at school, they may develop more empathy and compassion for others.[24] Children with a chronically ill sibling often develop more social maturity than others their age, and they show more prosocial behaviors (that is, doing things that benefit others).[25] Your child may discover their own capabilities through caring for their sibling, and this can enhance their sense of value as a person. If your family finds ways to work well together, with good communication and strong connections, everyone will benefit from the resulting greater family togetherness.

As we noted earlier, be careful that all the positive feedback your well children receive doesn't inadvertently encourage them to set higher and higher standards for themselves. They may start to feel trapped in these expectations and worry about their ability to manage it all. Let them know that your support doesn't depend on their performance. Make sure they have times and places to let go and people with whom to share all of their feelings.

Helping Siblings Manage Their Feelings

As a parent, you can do a lot to help your children express their feelings and learn to understand those feelings as normal, healthy, human responses to your family situation and to offset any tendency to feel bad about themselves. For example, if you're able to set aside a daily talking time with each sibling, like we described in Chapter 4, you could use those times to offer your full attention and self to any anxieties your children are having. Similar to the coping tip we offered to parents in Chapter 1, you could set a timer for 10 to 15 minutes. During this time you are all ears and warm hugs for whatever your child wants to express. When the timer is up, if they still have strong feelings and thoughts, you can invite them to "store" them in an imaginary feelings box in their mind or an actual box they create. Together you can reopen that box the following day when you are sitting together talking about feelings and thoughts.

Here are some additional tips for helping your well child manage his emotions:

- Prompt him and draw out his feelings by offering words that he isn't comfortable saying himself.
- Share some of your own feelings; this can help open the door.[26]

- If he doesn't want to confide in you—perhaps because he doesn't want to add to your stress—help him find a place where he can speak openly, perhaps with someone in the extended family, or a close family friend.
- Locate a support group of children facing a similar situation who can help normalize his experience.[27]
- Make sure he has accurate, age-appropriate information about his sibling's illness. Find online resources, videos, books, and coloring books to convey this information appropriately. There are many listed in the Resources for Your Journey at the end of this book.
- Include him in family conversations and strategy sessions.
- If possible, help him interact with the medical professionals on your team, giving him the opportunity to ask questions of them directly.[28]
- Help him find activities outside the home, through school, a local recreation center, or your faith community, to give him a place to develop strengths and explore the competitiveness he may be reluctant to express at home.[29]

BRINGING IN GRANDPARENTS

If you have a good relationship with your parents or in-laws, consider reaching out to them for support. A grandparent can provide a wealth of benefits to the family, especially when one of the children has a chronic medical illness. Some of the benefits they provide include

- emotional support for the whole family;
- a sense of security, safety, and love;
- a lived knowledge of the family history;
- child care and good advice about child rearing;

- practical help with errands, shopping, and transporting children to school, doctor's appointments, and other activities;
- unconditional love for the ill child, including those with disabilities;
- showing up for special events, like school trips, or giving support in the classroom; and
- providing financial help, if they are able.[30]

Because finding appropriate care for children with medical issues can be difficult, a grandparent's ability to provide it can be especially valuable.[31] Keep in mind, however, two things. First, if you have a poor or conflictual relationship with the grandparent, including them may lead to greater stress and poorer adjustment for the whole family. Second, remember that grandparents go through a lot of the same emotional reactions that you do, in dealing with a grandchild with a chronic medical illness—and they are watching their own child (you) suffer as well! They may be unlikely to share these feelings with you, wanting to be "strong" for the family. Their reactions may also be complicated by other losses of all kinds, both personal, and communal, that they may be experiencing.[32]

Probably the biggest obstacle grandparents face in their efforts to help, because of simple logistics, is the difficulty of interacting directly with medical personnel.[33] They may also have more difficulty finding outside support, although online opportunities have become more available.[34] Make sure that if you invite your child's grandparents to be part of your child's regular support team, they have the information and practical training they need to actually help out.[35]

Because of their wealth of life experience, grandparents bring resilience and emotional toughness to the table. Their ability to flow with the emotional ups and downs allows them to be steady when you are not. They tend to be accepting of the situation and focused on dealing with the immediate issues, rather than worrying about outcomes further down the road. They also have a wider view of the family, and they may notice which children need extra attention when you are overwhelmed. They often act as intermediaries of family relationships. They are ready to make the necessary sacrifices, sometimes including jobs, vacation, or retirement plans, in order to support the family. Their biggest concerns as they age are their waning abilities, such as diminished hearing, poor eyesight, or cognitive limitations, which may not be obvious to you. Keep in mind that they do want to be appreciated for their contribution.[36]

Grandparents who have a good emotional connection with you, their child, can be a valuable asset for everyone. Even those who live some distance away, or who aren't capable of providing the practical support we've discussed, can still provide emotional support and forge deep, positive connections with their child and grandchildren, through letters, emails, phone calls, and video chatting.[37]

STEPPARENTS: WHERE DO YOU BELONG—BACK SEAT OR FRONT SEAT?

Stepparenting is perhaps the most difficult job in any family: You are expected to step into a role that is blurry at best and often contradictory! You get respect, but you're not the authority. You act parental, but you don't replace the parent who is not there. The children may resent you, through no fault of your own, and blame you for their parents' separation even if you had nothing to do with it. Stepmothers, especially in heterosexual relationships, are often expected to take on a lot of the tasks that mothers "traditionally" handle, sometimes without the backup they need from their more "traditional" partners. It is a tricky needle to thread!

If you are a stepparent, you have probably taken a very hands-on role in the ill child's situation and likely feel comfortable in the front seat. If there is no parent in the picture, other than your partner, you are to be commended for stepping up and filling in the gaps. If there is an ex in the picture, and you are all working together without conflict, congratulations! The children, both ill and well, will be the beneficiaries. If the ex has been in the background, and you have been filling in the gap, be aware that, depending on the custody arrangement, that person may want to step up more, and that may change your role. Don't take it personally if you are asked to step back a bit. Most people agree that a child's original parents are the ones best suited to making decisions about their medical needs, and a parent who has been on the margins, regardless of the reason, may want or need to get more involved when a child is diagnosed with a chronic medical condition.

If you and your partner, the parent, are used to running the show, then an ex showing up and wanting to be part of things may feel like a particularly unnecessary complication. You may think the ex is manipulating the situation or trying to use it to reengage your partner. If you do see bad behavior, try not to get into the habit of criticizing the ex. If you feel your partner is not seeing something, approach the topic tentatively, perhaps with a question; otherwise you run the danger of creating a rift between the two of you when it is most important for you to work together. Support your partner when they criticize, but don't pile on, either. If your partner and his ex have to work together for the best interests of their child, it is better that they are able to do so with some level of calm and mutual respect. Sometimes, keeping silent is the wisest option.

Your partner's ex becoming more involved may be a temporary change, but even so, this could result in long-term shifts in the adult relationships. Your ability to be flexible, to step up and back as needed, will do the most toward keeping the situation calm and fulfilling your primary role of supporting your partner and all your children.

Any stepparent who is expected to perform medical procedures, or follow complicated medication regimens, should have some access to direct training by appropriate medical personnel. Whether you are the primary parent or the stepparent, advocating for this training is important for the consistent and appropriate care of the ill child.

If you are the ill child's parent, and are wondering what to ask of your new partner, the stepparent, start by letting them know what you need most in the situation: support, logistical help, hands-on medical treatment, or help managing the other children. If you are seeing your ex a lot as a result of your child's need for extra care, be aware this may make your new partner feel vulnerable. Be clear about their expected role, and reassure them of the value of their support. Let them know when you want their opinion, but be gently clear if you do not. Remember, they can be a repository of information, or a clear mind when yours is clouded by worry and concern, so encourage their involvement when it seems most fitting. You also may need to be respectful if they want to step back, for their own reasons. Remember, this is your child, and you hold primary responsibility here!

Be sure to let your partner know about any issues bubbling below the surface of which they may not be aware. For example, you can tactfully fill them in on your ex's sensitivities about the relationship, which will be keener if the stepparent played a role in the breakup or came into the picture soon after. Suspicions, fears, and resentments may be affecting your ex and how they are responding to changing family needs. A child's diagnosis of a chronic illness, especially a serious or life-threatening one, brings out all the vulnerabilities a parent may have, even if they are not grounded in the facts of a given situation. Try to be alert and sensitive to these feelings.[38]

NEXT STEP: BE FAMILY FOCUSED RATHER THAN ILLNESS FOCUSED

Family functioning tends to fall into patterns, and looking at the various ways families respond tells us much about which patterns are most supportive of families and which patterns are less helpful, adding to the family's problems rather than alleviating the stress everyone is under. In fact, research strongly suggests that these family variables—specifically, how the family responds to and adjusts to the child's illness—are more powerful predictors of outcomes for the ill child than the disease or its severity.[39] In particular, the lack of conflict, the level of cohesion, and the opportunities available for family members to express their feelings to one another are often related to better health outcomes for the ill child, resulting in fewer crises and less severe symptoms.

Dealing With Ambiguous Loss

One of the potential effects of discovering that your child has a chronic illness is the experience of "ambiguous loss."[40] This occurs when a family member is either emotionally present but physically absent, such as a child who must spend extended periods in a hospital or other treatment facility away from home, or when someone is physically present but emotionally absent, as may occur when a child is at home but so incapacitated by the illness they have difficulty interacting with other members of the family. This leads the family members to wonder whether the ill child is still really a member of the family, and this uncertainty can affect their feelings about and relationship with him.

When an illness is diagnosed very early in a child's life—say, soon after birth—or if it has very serious, even potentially fatal, consequences, a parent or sibling may not want to develop a strong emotional connection to the child so as to avoid being hurt. They may feel guilty about these feelings, and/or feel embarrassed to disclose them, and thus begin to weaken their connection to other family members.

Try to remember that when it comes to feelings, there is no right or wrong. Being able to speak with someone you trust about your reluctance to connect with your child is the first step in addressing the situation. Understanding and vocalizing what has been lost for the family and the people in it will let you begin to see what is still there, the family connections that can still be enjoyed. How you make sense of the situation depends on your own upbringing, your ideas about the world and how it works, and your spiritual values and beliefs, as well as whether you tend to be an optimistic or pessimistic person.[41] Some of your ideas will have been challenged by the situation, and you may struggle to come to terms with this.

> *The grieving we've had to go through, the loss of the idealized child, the loss of a life we thought we would have, there has to be grieving and a letting go of that, and a reconciliation with that fact. Once the grieving is over, it's time to pick up and it's time to move on.*
>
> —Mom of a 16-year-old with epilepsy

Coming to terms with a child's diagnosis—that is, finding a way to accept it as a fact and being able to move forward to address the needs of the child and family, with a focus on the present and the future rather than the past—can have a positive impact on families and even on the illness itself. Without finding some kind of resolution like this, stress and family conflict can increase, reducing the sense of connection and the opportunity for everyone to express their feelings about what is happening. Getting stuck in this way can be due to either an emotional cutoff, in which a person's feelings are being ignored, or an overwhelming grief process that has not diminished. Most likely, you will feel a lessening of your sadness as you deal with the realities of illness management. Although families may continue to function sufficiently well even with these obstacles, finding a place to talk about how everyone is feeling, either with one another, trusted friends, or a mental health professional trained in dealing with family groups, can ease the strain and increase everyone's ability to continue to enjoy the life you have together.

Being Family Focused Rather Than Illness Focused

One pattern that often arises is when the family organizes itself around the illness and the ill child. When there is a severe illness, with a great deal of extended care needed, you will naturally become more invested in your child's medical tasks and may let other aspects of life drop away. This will be inevitable at the beginning, as your family undergoes its reorganization process, or during times of crisis or intensive treatment. However, we recommend preserving a place in your family for joy as much as possible. Keep noticing and marking milestones in your family and celebrating accomplishments outside the illness. Stay in touch with all your children's personality quirks, and pay attention to skills they are developing or interests they enjoy. If you are "organizing around the illness," these things may get pushed to the side as you focus on the difficulties of managing both the illness and the family. While you are working hard at the tasks required, an "illness orientation" may lead you to doubt your ability to be effective in your efforts.[42]

This pattern tends to be more likely with children who were first born, "one and onlys," or a highly anticipated birth, perhaps after years of infertility treatment, and may inspire in parents a sense of mission. It may also be more likely with a single parent. Families who orient around the illness also tend to be what we call "closed systems," meaning they don't share much outside the family. That can add to a sense of isolation and a feeling of uniqueness—the sense that no other family has had to deal with this exact situation.

If any of this describes your family, it's possible that instead of relying on other family and friends you tend to look to health care providers for emotional support and comfort. When your family system runs in this pattern, siblings may feel forgotten. You also might overlook your ill child's need to develop age-appropriate autonomy and separation from the family unit as they mature.[43] In these situations, the ill child can feel a lot of pressure, for example, that she is responsible for keeping the family together.

If you feel that you or your partner is too hyper-focused on the ill child and her condition, gently encourage some outside involvements, whether it be taking in a movie, having coffee with a friend, or engaging in a hobby. Even just taking time to do some reading or listening to music by oneself can ease the stress. If it is your partner who concerns you by an excessive focus on the illness, make sure he knows that you will be fully responsible for and capable of executing the necessary tasks of caring for your ill child while he is unavailable. Give him an opportunity to talk about feelings, concerns, and worries that may be part of the hyper-focus you are observing. If you notice a hyper-focus in yourself, find someone you trust that you can talk to, whether your partner, a friend or family member, or a mental health professional. Learning how to live with intense illness is a skill that can be learned, but it takes emotional guidance and an ability to learn how to cope with the unknown.

As an alternative to a hyper-focus on the illness, you can practice what's known as "balanced coping." Balanced coping involves "putting the illness in its place" and "seeing the whole child in the whole picture."[44] In other words, it means you keep recognizing the needs of the whole family, and you recognize the ill child's qualities outside the context of her illness.[45] Family members acknowledge the difficulties the illness presents, but accept them. They assume roles and jobs that might be different from before the illness, but they are flexible because they know they are valued beyond just what they can provide for the child. They effectively integrate the requirements of the illness into their daily life, seek help, look for solutions, and trust their health care providers.[46]

How to Get Everybody on Board

Some of the qualities that seem to be most important in reducing family stress and enhancing the ill child's adjustment to his disease are the family's sense of togetherness, open communication among the members, and the presence of opportunities for everyone to express the many emotions they may be experiencing. You may be asking, "How do you do that?" There are lots of different ways of connecting the family in a stronger way, depending on the ages of the children involved. We provide a partial list here:

- Plan age-appropriate activities the whole family can enjoy together so everyone can feel part of the bigger picture. This can include things like board games or jigsaw puzzles. Find activities that fit the developmental levels of all the children.
- Work in teams—as long as the rivalry remains friendly!—to integrate younger children who may not be at the developmental level of a game chosen for older children. There are also a lot of new cooperative board games in which the whole group works together, taking different roles in addressing some situation. This can be especially helpful when the children seem to be overly competitive with one another. There are even

video games now that address the issue of a child's illness in the family.[47]

- Watch television and movies together. This gives everyone a chance to talk openly and share their feelings.

- Find a TV show, a dramatic film or documentary, even a cartoon, that somehow touches on the topic of illness in a family. Then you can all talk about the people in the movie or the TV show and what they might be feeling, without having to confront one another directly. By sharing what they imagine the characters in the show might be going through, ill children can talk about feeling different and left out, siblings can voice resentments and guilt, and even parents can share feeling sometimes overwhelmed by all they have to do. Be sure that you are familiar with the content ahead of time, or prescreen the show, if possible, to make sure it is appropriate for all the children and not too distressing for anyone.

- Talk about a movie or show you have watched together, even if it has nothing to do with an illness. Simply talking about human situations of all kinds provides an opportunity to remind people that all feelings are okay, to explore what to do with these feelings, and to develop the collective wisdom of all family members. Knowing that what they feel is not wrong, and having opportunities to share their feelings safely, often relieves children's confusion and distress.

- Look for opportunities to laugh together, which may mean a funny movie or show, playing silly games, or just being goofy together. Nothing relieves the tension like a good laugh!

- Once family members can process their emotions, it's easier to move into action. Talk about actions the family might take to resolve problems or explore something new, reflecting on how the actions reflect the feelings and values you hold as a family.

- Brainstorm solutions to family issues together. This will result in a plan that will have the support of everyone because everyone has made a contribution. Even a 5-year-old can give Mommy or Daddy a hug.

Be Creative

Integrating the illness into family life without having it take over can be a tricky balance, and there will be times it does take over. Developing creative projects can help in many ways. Drawing pictures and writing a simple story about how illness has affected your family provides an opportunity for everyone to participate. Nothing helps us integrate our experience better than the creative process. It can increase everyone's knowledge, for instance, if you invite family members to do research as part of the project. It also provides a creative outlet that can be adjusted according to the developmental needs of individual family members.

Perhaps there is a service project your family wants to complete, as a reminder of the challenges you are facing and a celebration of what you still have as a family. Engaging your ill child in a project that addresses something larger than herself can reinforce a sense of worth that may have been challenged by the limitations of her illness. Brainstorm other ideas with the family, and invite everyone to think creatively about what makes sense given your particular family dynamics, traditions, and values.

CHAPTER 7

MECHANICS OF WORKING WITH THE MEDICAL TEAM

Over the course of your child's illness, you will work with a variety of medical personnel. You may be able to choose who leads your child's care team and perhaps some of the professionals who provide testing and other support functions. Alternatively, your child's medical team may primarily be decided by participation in your insurance plan. If you are just starting out, we encourage you to do your homework as much as possible, by speaking with other parents and contacting the national organization for your child's particular disease or condition (if such an organization exists) for referrals and information about experts on your child's illness.

When we spoke with parents and patients while preparing this book, they said that the most important factor in choosing health care providers is the doctor's expertise. They also noted that communication and trust are equally important for treating and managing chronic illness.

In this chapter you will learn about communication and building trust with your child's medical team. Often when we talk about the medical or care team, we're referring to doctors, nurses, and other professionals who manage the medical care. But the team also includes you and the child's other parent or additional caregivers

> *My child's doctor had a personality of a wooden chair. He had no feelings. He was horrible with returning phone calls. There was no warmth or empathy. As much as this was annoying, I accepted he was brilliant and he knew his stuff. At the end of the day, we didn't care about his bedside manner. We just wanted our child well.*
>
> —Mom of a child with cancer

who help manage their treatment at home. First, we'll talk about what you can expect from doctors and different members of the medical team and how to persist with questions when you feel you're not getting enough or the right kind of information. Then we'll look at what you, the parent, can do to build medical providers' sense of trust *in you.* Your child's care team needs to know that you are following through with at-home treatments and medications. Your child needs your loving support for at-home care as well. Sometimes this simply means that you keep on top of medication dosages and times and set up a consistent routine. Other times it means you need to teach them to cope with challenges such as swallowing pills and receiving injections. We wrap up the chapter with tips and encouragement for helping them understand and take ownership of their medical care. As they take on more responsibility for self-care and self-advocacy, your child will eventually be ready to "get in the driver's seat" and take over the wheel from you.

WHO IS ON YOUR CHILD'S MEDICAL TEAM?

In the world of childhood chronic illness, you may have to speak and interact with many medical personnel from various disciplines. It can be difficult to keep track of and remember all the names, much less what everyone does! If you do not know what someone does, or how they can be of help to your child or to you, do not hesitate to ask. As you gain knowledge of who the players are in your child's care, you may feel less overwhelmed and more comfortable during their hospital stay or during a specific procedure or appointment. With these professionals, it is important that you understand what they are saying and build trust and rapport. They are taking care of your child, who is your love and your heart.

In Tables 7.1, 7.2, and 7.3 we share descriptions of some of the professionals with whom you and your child may be interacting. You may be familiar with some or most of them. Please note that some of these professionals may or may not be part of your child's care team or available in your hospital or other care setting.

COMMUNICATING EFFECTIVELY WITH THE MEDICAL TEAM

Once your child has been diagnosed and referred to specialists, we strongly suggest that you reach out to those specialists, before your first appointment, to introduce yourself and your child and ask some basic questions, such as what to bring to your child's appointment and what will happen. This is a very important time in the relationship with health care providers because trust and rapport are being established. If anyone on your child's medical team is not explaining things in a way you understand, not making time for you or your questions, talking down to you, becoming frustrated with you or your questions, or not returning phone calls, it is wise to reconsider working with this professional. Given that your child's illness is chronic, you will be interacting with these professionals for a long time. Lack of communication and a poor professional relationship with health care providers add to your stress and can

TABLE 7.1. Medical Staff You Will Encounter at the Hospital

Title (degree/abbreviation)	Focus of work	Additional information
Physician staff		
Attending physician (MD)	Oversees child's care in hospital	Oversees residents and interns Manages health care team
Fellow (MD)	Sees the patient, talks with families, brings questions back to the attending physician	Has completed residency and works under supervision to obtain additional training in subspecialty
Resident (MD)	Same as Fellow; works under attending physician	Has trained in a specialty area for 3 to 7 years, then takes exam to become board certified
Intern (MD)	Same as Fellow; supervised by residents	Has completed medical school and is in first year of residency
Physician assistant (PA)	Can conduct exams, order and interpret tests, diagnose and treat common illnesses, write prescriptions, assist in surgery	Works under supervision of an MD Has a 4-year college degree plus 2 to 3 years of medical training

Nursing staff

Role	Responsibilities	Education/Requirements
Nurse manager (MSN)	Supervises whole nursing staff In charge of treatment and discharge planning for patients	Master of Science in Nursing
Nurse practitioners (APRN—Advanced Practice Registered Nurse)	Diagnoses and treats illness Prescribes medication, with or without MD supervision, depending on state	Master's degree, may have additional training in specialty areas, such as pediatrics or neonatology
Charge nurse (RN—Registered Nurse)	Cares for patients but also in charge of a particular ward, such as neurology or pediatric oncology Coordinates patient care with RNs, MDs, and hospital administrators	RN with 3 to 5 years clinical experience
Bedside nurse (RN—Registered Nurse)	Bedside nurse; provides direct patient care, including administration of tests and medications, performing blood draws, changing bandages, and taking blood pressure/pulse	Associate's degree or 2-year nursing program plus passing national exam; some have 4-year degree
Licensed Practical Nurse (LPN)	Provides practical assistance to patients, including changing bandages, administering medication, taking vitals, and inserting IVs	1 or 2 years of training, must pass national exam

TABLE 7.2. Other Medical Specialists and the Organs/Systems They Treat

Title (degree/abbreviation)	Function or organ/system treated	Additional information
Anesthesiologist	Administers medicines to put patients in a relaxed state or to sleep for procedures	Remains in the operating room throughout the procedure, monitoring patient
Allergist/Immunologist	Treats allergies and immunological disorders	Diseases like asthma, AIDS
Cardiologist	Heart and circulatory system	Includes all blood vessels
Developmental–behavioral pediatrician	Addresses effects of disease on development and behavior	Diseases like cerebral palsy and effects of behavior issues on treatment of other conditions, such as cancer
Endocrinologist	Glands and their secretions (hormones), also metabolism	Diseases such as diabetes and growth issues
Gastroenterologist	Digestive system: esophagus, stomach, intestines, liver, gall bladder, pancreas	Diseases like Crohn's, irritable bowel syndrome, and ulcerative colitis
Hematologist	Blood disorders	Sickle cell disease and others
Neonatologist	Treats premature or critically ill newborns	Pediatric specialty

Nephrologist	Kidneys	Kidney failure, spina bifida, and others
Neurodevelopmental pediatrician	Addresses effects of disease on the development of the brain and nervous system	Seizure disorders and other conditions
Neurologist	Brain and nervous system	Seizure disorders, hydrocephalus, and others
Oncologist	Cancer	Usually specialize in cancer of a particular organ or system
Osteopathic medicine (DO—Doctor of Osteopathy)	Physicians with a whole-person approach who operates in all areas of medicine; they attend different medical schools than MDs do but train in same facilities	Focus on disease prevention, impact of environment and lifestyle on health Special training in musculoskeletal system (muscles, bones, nerves)
Otolaryngologist	Ear, nose, throat, and neck	Diseases like asthma
Pediatric palliative care specialist	Heads team providing comfort care to child Addresses symptoms and side effects, especially in cases of medical complexity[a]	Also provides supportive care to entire family Referral available upon diagnosis Discussed further in Chapter 10

(continues)

TABLE 7.2. Other Medical Specialists and the Organs/Systems They Treat (Continued)

Title (degree/abbreviation)	Function or organ/system treated	Additional information
Psychiatrist	Mental/emotional disorders	Provides medications; some conduct psychotherapy
Pulmonologist	Lungs and respiratory system	Diseases like cystic fibrosis, asthma
Radiologist	Diagnose through imaging; perform minimally invasive surgeries; provide radiation treatment for cancer	Performs x-rays, magnetic resonance imaging (MRI) scans, computed tomography (CT) scans, etc.
Rheumatologist	Joints, muscles, and bones	Also treats autoimmune diseases
Surgeon	Performs operations	May be "general" or focus on a specific organ/system
Urologist	Genitourinary tract, including kidneys, bladder, adrenal glands, urethra, and male reproductive organs	Treats tumors and malignancies of the kidney, bladder, and testes

Note. This list is not meant to be comprehensive but to include the likeliest referrals.

[a]"Medical complexity" refers to having a moderate to severe illness, more than one chronic condition, or a condition that affects two or more organs or systems of the body. Ask at the time of diagnosis for a consult to determine whether such a team would be helpful to your family.

TABLE 7.3. Nonmedical Specialists Whose Services You May Need

Job title (abbreviation)	Focus of work	Additional information
Interpreters	Ensure you understand what the doctors are telling you and that they understand your questions, concerns, and answers	May be supplied by a medical facility or may be hired by you
Professionals who address physical needs		
Audiologist (F-AAA—Fellow of the American Academy of Audiology)	Addresses issues related to hearing	Treats hearing, balance, and related problems
Registered dietician (RD)	Plans meals based on medical needs when patients are in the hospital	Gives guidance about diet for family to support patient at home
Occupational therapist (OT)	Helps with skills of daily life, such as bathing, dressing, eating, playing, and self-care	Helps with motor skills and coordination May specialize in a body part/system

(continues)

TABLE 7.3. Nonmedical Specialists Whose Services You May Need (Continued)

Job title (abbreviation)	Focus of work	Additional information
Pharmacist (RPh, PharmD)	Reviews and fills prescriptions	Expert on drug side effects and interactions
Physical therapist (PT)	Works with patients to improve their mobility and strength	Uses exercises, stretches, and other targeted techniques
Respiratory therapist (RT)	Treats breathing issues and heart issues that affect the lungs	Subspecialties include CRT (Certified), RRT (Registered), and NPS (Neonatal/Pediatric)
Speech therapist or speech–language pathologist (SLP)	Difficulties in speaking, such as stuttering, expressive language, or articulation disorders	Can also help with swallowing and feeding issues

Professionals who address psychological and emotional needs		
Certified Child Life Specialist (CCLS)	Helps children lower stress and anxiety and adjust to the hospital setting	Supports families in dealing with difficult procedures and talking about illness See Chapter 10 for more information
Marriage and family therapist (LMFT—Licensed Marriage and Family Therapist)	Provides psychotherapy, specializes in couple and family dynamics and children	Master's level See Chapter 3 for more information
Play therapist	Helps children open up and express feelings through the use of games, toys, puppets, dolls, dollhouses, art, clay, books, sand play	Credentialed Often utilized by other mental health or school counselors
Psychologist (PhD, PsyD)	Provides psychotherapy Treats emotional and behavioral disorders Conducts psychological testing	Doctoral level See Chapter 3 for more information
Social worker (LCSW—Licensed Clinical Social Worker)	Provides psychotherapy Helps with coping strategies and emotional support Connects family members to community resources	Master's level In the hospital, helps with coordinating health care and discharge planning

compromise your child's care. Here are a few tips to help you avoid or lessen that stress:

- When communicating with medical personnel, if you don't understand what they are saying, ask follow-up questions; for example, "I heard you saying that we need to [restate instructions in your own words]. Is that right?"
- Before your child's appointments, write down your and your child's questions. Brainstorm questions and concerns with the people who share parenting duties with you. If possible, send the medical office your questions ahead of time so they have time to read and understand your concerns and can be prepared to talk about them when you come in. Send your questions by email, fax, or a patient portal.
- Consider bringing another adult, who is not a coparent, to your child's appointments. Task this person with taking notes during the appointment. When you are stressed, it is difficult to talk, listen, and write at the same time. Make sure your helper writes down information about medications, dosages, and frequency; names and phone numbers of other specialists; and any other important directions. You may have to sign a consent giving permission for other adults, depending on their legal relationship to your child, to receive clinical information about your child.
- Some medical practices and health care facilities offer secure, confidential online patient portals that enable patients and parents to send messages to their health care providers; schedule routine checkups; and keep track of health care information, such as test results, lab reports, appointments, and such. They provide an excellent way of communicating with your medical team and keeping your records at your fingertips. Regular email may not provide the protections that medical systems' portals do;

in other words, it may not be compliant with the privacy rules set forth by the Health Insurance Portability and Accountability Act of 1996 (HIPAA).[1] HIPAA provides specific protection regarding the sharing of patients' medical information whether it be through electronic, written, or oral means. For an easy-to-understand guide to HIPAA, see **https://www. hipaaguide.net/hipaa-for-dummies/**.

One of the frustrations patients and parents often express to us is having to repeat themselves at medical appointments and in the hospital. You may have to tell your child's story to the triage nurse, then the nurse assigned to your child, then the resident, and then the doctor. This can be extremely frustrating, but it is important to make sure everyone has the proper information to provide the best care. The best way to prevent repetitive questioning and other challenges in communicating with medical professionals is to be proactive. In the sections that follow we offer suggestions to help you communicate with doctors and other providers on the medical team. Some of these tips may be common sense; however, when people are stressed, common sense can sometimes get lost along the road.

Get Organized and Map Things Out

The first thing to do is make sure your doctors and specialists accept your health plan, because many insurance plans have restrictions. Insurance plans are varied and have different names. Your insurance company may be a health maintenance organization (HMO) or a preferred provider organization (PPO). Check your card, and tell the receptionist exactly what type of insurance you have—that way, you'll know whether the doctor accepts that particular insurance or whether you need a referral before coming to the office. Make sure you have your insurance card with you at all times.

Because you'll probably have a short window of time to speak with the doctor or specialist, you will want to make the most of that time together. As you prepare for the appointment, write down your questions or put them into the note app on your device. Look online to see what other parents have had questions about, and do an internet search to help you find questions to ask. During the appointment you may be able to audio record information using your phone, but always ask permission before doing so.

Request copies of all reports and tests. If you can obtain digital copies of medical tests, that is even better. These may be stored in an online patient portal, as mentioned earlier. It is your right to have copies of all of your child's medical history; however, some doctors and facilities may charge a fee for copying, faxing, and mailing charts and other documents. We also advise you to keep the medical information in a binder, a folder, or on a computer. Create a summary of your child's medical issues and medications and any supplements they are taking. This helps you put your thoughts together and quickly cover the key points you want your doctor to know.

When working with different professionals, the goal is to get everyone on the same page. If you feel it is important for certain professionals to speak to each other, sign appropriate consent forms for each person (required because of privacy laws) and insist that they communicate clinically with each other. Ideally, someone will take the lead and have everyone work together as a team. This will be more challenging when you have doctors and specialists all over the country. To ensure that the continuity of care for your child doesn't suffer, make sure everyone is communicating.

Share Family Information

When you meet with a new medical provider you may want to share all of your child's current symptoms at once. However, what may be most helpful for providers is for you to list which symptoms, problems, or challenges are the most concerning to you and your child and describe other issues in order, from medium to lower levels of concern. For example, if you are visiting the pulmonologist, you should focus on which of your child's breathing issues are most concerning—however, if your child also experiences pain, note whether you think her pain and breathing might be linked (for example, taking shallow breaths to brace against pain). Be sure to also share how your child is doing in other areas of their life, such as school performance; social functioning; and activities of daily living (ADLs), such as dressing, bathing, and doing tasks. Talking about symptoms and challenges in priority order will give clinicians valuable insight into how they can be of most help to you.

In addition to information about how your child functions at home and in other spheres, include any family history regarding physical and mental illnesses. Often mental issues get pushed aside or are not deemed important when giving a medical history. For example, a professional should know if someone in the family has struggled or is struggling with substance abuse and how that may affect the child. Provide information about siblings and any issues they may have. Perhaps a sibling also has a chronic illness or another condition, like depression or autism spectrum disorder. Genetics and environmental factors can both play a strong role in illness, so it is important that the medical team knows about you, your copilot, and other family members.

If there have been any changes in the family or the home, share this with your doctor. Examples of changes might be a divorce or separation, a death of a family member, the birth of a child, and the loss of a job, among others. When there are changes in the family system, the medical professionals will need to know what information is allowed to be given to which family members. Medical professionals are legally bound by the HIPAA legislation to maintain privacy and confidentiality of health care information. HIPAA mandates data privacy and provides standards for secure procedures for protecting this information. It is important that the medical team know who has legal responsibility for the child as well as who is involved in her care. Grandparents, nannies, and babysitters all may be providing direct care for your child. You will need to provide consent for the medical team to give these individuals information in an emergency in the event you are not available.

Manage the Stress of Waiting

Having a child with a chronic illness means you will be spending a lot of time waiting in medical offices and exam rooms. Waiting is stressful, frustrating, boring, and anxiety provoking. If you are in waiting rooms often enough, you have read every magazine there, even if you're not interested in the subject matter. In addition, you are sitting among strangers who may also be sick or coping with some illness and/or treatment. The tension in a waiting room can be as thick as pea soup.

The staff behind the glass wall can also exacerbate stress. They may not be friendly but instead rather curt and businesslike: "Your copay is $50, and you have an outstanding balance of . . ." (spoken in a monotone, sometimes annoyed voice).

Offices that have waiting rooms with comfortable and ample seating, TVs, pleasant music, and friendly staff can go a long way toward decreasing stress; however, you have no control over this. Without those comforts (or to add to those comforts, if you're lucky enough to have them), there are steps you can take to reduce the stress of waiting:

- Bring your own reading material for you and your child to the waiting room, perhaps something light or uplifting. It should be something both of you enjoy, to serve as a distraction.

- Many medical offices do not have toys, to avoid germ sharing. Allow him to bring one or two favorite toys or an electronic device (as long as it can be used with headphones or set to silent, so as not to disturb others).
- Bring snacks to curtail hunger. Being "hangry" can add to stress.
- Bring some relaxing music, and earbuds so only you can hear. Listening to guided meditations or just focusing on your breathing can help. This would also work with your child!
- Consider bringing a blanket for you or your child if there are long waits in a cold treatment room.
- If your child has a comorbid diagnosis of autism spectrum disorder, Down syndrome, or a physical disability, help him cope with unfamiliar or overstimulating environments. In addition, he may need special care to deal with pain, anxiety-provoking procedures, and strangers. Here are some suggestions:
  - Make sure his diagnosis is clearly flagged in his chart.
  - Request that he be seen first, if multiple patients are scheduled for the same time slot.
  - Take him to a quiet space in the hallway, or outside, rather than sitting in a busy waiting room. The staff can get or text you when the doctor is ready for your appointment.
  - For children who are prone to sensory overload, consider using sunglasses and noise-canceling headphones.
  - For nonverbal children, ask about ways to assess pain through rating scales and using communication boards.
  - Discuss your child's needs with the medical team and with the office manager ahead of time to make sure his needs are met.

Above all, be gentle with yourself. When you and your child are in the cold, sterile exam room your mind may wander, which is natural. You may start to think about your child's future: "Is this the way my child's life is going to be from now on?" You might have pangs of guilt. Don't let them consume you! When you are having "big" thoughts like this, focusing on smaller things that are more under your control can help. For example, talk with your child about specific issues they want to ask the doctor about. Or play a centering game with your child—think of five things you can see around you, four things you can touch, three things you can hear, two things you can smell, and one thing you can taste. The goal is to remain calm, because your child can pick up on your feelings. Your emotional experiences may be mirrored onto them and vice versa. If you're able to make some accommodations for them and take one or more of the steps noted above, your appointments with your child's care team will be more pleasant, and you both will feel less stressed.

AT-HOME TREATMENTS AND MEDICATIONS

When your child has a chronic illness, she will often need to take medications on a regular basis. This isn't easy. We've all had medications that tasted awful. Pills can be big and difficult to swallow; some children have strong gag reflexes that may cause them to throw up. Also, some medications have to be administered through the nose or a peripherally inserted central catheter (a PICC line), intravenously (IV), by regular injections, or in the form of infusions that can last several hours.

> *I hate having to give my teen shots. My doctor says this new medication will help him with his illness. I'm so conflicted, and I feel the pain for my kid. It's horrible that we have to do this. Isn't there a better way?*
>
> —Mom of a child with Crohn's disease

You, the staff at your child's school, other caregivers, and health care providers play crucial roles in helping your child adhere to their medication and treatment plans. The World Health Organization defines "adherence" as "the extent to which a person's behavior taking medication, following a diet, and/or executing lifestyle changes corresponds with agreed recommendations from a health care provider."[2] Sticking to medical regimens is one of the most common problems in managing childhood chronic illnesses.

It has been reported that approximately 50% of children do not adhere to their medication treatments; this figure has been documented to be as high as 75% for adolescent and young adult patients.[3] Research also indicates that patients with chronic illnesses, such as epilepsy, asthma, and diabetes, exhibit poor adherence because the duration of their treatment is long, they often take multiple medications, and they have periods of symptom remission.[4] Poor adherence not only leads to worse medical outcomes but also complicates the relationship between the medical team and the patient (and between the medical team and the patient's parents).

What causes people to not maintain a routine or stick to their prescribed medical treatment plan? The demands of a busy work and family life, other commitments in the schedules of parents and children, stress, and typical family conflicts are noted as the greatest barriers to medication adherence.[5] Other reasons include parents' lack of understanding of the diagnosis and misperceptions of the severity of the disease, concerns about the effectiveness of medications, fear of medication side effects, and the benefits of treatment. Age, socioeconomic status, race, and other family attributes can also influence a child's adherence to medication and treatment,[6] as can the necessity of taking multiple medications versus being on a single medication, the quality of communication between health care providers and family, language barriers, and poor health literacy.[7] In our experience, parents sometimes give in to the fear and resistance children have about taking medications.

Money also plays a pivotal role in medication adherence. Parents have often remarked to us that they save money if they don't have to refill their medications as often. Perhaps you will save money in the short term by refilling your child's medication less often than directed, but long-term costs due to worsening of symptoms, hospitalizations, and nursing care can substantially increase the cost of managing the illness.

> We skip giving our son his medication from time to time. We are not neglectful parents. Our life is so hectic that sometimes we just forget. His medication is so expensive; it places a huge burden on us. If we give it every other day, it saves money and we have to have it filled less. Giving it to him every other day also cuts down on the struggles and meltdowns, because he doesn't like taking the pills. We know it's best for him and his health to take the medication daily, but it's so stressful for all of us.
>
> —Mom of a child with ulcerative colitis

If you simply cannot afford to buy the necessary medications for your child's illness, you're not alone. Medication costs have soared, and insurance may cover only a fraction of them. Doctors are aware of this, and they will not judge you if you ask about costs of medications and whether there are lower cost alternatives, such as generic drugs. They may not be aware of exact drug prices or what portion of prescription costs different insurance plans cover, but you can help them out by bringing your insurance plan's current formulary (list of treatments and drugs the plan covers) to your child's visits. Doctors often have samples of medications they will give you at the office, which can save you some money. We have provided some resources in the back of the book (the Resources for Your Journey) on obtaining medications at a reduced or no cost if you qualify.

> *Between the medications, supplements, and other health care costs, we pay over $1,500 a month. Our insurance has changed, and we are paying more now than ever. We had to cut back on other things in our lives. I don't want to let my child know the costs. I don't want her to feel bad. She feels bad enough.*
>
> —Mom of a daughter with multiple medical diagnoses

Medication adherence isn't all on your shoulders, though. Physicians and other health care providers should take the time to thoroughly educate you about your child's medications and treatment plan. Remember, this is all new to you, so go easy on yourself. Learning a new at-home procedure can take a lot of energy; going over it step by step with the doctor will save you frustration and worry later. We encourage you to ask for written instructions. You may have questions like, "Why does she need to eat before the medicine?" or "What if we forget a dose?" Ask whom you should call if you have follow-up questions or problems. If you don't understand something, say something.

The communication skills you hone while interacting with your child's providers and other medical staff will help you in other situations as well. As the parent, you may have to orchestrate communication about your child's medications with school nurses, pharmacists, teachers, guidance counselors, school social workers, school administration, and child study teams. (Check Chapter 8 for ideas about developing a school medication management plan.)

Improving Adherence

Nobody knows your child better than you do. You know what works and what doesn't, what motivates him and what leads to meltdowns. When it comes to giving your child medication on a consistent basis, though, all bets may be off. When children are required to receive medication in uncomfortable ways, it can bring on anger, fear, and anticipatory anxiety reactions. How can you blame them? Aside from the taste and size of medications, or the possible pain induced, it's also an interruption in their lives. As one young patient stated, "I hate having to pause my video game to take my stupid pills!" Children have shared that they feel embarrassed that they need to stop at the school nurse's office before or after lunch, and upset that it will limit their meal or playtime. It also sets them apart, making them feel different from the other children. They may already feel this way because of their illness, but medication is another reminder that engenders anger and fear, among other feelings.

When we think about how to improve our children's relationship with medication, we need to start by taking a look at ourselves. Remember when we discussed in Chapter 1 about the feelings you had when you received your child's diagnosis? If not, you may want to revisit that chapter. The feelings that were discussed may percolate again in regard to giving medications to your child. Ask yourself the following questions:

- "How do I feel about giving him these medications?"
- "How do I feel about the caregivers who are taking care of his medical needs?"
- "Am I sending a message to him that I'm anxious, uncomfortable, doubtful, or sad about giving medication?"
- "Do these medications really help him?"

- "Are the side effects worth it?"
- "Do I really understand the benefits of these medications?"
- "What are the long-term effects of these medications on his health?"
- "Is there another way of taking the medication that may be less stressful?"
- "Are there alternative treatments we haven't explored?"

If you have any doubts, concerns, or confusion, we encourage you to speak with your medical team. Ask questions. Get answers! There are no stupid questions. The more you know, the better you might feel about the decisions you make regarding your child's care.

So, how can you improve medication adherence? When considering how to approach this with your child, you must first consider their age. Interventions and suggestions are quite different for school-age children versus teens. Along with age, you need to think about their unique personality. You know how they react to newness or trying something different. As stated earlier, you know how to read their moods, their feelings, and their behavior.

For young school-age children it's advisable to pay attention to the taste of the medications. We all have certain preferences for different flavors: Some people like sweet, some like sour. Pharmacies can make liquid medications in different flavors. Several reports have found that chocolate flavoring or other different flavored "chasers" are preferred to improve adherence because they mask the taste of bitter medications.[8]

Chronic illness is difficult at any age, but it seems particularly challenging during the tween and teen years. Developmentally, adolescence is also a time of increased risk-taking, which may include experimenting with substances. The interactions of alcohol and other drugs may have negative effects on prescribed medications. Adolescents may be resistant to going to their doctor appointments on a more frequent basis, and they may stop taking their medication because of certain side effects they especially want to keep secret from you.

> *I don't like taking one of my meds. It prevents me from getting an erection, and I am not able to ejaculate for a long time.*
> —A 17-year-old male patient

Adolescents like to feel in control of their lives and may reject the advice of authority figures. However, they need to learn how to manage their own medications as they prepare for young adulthood. Although following treatment plans and taking medication is non-negotiable at any age, giving your teenager some say in when and how to take the medication will give them a sense of control.

In addition, research on medication adherence has identified interventions that will assist parents in administering medication and following their children's treatment plans. The interventions have been identified as *educational, behavioral,* and *organizational* approaches.[9,10] The organizational approach is one that parents have little control over and is directed more at health care providers and medical settings, so in the following sections, we will discuss the educational and behavioral approaches as they apply to parents.

Take the Educational Route

During doctors' appointments, you can get overwhelmed quickly. Doctors may be speaking fast, using words you've never heard before. Feelings of anxiety and stress can cause you to not hear and understand everything the doctor is telling you. If your doctor has an accent, or if there is a language barrier between you, this may reduce medication adherence. To overcome these problems, you can increase your and your child's knowledge and skills by asking questions and doing research about the illness, the treatments, and the benefits and side effects of medications.

This route invites you to ask questions of medical staff on treatment procedures, such as how to give an injection, use an inhaler, or check blood sugar. As we discussed earlier, ask for brochures or other written materials to make things more understandable and serve as references to access at any time. Pharmacies routinely provide drug information when they dispense medications, and most pharmacists are available to answer questions.

Take the Behavioral Route

A behavioral route involves setting up a behavioral program that focuses on positive reinforcement schedules to reward children for complying with taking their medication. As we discussed briefly in Chapter 4, a behavioral program normally consists of creating behavior or reward charts, such as sticker charts. These charts are often used with young children. We recommend behavior contracts for older children and teens. Creating the behavior chart or contract and brainstorming rewards together will help them increase adherence. Templates for behavior charts and contracts are easily found online.

We recommend that medication behavior charts be broken up by different times of the day, for instance, morning, afternoon, and evening periods, with rewards given for each period or at the end of the day. Breaking up the chart into different times of the day may be particularly helpful for complex medication regimens or when some of the chart may need to be completed by other individuals, such as the school nurse.

Effective and meaningful rewards are an important component of behavior charts. Rewards can range from smaller, daily ones (for example, extra electronics time) to larger, weekly ones (for example, receiving a "no-chore" pass). In Frank's practice, he recommends parents take their child to the dollar store or a store where all items are below $5. He encourages parents to let the child select the prizes they want to earn and to place the prizes in a box or a bag (such as a large pillowcase), and keep it in a place away from them. When children are able to select prizes, they are more motivated to work for them. You can also create "Behavior Bucks" that translate into actual cash that children can use to purchase something, and "Behavior Coupons," such as more video time, an extra snack, a later bedtime, or extra reading time. I discourage parents from promising prizes such as a trip to the toy store because this can make it expensive for you; having an illness is costly enough. It may also not be logistically possible to promise a trip to the store because of your schedule, weather, or how your child is feeling. Failure to follow through will hinder the consistency that is critical to the success of the behavior chart.

When giving stars or stickers on your child's behavior charts, it is important they be given immediately, along with praise for the specific behavior. The chart should be displayed so that your child is able to see it and be reminded about it. However, to maintain privacy, you may want to consider temporarily taking it down when company comes or when play dates are occurring in the home.

Consistency is important in behavioral systems. Sometimes parents will forget to place a sticker on the chart or supply a reward when earned. Sometimes one parent takes the chart seriously and one parent does not. As parents, we set the tone, the rules, and the structure in and out of the home. Parents, other caregivers, and children need to be clear about what the expectations are and what the consequences are going to be for nonadherence to medication regimens. Following through with these consequences is a key component of this route.

Some other behavioral interventions for medication adherence may include leaving visual reminders (for example, leaving Post-It notes on a mirror, on a computer) as well as setting reminders on phones or watches. Combining medication behaviors with other activities (such as before or after breakfast, after brushing teeth, etc.) may also help with adherence.[11] You can even include other family members on these charts by creating separate charts for other children based on their needs. Extending it to other family members can help keep it from becoming a source of conflict. It can help make the child with the chronic illness feel less different from their siblings. If the ill child does not get more attention or rewards than others, giving each child a behavior chart may decrease feelings of jealousy and resentment between siblings. We discussed siblings and their feelings in detail in Chapter 6.

Like anything in life, "one size doesn't fit all." Depending on the child's age and medical regimen, they may require different approaches and strategies to help them take their medications regularly and their treatments seriously. Thus, we think it's best to take ideas from all the paths discussed and use what works most effectively for your child and family at the moment.

Children are really savvy. As parents, we have to be one step ahead of them. When kids don't want to do something, they come up with creative ways to avoid it. Remember pushing vegetables around the plate to make it look like you had eaten more than you did? Check to ensure that your child is truly adhering to their medication regimen before offering any reward or praise. Make sure that pills are swallowed and not "cheeked" and disposed of later. Reflect on the intervention approaches you are using to determine what adjustments should be made, what questions should be asked, and where you might find new ideas to approach the behavior. Talk with a mental health professional who specializes in behavior psychology for additional guidance on creating and implementing behavioral charts and contracts.

MAKING PILLS MORE MANAGEABLE

Taking medications in the form of a pill can be a daily occurrence in the life of a child with a chronic illness. It is quite common for children to have a difficult time swallowing pills in various forms depending on the coating, shape, and taste of the pill. An inability to swallow pills may interfere with medication adherence. Chronic illnesses, such as cancer, may cause your child to experience dry mouth or excessive drooling, both of which complicate the process of swallowing pills effectively.

> *Every time I gave my child his medication, he would gag and eventually throw up. It was horrible to watch my child go through this! I found myself frustrated with him, but he was frustrated too. My doctor was of no help and offered no solutions.*
>
> —Mom of a child with a chronic illness

Inability to swallow pills is a common problem. But don't panic! We will offer some guidance based on research and best practices.

First, check with your physician to see if there is an alternative method to taking the medication that does not include swallowing a pill. Perhaps the medicine comes in a liquid form that can be flavored. Some medications can also be administered via a *transdermal patch*, an adhesive patch by which the medicine is absorbed slowly into the body through the skin. Although transdermal patches are not as common a method of administering medication, always ask your physician or pharmacist. If the medication must be taken in the form of a pill, ask if the pill can be crushed or given in food or if there are any other strategies to help your child swallow it. Be cautious about crushing your child's medication because some are time released—the medicine needs to be released a little at a time in the body. Also, some pills have special coatings to prevent stomach acid from breaking the pill down too soon and therefore cannot be crushed.

Several factors affect the ability to swallow pills effectively: a child's developmental stage, fear, anxiety, and intolerance of unpleasant flavors.[12] Furthermore, pill-swallowing problems are especially pervasive in children with autism spectrum disorder, hyperactivity and impulse control problems, respiratory diseases, HIV, or developmental disabilities.[13]

When it comes to swallowing pills, never threaten or punish your child to get her to comply. You need to remain in control and *calm*. Your agitation and frustration will not help the situation and can make her feel even worse. Never force medication into a child. Physically forcing the medication can lead many children to develop anxiety and/or a hatred of pills, may hurt your relationship with your child, and may physically harm her. We want our children to comply with treatment, not develop anxiety from it. Moreover, do not hide the medications. If your child believes you have snuck something into her food, she may have a difficult time trusting you in the future. In addition, placing medications in foods may create future food aversions. We want our children to get the treatment they need, to know that we are there to help them, and that they can rely on and trust us.

Anxiety can be a factor in pill swallowing. Children may have a fear of choking or vomiting when they take pills. Most medical studies that have looked at this problem have used behavioral interventions that involved practicing pill swallowing by using placebo pills, small candies, and ice chips.[14] In those studies the researchers gradually increased the size of the item to be swallowed until the target pill or a larger pill was swallowed effectively. Modeling by a therapist, teaching children relaxation techniques like breathing exercises, and rewarding the child after each step of the procedure have been found to help maintain children's motivation and encourage success in pill swallowing.[15] Cognitive techniques, such as positive self-talk and cognitive restructuring, were also used in the research.[16] Cognitive restructuring involves teaching someone to recognize and change their unhelpful thoughts with more adaptive, healthier thoughts. Examples of unhelpful thoughts might be "I can't do this," or "I'll never learn this!" These thoughts can be restructured as "I can do this" and "This is hard, but I got this." Teach children positive self-statements and practice with them. Put them on Post-It notes and stick them to mirrors, computers, and other areas to remind children of these positive statements. Practicing both physical behaviors and positive thinking will help your child be more successful and confident in following their treatment regimen.

There are several helpful resources to help children swallow pills. For example, Alberta Children's Hospital offers training videos that contain step-by-step instructions on how to teach children to swallow pills.[17] Several doctors and families we have spoken to recommended specific pill-swallowing cups. These cups are designed to use the natural swallowing reflex to help individuals swallow medications. Before using these resources, talk to your doctor and to your pharmacist to determine whether these tools would be appropriate for your child and the type of medication they are taking.

NEEDLE FEARS: A STICK-Y SITUATION

When children are on their way to the doctor's office, they commonly ask, "Am I getting a shot today?" It has been noted that needle fears and phobias begin in children around age 5 1/2.[18] Needle procedures are among the most feared experiences children have.[19] However, children with chronic illnesses are particularly at risk when acting on their fear of needles because avoiding or refusing treatments that involve needles can lead to poorer health outcomes that may possibly be life threatening. Children who develop this fear may, as they grow older, refuse to get vaccinations, flu shots, or take insulin when they need to, leading to worse health outcomes.[20]

If your child experiences challenges during needle procedures, such as fainting, bolting out of the room, temper tantrums, or uncontrollable crying, we feel for you! This is so hard, and it can lead to a potentially traumatic experience for the child and for you. Whenever possible, be present during needle procedures and hold your child in a comforting position as opposed to restraining them or having medical staff restrain them. There are helpful resources for parents and professionals on ways to support children through procedures—for example, we like the ONE VOICE[21] approach and others like it that aim to make the medical environment less threatening.

Does your child have a needle fear or a needle phobia? They are two distinct things. Children can develop a needle *fear* from their own experience—their brain will pair the needle with a pain response quite naturally. The fear may also develop by watching others, like their sibling or you, receiving a needle and witnessing a negative reaction (for example, screaming, crying, pulling back, etc.). For instance, the medical literature notes a positive correlation between child distress during blood tests and a parent who is anxious while watching the child's procedure; put more simply, the more anxious the parent is, the more distressed the child will become.[22] If this is an issue for you, find strategies to help you manage your own worries or fear about your child having needle procedures. You want to be fully present to help him cope.

A *phobia*, on the other hand, is a fear that has become excessive and interferes with a person's ability to function. It is usually connected to a specific object (that is, a needle) or a specific activity or situation (for example, getting blood drawn). Phobias lead to intense avoidance of a particular object or thing, such as heights, dogs, or elevators. Typically, there is a strong reaction and the fear is out of proportion to the possible or imagined danger. If this describes your child, consider getting a mental health professional to help them face the phobia and learn how to cope with it.

Even without a needle fear or phobia, most children with chronic illnesses will need practical ways to deal with frequent needle procedures or infusions. The good news is, needles don't have to hurt. Yes, you read that correctly. Physical interventions such as numbing creams and ice can help; we discuss some of these below. However, you might be surprised to learn that research has shown that a very simple technique—distraction—appears to be the most effective strategy for decreasing pain or distress during needle procedures.[23,24] Many studies have shown that distracting a child's attention from a needle procedure helps him experience less pain and distress because it taps into his cognitive (mental) resources in a way that affects his body (a slower heart rate or other changes) and behaviors (less tensing up).[25]

You can distract your child with electronic devices so they can watch videos, listen to music, or play games. Other, nonelectronic options include reading them a book or having them blow bubbles, squeeze a ball, or sing a song. You know your child and what method would work best for them. It is interesting to note that a research study demonstrated that although distraction is connected to improved child coping, verbal reassurance offered by an adult, such as "It's okay," resulted in higher levels of distress in the child.[26] Attempting reassurance by telling children they are fine ("That didn't hurt at all, right?" or similar statements) can actually backfire and exacerbate the fear. Remember, when we don't tell children the truth, we lose their trust.

When your child must receive a needle procedure, take into account their age, developmental level, and their maturity in determining the best strategies to help alleviate her fears or aversions to needles. Not all 5-year-olds, 8-year-olds, or 13-year-olds are alike. What we do know is that younger children tend to respond better to behavioral coping strategies. Younger children also rely more heavily on their parents. Older children and teens, on the other hand, are more independent and tend to use more cognitive strategies (for example, "This is necessary. It hurts, but I can get through it").[27]

On the basis of how your child handles anxious situations, use your best judgment to determine how and when to tell them about any upcoming needle procedures. We recommend not disclosing too much information prior to the office visit. If you tell them too early, you run the risk of your child thinking and potentially worrying about the procedure all week or all day. Their concerns about the appointment may affect sleep and schoolwork. Don't mention a shot unless they ask—and they *will* ask. If you don't know whether your child will be getting a shot, it's best to say, "I'm not sure. We'll have to ask the doctor when we get there." Be brief and don't over-talk it. Too much talk equals too many questions, which equals too much worrying.

In addition to the studies we mentioned above, research on the use of pharmacological and nonpharmacological methods and products for diminishing or preventing needle pain for children continues to evolve. Amy Baxter, an emergency pediatrician and pain management researcher, has developed several products to solve the problem of pain for children.[28] You can also apply an anesthetic cream, such as lidocaine, onto the skin for about 20 minutes before the shot. Talk to your pediatrician about what brand they recommend. After the shot, apply ice to the area. The coldness of the ice may serve as a distraction because it offers a different physical sensation. We encourage you to ask your health care team about these methods.

Regardless of which coping methods your child uses for procedures involving needles, be sure to give him plenty of loving statements and positive praise when it's over. Use soothing, encouraging words, and express your empathy:

- "I know that was really difficult for you. It's over now. I'm proud of you."
- "I am so proud that you were brave when you got the shot. I know the needle hurt you."
- "It's okay that you cried. Our tears tell us something hurts."

If your child knows about the procedure ahead of time, or it is scheduled, you can set up a behavioral reward system like the ones we discussed earlier. You can offer a reward after the procedure for being brave, for not giving the doctor a hard time, for not giving you a difficult time, and for using the techniques you taught them on how to handle their fears.

All the coping tools in the world may just not work for your child. If she continues to experience great distress, and needles are a central part of her treatment (i.e., frequent needle pricks, infusions, or IV therapies), it may be advisable to seek the assistance of a mental health professional or, if your child's appointments are in a hospital, ask to have a child life specialist present to help you and your child navigate the use of needles for upcoming appointments.

NEXT STEP: GIVING YOUR CHILD MORE RESPONSIBILITY FOR HEALTH CARE COMMUNICATION

It is likely that, up until the teen years, you have been responsible for all the decisions about your child's health and well-being. Adolescents want more say and more autonomy when it comes to their lives, including their health. This can be scary, for various reasons. One reason is you might not be ready to give up control of decisions for your child. Discuss what you are comfortable with them managing and what you are not. You will get more "mileage" from your adolescent and your relationship with them if you keep communication open, setting boundaries and expectations ahead of time.

Your adolescent's ability to follow through can be an issue as well. In Chapter 4 we discussed allowing some flexibility in adherence to medication, in coordination with the medical team, and when the natural consequences of failure to follow through aren't severe. This is potentially dangerous for some conditions, however, so it is important to follow up, provide gentle reminders, and encourage your child to keep up with their treatments. You may get plenty of resistance, arguments, eye rolling, and requests to "stop nagging me!" Communicate with your teen and help them understand that trust equals freedom. If they betray your trust, this will lead to more restrictions on their freedom regarding their health care and in other areas of their life, such as driving and curfew.

You may want to begin with assigning your child small health-related responsibilities and building from there. We described a few of these responsibilities in Chapter 4. You know your child's strengths, weaknesses, maturity level, and what she can handle. Sometimes our children surprise us with what they are capable of doing. Chronic illness can sometimes make us forget about that. Children, teens, and parents feel disempowered by an illness they did not ask for. Fostering more responsibility and autonomy brings

233

some of that power back to all who are involved. In addition to the "jobs" you've given your child so far (such as creating a healthy menu, or inhaling and exhaling to the count of four during a treatment), here are some things you can do to help them deepen their ownership of their health:

- Assign small responsibilities, such as calling in a prescription and going to the pharmacy and picking up medications.
- Encourage your teen to spend some time alone with their doctor or other health care provider. This will help foster a trusting relationship between your child and the provider. Adolescents and even younger children may have questions they are embarrassed to ask in front of you. Allowing our children to have privacy teaches them about setting and respecting boundaries. This is an important life skill.
- Teens or younger children with phones should keep as contacts the phone numbers of medical providers, emergency contacts, and whom to contact if they need medical supplies.
- As your child matures, she should be educated about her medical history, including medications, previous tests or procedures, hospitalizations, or any other treatments. Adolescents should be knowledgeable about any family history that may be relevant.
- You can show your child how to access their medical records— those you keep filed at home, whether in a paper file or computer, or on their medical provider's online portals. Note that, under HIPAA, there may be some instances where children under age 18 can withhold their consent for parental access to their records. Depending on state law, the age may be as young as 10.
- It may be helpful to teach older teens about the family's insurance provider, give them the numbers for the insurance company,

and discuss how to speak with an insurance representative. Have your teen sit in with you during phone calls or meetings and learn what questions to ask and how to handle filing claims and following up on payment.

Before you know it, your adolescent child will be at the door of young adulthood. It is your job to prepare her the best way you know how to navigate the roads of chronic illness and her health care. Whenever you have the opportunity, involve her in learning health care information so she can make healthy decisions. This may test your patience because she may be reluctant about becoming involved in her health care. Sometimes resistance stems from fear, anxiety, and denial about what is happening to her. As you prepare your teen to advocate for herself and to take responsibility for her health care issues, reassure her that you are not going anywhere. Communicate that you are always there for support and guidance if she needs it. Sometimes—despite an adolescent's declaration that "I don't need you!"—it may be comforting for her to know that you are not far away.

CHAPTER 8

MECHANICS OF WORKING WITH THE SCHOOL TEAM

Attending school is a child's primary job. When your child has a chronic illness, it can interfere with learning. It can make any school-related stress and anxiety worse and can affect their social relationships. Studies indicate that children with chronic illnesses often have mixed school experiences and worse academic outcomes than children without chronic illnesses.[1] Research also shows that poorer school experiences and outcomes are linked to the severity of the disease, stronger medication side effects, and lower socioeconomic status.[2]

Prolonged school absences interrupt classroom time, homework, social lives, and extracurricular activities. When your child is absent for long periods, they spend a lot of time just trying to keep up. This game of catch-up can seem like a losing battle and only increases the child's anxiety, and they may think, "I will never get caught up." Medications and symptoms can impair concentration and attention, making learning difficult.

Teachers who demonstrate supportive attitudes and behavior toward children with chronic illnesses can have a big impact on those children's academic, social, and overall school outcomes.[3] The systems that direct how teachers and others in your child's school deliver education services also play a big role in your child's experience. The word "systems" refers to the school's technology resources, classroom aides, continuing education for teachers about special needs, and other types of support, and to policies and laws that govern how schools serve children and families.[4]

Our hope is that, despite the limitations chronic illness may impose on your child and his learning, you become an advocate for your child by taking steps to ensure his academic and extracurricular needs are met. In addition, we hope you will empower your child to learn to advocate for himself by teaching him how to tell school personnel and classmates what he needs to succeed. Regardless of your child's complaints about school, he does want to succeed.

Most children with illnesses report to us that they would rather be in school than in a hospital or undergoing some painful or uncomfortable medical test. Staying home and not feeling well gets old fast and leads to feelings of isolation, loneliness, and depression. Working with your school can help your student feel like they belong, rather than feeling on the outside of things. When schools work in conjunction with children, parents, health care providers, and others, children can thrive despite their medical issues. The goal is to establish and maintain a safe, supportive environment so that children with chronic illnesses are afforded the same learning opportunities as other students.

In this chapter you'll learn how to help your child get support in the form of Individualized Education Programs (IEPs), or a 504 plan, if they qualify.[5] We will also explore alternatives to traditional classroom schooling, such as home schooling and technology-assisted learning. Then we'll offer some tips for opening up communication around school refusal. Finally, we will walk you through bumpy sections of road you may encounter on your parenting journey—stigma and bullying—and show you some strategies to help keep you and your child from "spinning out" if you hit these bumps.

CIVIL RIGHTS LAWS THAT SUPPORT YOUR CHILD

When your child has been diagnosed, or when she needs to have a medical procedure, be sure to speak with your medical team to determine the length of time she may be out of school. Of course, health care providers do not have a crystal ball, so they are not able to predict this with 100% accuracy, but they should be able to give you a rough estimate so you and the school can plan accordingly. It is also important to ask your doctor how medications, treatments, and the illness itself may interfere with your child's energy levels, concentration and focus, stamina, and her overall ability to do schoolwork. This is important because sometimes children will use their illness as an excuse to avoid doing work or going to school. (We discuss the issue of school refusal in more detail later in the chapter.) When you discuss these issues with your health care providers you will have a better idea of what to expect and can plan accordingly with the school, Child Study Teams, tutors, and other support personnel.

Under U.S. federal civil rights law, a child with a chronic illness has legal rights connected to school, specifically under the Individuals With Disabilities Education Improvement Act (IDEA)[6] and the Rehabilitation Act of 1973.[7] IDEA entitles children with chronic or life-threatening illnesses to educational support and possible free services. The Rehabilitation Act of 1973 protects the civil and constitutional rights of people with disabilities. As with other aspects of managing chronic illness in children, to learn what services and protections can help your child, you will have to do research and start communicating about his needs. We'll describe this process next.

Individualized Education Programs

To help your child succeed in school, you may need an IEP or a 504 plan. An IEP is a legal document developed for a child who needs special education. A team of professionals called the "Child Study Team" develops the plan, and you and your child are involved in making recommendations and approving its implementation. The IEP acts as a map that lays out measurable goals and objectives for certain types of instruction and supports for the child and details specific services to help him succeed in the school setting. In order to get an IEP, there are two requirements. The first is that your child has one or more of the 13 disabilities listed in IDEA:[8]

1. *Specific learning disability.* This is the most common category under IDEA. These conditions affect a child's ability to read, write, speak, listen, reason, or do math.

2. *Autism spectrum disorder.* This disorder affects a child's social and communication skills. Behavior may also be affected.

3. *Other health impairment.* This is an umbrella term that covers conditions that impair a child's energy, strength, or alertness.

4. *Emotional disturbance.* Many types of mental health disorders fall under this category, such as depression, anxiety, and bipolar disorder, to name only a few. Some of these may also be covered under "Other Health Impairment."

5. *Visual impairment, including blindness.* This covers children who have partial sight or blindness. A child with vision problems who wears glasses does not qualify in this category.

6. *Speech or language impairment.* This category covers children with challenges in speech or language. Examples of this might be stuttering or problems with receptive language (the ability to understand what is said to them) or expressive language (the ability to express oneself to others).

7. *Deafness.* This category encompasses all children who have a diagnosis of deafness and children who cannot hear most sounds even with the assistance of a hearing aid.

8. *Hearing impairment.* This category includes children with hearing loss not covered by the deafness category. This impairment can change over time.
9. *Deaf–blindness.* Children who have this diagnosis have severe hearing and vision loss.
10. *Intellectual disability.* This is for children who have been diagnosed as having below-average intellectual ability.
11. *Orthopedic impairment.* This category includes children who lack function or ability in a part or parts of their bodies. Cerebral palsy and dystonia (uncontrollable muscle contractions) fall into this category.
12. *Traumatic brain injury.* Children in this category may have some brain injury due to an accident.
13. *Multiple disabilities.* This category includes children who have more than one condition covered by the IDEA legislation.

The second criterion for obtaining an IEP for your child is that the disability must affect the child's educational performance and/or their ability to learn and benefit from the general education curriculum.

Children who attend public schools are eligible for IEPs. Children who attend private or religious schools are not offered IEPs, but they are able to access special education services through what is referred to as a "service plan," also called an "individual service plan."[9] IEPs can be designed for children as young as age 3. Meetings are planned periodically to review progress and make adjustments and recommendations. It is important, as your child gets older, that they participate in their own IEP meetings; it helps them have a say in their education plan and teaches them to advocate for themselves. As in medical settings, when children participate they take more ownership of their care and learn to articulate their needs to the adults around them. This kind of self-advocacy is important because your child's school IEP will not automatically travel with them if they go to college. Students eligible for services can still get them through the college's disability services. Offices of Disability are on all college campuses.

To be eligible for an IEP, your child will have to have a full evaluation that addresses psychological, learning, social, and other areas by members of your school's Child Study Team. There are strict legal requirements about who participates in the testing and the formulation of the IEP. The team must consist of the following:[10]

- a child's parent/parents/caregiver/legal guardian,
- a minimum of one of your child's mainstream teachers,
- at least one special education teacher,
- a school psychologist, and
- a school district representative who has authority in regard to special education services.

Once the assessment is completed, the Child Study Team will review the results and create a program of different services that relate to your child's strengths and weaknesses. Within an IEP, an instruction plan will be created for your child. In addition to plans and services that will help your child improve in the academic arena, the IEP may include special accommodations, such as extended time for test taking, as well as special therapies such as speech or occupational therapy. The plan will also address how the school will monitor and track your child's progress or lack thereof.

If changes occur in your child's academic life, an IEP may need to be modified. After your child is initially evaluated, they typically are reevaluated every 3 years; however, this varies from state to state. IDEA does not define when reevaluations should be conducted. If you believe your child's needs change regarding instruction, supports, or services, reach out to the Child Study Team, in writing, to set up a meeting to discuss your concerns. Do not wait until the reevaluation time.

You can also ask your school district to have your child assessed by an outside expert. This is called an "independent educational evaluation" (IEE). Be aware, though, that the school district is not obligated to pay for an IEE and may not consider it in your child's educational plan. Outside assessments can be costly and may or may not be covered by your health insurance. Call your insurance company ahead of time to avoid any surprises.

When dealing with school systems, you may not be familiar with the laws and rights you and your child have. School systems can be intimidating. If you are feeling overwhelmed or confused by the jargon or the process, there are people who can help you. For example, you can hire an attorney who specializes in school law. Such an attorney works with the school on your behalf and gives advice about your child's legal rights. Lawyers will review education plans, write letters to the school, and prepare any legal paperwork. They will represent you in any mediation, hearings, or due-process meetings.[11] The school can bring their own attorney to meetings as well. We have been told that bringing an attorney to a meeting is often seen as confrontational; also, hiring an attorney can be costly. With health care costs and other medical out-of-pocket expenses, it may not be financially feasible. If you choose not to go down the route of hiring an attorney, you can hire an advocate who specializes in special education.

A special education advocate can help guide you through the special education process. Advocates may have been education specialists, teachers, or parents of children with special needs. They know the ins and outs of the law but may or may not have legal training. They also negotiate with the school on your child's behalf and give advice on education services and plans. They will speak for you in meetings and assist with recommendations of services and

243

specialists. They can help write letters for you and can represent you in due-process hearings, though their attendance at such hearings is permitted only in certain states.[12] Unlike attorneys, advocates cannot offer legal advice or prepare legal documents. Also, advocates do not possess any specific license or certification; however, some have completed specific training programs.[13]

Many school systems are receptive to having advocates attend meetings, and it is often seen as the norm. Most advocates do charge for their services; some charge by the hour, and others charge a flat fee. Depending on your child's situation and needs, you may not need to have an attorney or an advocate present at the school meetings. Speak with other parents. Call advocates and attorneys and find out if they believe having them present would be helpful. Go with solid recommendations. This is an investment of dime and time. Who has that to waste?

The 504 Plan

Section 504 of the Rehabilitation Act of 1973 applies to individuals with disabilities.[14] A 504 plan is developed collaboratively with you, the school, and the child. The plan typically lists any accommodations for your child so they will be treated fairly and have access to education equal to that of other students. In order for a child to get a 504 plan, they must have a disability.

Section 504 includes many different disabilities. The disability must interfere with your child's ability to learn in general educational classes, and it must greatly affect and limit one or more basic life activities.[15] If your child does not qualify for an IEP, she still may be eligible for a 504 plan. Many children with chronic illnesses have 504 plans because many illnesses typically affect at least one major life activity, such as learning, communicating, or thinking. The 504 plan applies to public schools but can also apply to private schools as long as the private school receives federal funding. There is no standard 504 plan; in fact, unlike the IEP, a 504 plan does not have to be a written document.[16] Typically, the plan includes the accommodations that will be made. Examples of some accommodations might be unlimited testing time, using the nurse/faculty restroom facilities, making up class time lost because of medical appointments or procedures, and tutoring. The 504 plan includes the specific supports or services that will be provided to your child. The plan should include the individual or individuals who will provide each service and the name of the person who will be responsible for ensuring that the plan is properly executed.

If you feel that your child would benefit from having a 504 plan, reach out to their school in person or make a request in writing. Obtain a letter from a doctor or health care provider indicating your child's diagnosis. Set up a meeting to discuss the accommodations you are requesting. Your health care provider and other professionals can be helpful in discussing with you what special accommodations, support, and services your child will need. We recommend speaking with other parents of children with similar medical diagnoses because they may be able to offer you insight into developing the 504 plan.

As with many illnesses, things can change over time. As a result, a 504 plan may need to be adjusted. Being open and transparent with the school will help your child deal better with the school and their illness. A 504 plan is good for 1 year, so keep in mind that a plan may need to be updated and reviewed each year even if there have been no changes in your child's health.[17]

In creating a 504 plan for your child, depending on the child's age and maturity, we recommend that they be involved in helping you articulate what accommodations they think might help them succeed in school. Go over the plan with them; parents often make the mistake of believing their child is aware of or utilizes the accommodations in the 504 plan when in reality they do not. Getting children involved teaches self-advocacy skills and lets them assume more ownership of the plan. When meeting with the school, be very specific about what your child needs. If things are vague or written on an "as-needed basis," they may not be implemented. Your child is entitled to a 504 plan even if she is a straight-A student or does not have any difficulties with academics.

Other Considerations

Follow up with your child and with the school on a regular basis to ensure that the IEP or 504 plan is being implemented and that everyone who interacts with your child, including coaches and administrators, knows your child's accommodations. This responsibility is not just that of the teachers and aides. Keep lines of communication open between you and your child, you and the school, and your child and the school. Set up meetings if you believe things are not working. Speak up at meetings; if you do not agree with any part of the plan you can suggest alternatives, and you can refuse to sign the plan until you believe it meets your child's needs. As we said earlier, schools can be an intimidating place not only for children but also for the adults in their lives. The bottom line is this: You don't ask, you don't get. There is no harm in asking.

If your teenager is taking the College Board exams, such as the PSAT, SAT, or the ACT, their school accommodations may or may not be approved by the College Board. One particular accommodation that is pertinent to these exams is extended time allotted to complete the test. If you think your child may need special accommodations from the College Board, we advise that you apply well in advance of the test and clearly communicate what, specifically, you are seeking. Your child's guidance counselor and even your medical team can assist you. Some medical practices may write letters to the board on your child's behalf. Medical personnel and even mental health professionals can be helpful in documenting your child's medical issues and how they may affect their performance on College Board exams.

If your teen cannot take the College Boards because of medical or other issues, or doesn't function well when taking standardized tests, there is good news! Some higher education schools have become "test optional." This means that certain schools do not require your teen to submit SAT or ACT scores for admission but will consider them if they are submitted. Search the internet about this possibility for your teen and to find out which schools participate.

THE ON-RAMP BACK TO SCHOOL

Because your child's illness is chronic, he may be absent from school for prolonged periods of time and may experience several challenges returning to school. He may be overwhelmed by the academic demands and fear falling behind in his schoolwork. He may be anxious about his social life and reintegrating with friends after lengthy absences. Many children and teens report to us having fears that their friends have moved on without them. Some children report that they feel self-conscious about having to explain their absences to peers, including disclosing their medical illness. Successful school reentry requires planning with your child's school and possibly the school district.

Working collaboratively with professionals may help ease your child's transition back into school. Some hospitals have a school reentry team to help with such transitions. The team may include a child life specialist, a social worker, and sometimes a nurse. This team can communicate with school administrators, teachers, and school counselors to discuss your child's needs in various areas.

When the team speaks with people in the school, the school administration can then assist the educators and your child's peers in understanding what's going on with her and what her specific needs are. Communication needs to be very clear; consider having your child be part of this process. If the hospital or medical facility does not have a school reentry team, seek out a professional, like a child life specialist, a social worker, or another mental health practitioner, either in the hospital or in private practice, to help coordinate your child's reentry into school. You should also educate the school district about her needs. Your child, in particular an older child, may have an active role in this process.

OTHER SCHOOL AVENUES

Despite having a 504 plan or an IEP, there may be times when your child will be unable to attend school on a regular basis. It is fortunate that now other options exist for how and where they can receive an education. Many factors come into play when thinking about the best solution for your child's educational needs. Those needs include not only academics but also the physical, social, and emotional aspects of school.

Some alternative educational options for your child might be in-home tutoring through the school district, homeschooling by a parent or other adult, or adjusting the school schedule. Although it's great that you have these options, know that they do not come without possible compromises in other areas, such as social–emotional development. Often children who have in-home tutoring or are homeschooled report feeling isolated, lonely, and different from other children. Your child might already be struggling with these feelings, and in-home tutoring and homeschooling may further affect her social life. Some school-run extracurricular activities may be available and accessible; however, your child may not be permitted to participate if she does not attend formal school. Check to see if this would apply to your child, because these rules differ from state to state.

Technology (discussed in more detail below) lets children participate in their classrooms online, but this is not the same as actually being in the same space as their fellow students. Digital classrooms provide a completely different experience, and you may have to contend with Wi-Fi unreliability, technical glitches, and delays in back-and-forth with the teacher. Finding the optimal situation for your child may take a lot of trial and error, and it may need to change as they grow and their illness and its symptoms fluctuate.

Along with advocates, lawyers, and school professionals, family therapists and other mental health providers can be helpful allies in finding solutions to balance your child's academics, school attendance, and social life. For example, Frank was once treating a girl who had Crohn's disease. She was a sophomore in high school. Because of her symptoms, she was unable to attend a full day of school. The abdominal pain from her disease, the fatigue, and the need to be in close proximity to a bathroom made it difficult for her to sustain focus and attendance in the classroom. As her psychologist, Frank was able to play a coordinating role with the school, the parents, and the patient so that she could receive tutoring in the library for part of the day. This allowed her to get out of her home, be in a school setting, and participate in classes and lunchtime with her peers when she felt physically up to it. There were days when she couldn't even go into the school for in-school tutoring; however, seeing her friends served as a motivator, and she reported feeling less alone, less isolated, and less different from others.

Use of Technology With School

In the past, parents had to go to the school and retrieve books and assignments from the teacher, or from many teachers, and then sit down with their child to go through the sometimes-cryptic notes about the week's assignments. Even before the COVID-19 pandemic that saw in-person learning at schools shut down across the country and much of the world, many teachers were using email and platforms such as Google Classroom to provide assignments along with links and other documents that students could access on a home computer. Because of the pandemic, we saw an explosion in the use of such tools. Being able to continue with learning while at home or otherwise outside the school setting became a must, instead of an option, for just about all students and teachers.

In addition to accommodations for in-person attendance, schools may provide what is called "distributed learning," which uses a variety of methods for delivering information and having students construct or demonstrate their knowledge on their own schedule.[18] For example, a distributed curriculum might include traditional print materials for the student to read, which the teacher will assess by means of a quiz delivered in Google Forms. The teacher could also provide links to an on-demand video, such as a documentary, or ask students to move at their own pace through "game-ified" content or tutorials that have tests, feedback, and extra practice built in.

Students can demonstrate their learning by collaborating with classmates in cloud-based presentation software that incorporates text, photos, and other types of media. This allows them to study when they are best able to focus and are not overly fatigued or experiencing distress as a result of an illness or a medical intervention. These approaches can even build in teacher explanations and the teacher's availability for office hours as well as individual or small-group video chats to go over specific questions. Still, these solutions do not address the social needs of students the way face-to-face interaction—or just having lunch or walking the halls together—can. In addition, catching up with the teacher during office hours to make sure all their questions are answered can be a logistical challenge for even the most diligent student.

When your child's primary mode of instruction is a live classroom format, missing out on the teacher's explanations makes things difficult. Teachers' abilities to gear explanations to students' needs, quickly assess who is following and who is not, and answer questions in real time are important for a full understanding of the material. Luckily, technology such as a tablet can be used to record teachers' lectures or explanations. There are also videoconferencing platforms that allow a student to see what is going on in real time, as long as there is a laptop or other computer hookup at school through which the student can view the teacher and the classroom. This synchronous technology, also called "information and communication technology," can allow a student to participate in classroom discussions directly and ask questions. Included in these technologies are interactive whiteboards (also called "interactive boards" or "smartboards"), which allow students to see what the teacher is writing on the board at the same time as they hear the explanation.[19]

Telepresence robots, which enable the user to interact with an environment that is far away from their physical location, may be an option for your child, although these require the cooperation of the school and teachers in the classrooms.[20] One type is merely an electronic tripod, providing access for the child but not showing their image. They can help children not only attend school but also go on shopping trips or other errands with a parent, or travel with the parent, and they may be especially beneficial for children who are regularly confined at home.[21] Other telepresence robots have a screen on which the child at home can be seen. The robot is operated by her from home, and other students may treat the robot as if it were the child herself, thus combating her isolation and normalizing her relationship with peers.[22] When families cannot foot the bill for a robot, private or public grant money may be available, or opportunities to beta test the technology for free. In beta testing, a family is provided an early model that is being assessed for functionality and to discover problems before mass marketing or production.

These kinds of technology enable the student to access the full experience of the classroom, or as closely as possible without physically being there. However, the use of these technologies presents logistical and privacy issues for you and your family as well as for the teachers and the other children in the classroom. If a particular technology enables recording, for the student to access at a later time, you would need to get permission from the school, the teacher, and the other students who might be recorded, or their parents. What a particular school district is prepared to use, and how that can be accomplished, may differ significantly between communities, so the first step is to communicate with your child's teacher and, beyond that, with the superintendent, principal, or technology liaison to determine what steps need to be taken so that your child can get the most out of school, even when he must be absent.

Technology changes rapidly and continually, so by the time you read this book, some of this information may already be out of date. Your own research on improvements and innovations that have been made will show you what may be available now, where you live. Regardless, having a conversation with the teacher and the school is essential to determine what works for the school and teacher(s) involved. Schools receive state and federal funding based on the attendance rates of their pupils, so it will be important to determine whether your child's telepresence or other online engagement counts as school attendance. Teachers may or may not be compensated for the time spent using the required technology, and they may lack the expertise or resources needed to use it effectively. Close collaboration is essential to find the best fit for your family and the school and school system in question. If your current school cannot meet your needs, others may be better equipped to respond; doing some research and checking with other schools, even those nearby in the same district, may lead you to more of what you need.

The Homeschooling Path

When a child has a compromised immune system or is receiving chemotherapy, being exposed to germs poses a danger to her health. Of course, you cannot keep your child in a bubble, but schools can be breeding grounds for germs and make her more vulnerable to infections and other illnesses that may compromise her health further. Moreover, classrooms can be crowded, and teachers cannot always devote all their attention to monitoring your child's health issues. In these circumstances, through a 504 plan or IEP, an aide can be requested and assigned to monitor her, help keep her on task, and assist her with their academics. However, if your child is missing a great deal of school, you may consider homeschooling, which is a viable alternative when she cannot participate in traditional school settings.

Parents and children have told us that the thought of homeschooling is a defeat for them and a win for the illness. On a more practical level, some parents are simply afraid that quitting work or cutting back on hours to be their child's primary at-home teacher will mean losing income or missing out on adult connections. Some parents and children like the idea of homeschooling because it affords flexibility in one's day. Either way you look at it, it is not easy to manage and balance out your child's health and academic needs. Now you may be responsible for administering medical treatments *and* teaching math skills you have not used in years. How will you manage your time—helping your child get their work done while running around for different appointments and procedures, perhaps balancing your job and other family members' needs? Teaching your child and managing their health is a full-time job.

Some public school districts and some private schools may offer help by means of tutoring, although for public schools, laws and regulations on homeschooling vary widely. The U.S. Department of State's homeschooling and online education website, while mainly geared to families of embassy officials working abroad, offers an extensive list of links to resources you may find helpful.[23]

You know when your child is not well enough to function in a school setting. Many children with chronic illnesses have symptoms that interfere with their ability to focus and learn in a formal school setting. Symptoms that may get in the way include, but are not limited to, headaches, fatigue, gastrointestinal distress, nausea, an inability to sit for long periods of time, increased irritability, and pain. When you are deciding whether or not to homeschool your child, you should consider how their illness affects them. You also know when your child can do their best work, given their illness and the effects of their medications. Some children function well in the morning; others do better in the afternoon. Times for learning may be arranged around the schedules for medications, procedures, appointments, or fatigue.

Sometimes the choice for homeschooling is an option you have, and sometimes it is an option that is forced on you. Parents always feel better when they are in control of their decisions and can make informed choices. Do your research and speak to parents, educators, and your child's medical team about what is best for your child and family. Ideally, you and your school district, or private school, can work collaboratively on behalf of your child to provide the best solution to educating your child and helping them thrive in both academic and social arenas.

When your child is ill, school still has to be a priority for her. To combat isolation and loneliness, arrange for play dates and get-togethers with her friends. If feasible, help her get involved in extra-curricular activities, such as clubs, hobbies, and sports. This helps her stay connected to the outside world, and it fosters and maintains interpersonal relationships. If activities are a strain on her body, or if finances or transportation are a concern, see what you can do to keep her top activity part of her week, assuming your doctor advises continuing with it.

We recognize that children will become disappointed and angry if they are denied a special activity because of their illness. They may act out or displace their anger onto you or their siblings. This is where you need to set boundaries around acting out and balance those boundaries with empathy and a good listening ear. Your child didn't ask to be sick. Not being able to do something they love only drives home their negative feelings about their diagnosis.

As we discussed earlier, you could suggest that they continue participating in the activity but perhaps in a different capacity, such as a scorekeeper, member of the stage crew, an assistant coach, or a broadcaster at an event. We recognize that this is not the same as playing a sport or being in the school play, but try to encourage the concept of "team." The goal is to keep your child interacting with peers. Moreover, if your child continues to play a sport or other activity, be sure to speak with coaches or teachers. Often children will get benched in a game because they missed practice or a game. This cannot be helped if your child is not feeling well or has a medical appointment or procedure.

Balancing Your Child's Needs With Your Own Self-Care

Remain flexible in regard to attending school and doing school-work with your child.[24] Illnesses can be very unpredictable, and your child's condition can change quickly. One minute they may be energetic and attentive, and the next moment they are exhausted and running a high fever. It's important that you learn to be able to switch gears, plan less, and prepare more.[25] What does it mean to plan less and prepare more? It means to be open to as much change as possible and to let go of some of the control. You can't live your life waiting for a shoe to drop.

Even when things shift gears on you unexpectedly, it is important to factor in some time for *you*. This circles back to the self-care and mindfulness practices we discussed in Chapter 2. These practices can help you stay in the moment when you're tempted to make inflexible plans for the long term. If you approach unpredictability with an openness and acceptance, you may be less likely to experience frustration and disappointment. This is an important lesson for your child as well.

You also have to keep in mind not to take things personally.[26] Sometimes this is difficult to do. You do everything for your child. You are going through so much yourself. When your child is sick, they may take things out on you in action or with words. Ask yourself, "Is this my son talking or the illness talking?" Be sure to remind others in your child's life, including teachers and other school personnel, to reflect on this as well. It makes things much easier when you help your child and the children around him understand that his words and actions are the disease talking and not to take it personally. However, it is always important to set limits and boundaries and give consequences for abusive, harmful, and hurtful behavior and words.

WHEN YOUR CHILD REFUSES TO GO TO SCHOOL

Most children feel, at one time or another, that they do not want to go to school. School can be seen as boring, annoying, difficult, and a frustrating place for many children. "School refusal," the general term for chronic absenteeism resulting from truancy, separation anxiety, and school phobia, is when a child will not attend school and/or has difficulty attending classes for the full school day.[27,28] The definition of school refusal includes being absent a full day, having sporadic absences from school or from select classes, or persistent tardiness. School refusal can also refer to instances when children report anxiety or bodily symptoms in an attempt to miss school.[29]

School refusal is often more prevalent among children who are beginning a new school, such as children entering preschool or kindergarten or transitioning to middle- or high school. Children who refuse to attend school often experience anxiety surrounding social or academic functioning, have depression or suicidal ideation, report more fatigue, and present with physical body complaints.[30] School refusal is also evident in children who have higher levels of defiance against authority, higher incidences of aggression, and/or clingy behavior toward caretakers, and children who are impulsive and prone to avoiding situations that cause them discomfort.[31] Sometimes this behavior exhibits itself with no known cause.[32]

Having a chronic illness can certainly make going to or staying in school more difficult, and its symptoms may serve as a trigger for school refusal behavior. How do you know when your child is really not feeling well or just wants to avoid school?

As we have been saying throughout, you know your child best. You know when they are faking illness. However, this can be challenging when your child has an invisible illness, such as lupus or inflammatory bowel disease, because they may look healthy but feel ill on the inside. They may test limits and push boundaries about staying home. You may have a child who has "cried wolf" so often you have difficulty trusting them. When your child comes to you and tells you they are too sick to go to school, here are some things to consider and ask yourself:

- What's going on in my child's life? Does she tend to report symptoms before a test or when a project is due? Before a sports game or other extracurricular activity? Some degree of anxiety is typical before a test or a big game. Some children will report anticipatory anxiety about doing well, fearing they will make a mistake, or being humiliated.

- Is it Sunday night or just after a holiday break? Is your child fine on Friday and Saturday nights but ill on Sundays? Getting back into the routine of things can be difficult, even after a short break. Many children (and adults) experience the "Sunday Scaries" or the "Sunday Blues." Children start to think about the responsibilities and demands of school. Sunday nights may also be dreaded if procedures are scheduled in the upcoming week. Children like and need structure, and when it is disrupted it can be difficult to return to school.

- Listen for bodily complaints. Many children will report headaches, stomachaches, and other physical complaints. If your child reports symptoms of stomachaches but is still eating and drinking regularly, and you have applied pressure to the abdominal area with no resulting discomfort, chances are there is nothing seriously wrong. Some children will report they vomited or had diarrhea. In the cases of certain gastrointestinal diseases and/or side effects of certain medications, it is not uncommon for your child to have gut pain, diarrhea, nausea, or vomiting. In these cases, both parents should inspect to determine whether the child actually had these symptoms.

- Headaches are also a common somatic complaint. Headaches are not typically an indication of something seriously wrong if the child does not have a fever, stiff neck, or discomfort at loud noises or bright lights. Unless he has a neurological condition, such as hydrocephalus (excess fluid in the brain), see if you can help your child push through the headache. Headaches can also be caused by dehydration from not drinking enough fluids, or as a side effect of a medication. Any concerns regarding side effects from medications or treatments should be directed to your medical team.

- Look at their appetite and energy level. This may be difficult to assess because decreases or increases in appetite and increases in fatigue and lethargy are often associated with many chronic illnesses and can be side effects of medications. If your child reports these symptoms and then their behavior suddenly changes when you make the decision to keep them home, be suspicious. If they are running around the house, requesting all kinds of food, your child may be using their illness to stay home.
- Does your child spend a lot of their school day in the nurse's office complaining of not feeling well despite the absence of any medical symptoms? Frequent trips to the nurse may mean your child is feeling anxious. Talk with the school nurse and other school personnel on how to develop a plan to help your child.

Moreover, if your child is staying home because they are sick, this should not mean the day is all fun and games. It should not include endless video game playing, television watching, and running around doing errands with you. The day should be filled with resting. If they have some bouts of energy, then they need to do schoolwork. If your child is faking their symptoms to stay home, the direction to stay in bed and rest, without electronics for the day, may be just the trick. Try to watch them when they are not looking, because they may be pretending when you are around. It is important to note that if your child is faking illness, it may be indicative of something else. Don't brush off this behavior. Perhaps they are anxious about school and want to avoid it.[33] Maybe they are struggling not only academically but socially as well. Perhaps they are getting bullied at school.

We suggest opening the door to communication with your child without accusing them of faking illness. If appropriate, seek a mental health professional to discuss possible underlying feelings that are driving their school refusal or making it worse. Your child may already be missing a lot of school, and they can't afford to continue this pattern of school absenteeism. Not every answer will be found on a thermometer. There are many invisible illness symptoms, not to mention emotional or relationship problems, that cannot be seen or measured with an instrument. Taking the time to talk with your children and to figure out what is going on with them will go a long way toward helping your relationship with them and figuring out the best solution.

DEALING WITH STIGMA

Children with chronic illnesses often feel bad about themselves. They may dislike the way they look, be upset about taking medications with negative side effects, and undergoing treatments. They feel alienated from friends and activities. No one, and certainly no child, likes to look and feel different. Because of their condition, your child may be much more sensitive to feeling different in comparison with their well peers. They may lack the coping skills and emotional strength to navigate the roads of chronic illness and everything that comes with it.

Children with chronic illnesses may experience social stigma or "health-related stigma" whereby they are rejected, excluded, or blamed by others because they are different or sick.[34] This is often evident in schools and extracurricular activities. Your child may be labeled in a hurtful way and made to feel ashamed of who they are. Being stigmatized can have a profound impact on a child's self-esteem. Other children often misunderstand chronic illnesses, and stigmas come from ignorance. School personnel—teachers, health instructors, school nurses, and guidance counselors—can be helpful in educating your child's peers about illness issues without having to disclose personal information about him.

We have heard of parents who discouraged their children from having play dates or get-togethers with an ill child. Perhaps these parents feared upsetting their own child with another child's illness, or maybe they felt awkward in having to explain the illness to their child. You yourself may harbor similar concerns, but be careful not to stigmatize your own child by being overprotective and limiting her participation in school or other activities for fear of getting her sicker. Although you want to keep your child in a safe "bubble," you may be projecting your own fears and anxieties onto her and making her social situation worse.

Many chronic illnesses can be invisible. As we discussed in Chapter 4, this means a child may look healthy on the outside but her body is struggling on the inside. Invisible illnesses are often misunderstood, and people can say things that are hurtful, infuriating, and off-putting. Statements like "But she looks fine"; "Why can't she play softball? She looks great!"; and "Maybe she is just stressed out" can make your child feel worse about herself. When people say things that are stigmatizing, they may be projecting their fear onto your child, which can be hurtful. They may appear to be blaming her for being sick. They also may seem to be saying that you are not doing a great job or that you should have done more. It is important that you set firm boundaries with others. When necessary, assert yourself on your child's behalf and let others know how they are hurting her. Also teach her to stand up for herself. We offer more tips about this in Chapter 9.

Help your child cope with potential stigma by suggesting that he connect with peers who may be experiencing similar problems. As we mentioned in Chapter 4, your child or teen may benefit from joining a support group or attending a camp focused on the same medical issue. Some children and teens love the connections; however, some will say they want nothing to do with anything regarding their illness. Some kids report that they don't want to hear stories and struggles of others with an illness. This is usually generated by fear and anxiety.

Our patients have conveyed they are afraid to listen to others who are worse off than they are and to hear stories about poor prognoses and/or treatments they do not have to undergo. Some children just don't feel comfortable sharing with others because it is embarrassing. They may want to surround themselves with as many children as possible who are not sick. If this is the case for your child, he may be in denial or, more likely, he just needs a break from dealing with and talking about his illness. It's important that we respect children's wishes; however, when they are confronted with social stigma and other hurtful behaviors, seeking help from a mental health professional may be necessary. This may also prove challenging because there is stigma attached to seeing a mental health professional. Sometimes the stigma of getting mental health care can be greater than that surrounding chronic illness. This is one of the reasons why many people do not reach out for mental health care help despite its proven benefits.

In addition to social stigma, children with chronic illnesses may stigmatize themselves. When children do this, they have internalized the stereotypes associated with their illness. This can lead them to agree with the stereotype and apply it to themselves. Examples of this might be a child with asthma who feels he is lazy because he can't run extensively, or a child with diabetes who thinks she got the diagnosis because she ate too much sugar. This self-stigmatization can damage your child's self-esteem, contribute to feelings of worthlessness and depression, and lead to social isolation.

BULLYING

Bullying—repeated aggressive behavior with the sole intention of hurting and intimidating an individual—continues to be a huge problem in our culture. Bullying can be verbal, physical, or relational, and the perpetrator can be a group, rather than one individual—this is known as "mobbing." It is pervasive on and off the playground, in and out of school, and on the internet and social media. Bullying can affect a child's mental, physical, academic, and overall health, and, unfortunately, it can be difficult for children to avoid. Cyberbullying has become prevalent because it poses an easier way for people to bully others. The bully can remain anonymous and it's difficult to locate the source of the bullying. One tool that may be helpful for parents is an app called "MamaBear." This app not only tracks where your child is via their device but also alerts you when they are tagged in a photo, use foul language, or are being bullied online.[35]

Bullying is completely unacceptable, and it's unfathomable to us that any child would be bullied because they have a chronic illness. Children with chronic illnesses already have a full plate of many challenges. Prolonged absences from school and extracurricular activities may limit their peer connections and create social uneasiness. One would think that other children would have empathy for these children and not engage in bullying behavior. The reality is that they may not.

NEXT STEP: TAKE ACTION AGAINST DISABILITY HARASSMENT

Children who are different are targets for bullying. Remember our earlier discussion of IEPs and 504 plans? They are tools you can use to take action against bullying and disability harassment. You can request that your Child Study Team include in the plan ways to prevent and respond to bullying should it become an issue. Children with medical disabilities are protected from harassment under civil rights laws. The U.S. Department of Education defines "disability harassment" as "intimidation or abusive behavior toward a student based on disability that creates a hostile environment by interfering with or denying a student's participation in or receipt of benefits, services, or opportunities in the institution's program."[36] Bullying falls into this category. According to **https://www.stopbullying.gov**, bullying may be considered disability harassment if a child with a medical disability is bullied because of the disability, something that is prohibited under Section 504 of the Rehabilitation Act of 1973 and Title II of the Americans With Disabilities Act of 1990.[37,38] Similar to bullying, disability harassment can be executed verbally, physically, or in written form and can occur in various locations in and outside the school. Disability harassment can also occur during school-sponsored events such as dances, sporting and theater events, and club activities.

In the United States, each state, including the District of Columbia and other U.S. territories, addresses bullying differently. Some have enacted laws, whereas others have established policies. Most states require that school districts implement anti-bullying policies and procedures investigating and responding to allegations of bullying in their schools. Some states require bullying prevention programs and staff development. In 2010, the U.S. Department of Education developed a framework of common components found in state laws, policies, and regulations focused on bullying.[39] This framework provides information on how schools are to take action to prevent and respond to bullying. Visit **https://www.stopbullying.gov** and click on your state to learn about its anti-bullying laws and policies. Talk with the staff of your child's school and learn about their anti-bullying policies, procedures, and regulations. Addressing the issue of bullying involves everyone—parents, children, schools, and community officials—coming together. No child should be bullied for any reason, and certainly not for having a chronic illness. We should be cultivating the virtues of kindness, civility, empathy, and respect for all.

CHAPTER 9

THE CONE ZONE: SETTING HEALTHY BOUNDARIES

Does it ever seem to you that people sometimes speak without thinking? Let's say you are talking with an acquaintance—another parent from your child's school. You mention that this morning your son had a flare-up of his Crohn's disease, and as a result you are on your way to the pharmacy to pick up a new medication prescribed by his doctor. After a brief explanation to this person about what Crohn's is, and why hyperactivity isn't the reason your son is rail thin, she says, "God I wish I had Crohn's. Then maybe I could lose weight."

What do you say in response? Go ahead and shout out your answer if it makes you feel better! Let your eyes roll. Make a face to signal that the conversation is over: perhaps the one where you raise your eyebrows and lean back slightly as if to say, "Wow, I'm stunned into silence. Maybe you should rethink your weight loss plan, or at least the way you talk to me about it."

Here's another scenario you may know only too well. Your teen has to be in the hospital for a number of weeks. You're in the hospital room settling him after a procedure, making sure he understands how to use the device that lets him self-administer pain medication. Suddenly, your text inbox blows up. Messages from family members you haven't seen in months are flooding your phone. Friends outside your inner circle are also texting: "Are you OK?" "Do you need anything?" "Can we come by the hospital for a visit?" "We want to bring food—what would you like?" During this you've been concentrating all your energy on making sure your child is comfortable. Although these people mean well, you don't have time to respond individually to all these messages. Even if your responses would enable others to help out, you just don't have the bandwidth to do it right now. And visits at the hospital, even on his best days, are limited to a handful of people, namely, the ones who can handle you at your most raw, angry, or tearful. People should know that, shouldn't they?

What about the person who is the "know-it-all"? These individuals believe they know as much as doctors despite the fact that they don't have a medical degree. Perhaps they saw a show about your child's illness or read an article online, and suddenly they are the experts! Have you encountered the person who has heard of someone in a somewhat similar situation and lectures you on how to handle your situation? Or the person who doesn't know what to say and offers a generic "Everything happens for a reason"? All these individuals do nothing to assist you during your challenging time; instead, they are detours or dead ends in your path. When construction work or dangers are present on the road, cone zones are placed to create a boundary to keep you and the workers safe. To help you safely manage these people and their inappropriate comments, we encourage you to set up your own cone zones.

So, in this chapter we'll explore one of the trickier communication skills you learn as the parent of a child with chronic illness: how to interact with people who aren't directly involved in your child's care. We discussed some commonsense cautions you might need to take with employers in Chapter 3—for example, how it may not always be in your best interest to divulge too many details about your family's situation. And in Chapter 8 we touched on how to deal with stigma and bullying. In this chapter, however, we deal mainly with the people in your life who want your friendship and who genuinely care about your child and your family. These could be members of your faith community, your child's sports team, neighbors, or others who may casually check in with you from time to time, people who, if they knew the right way to ask, would gladly run an errand for you or offer after-school rides to your other children. We also include in this discussion people who seem totally clueless about your feelings and your needs. With this type of person you will need to set clear boundaries. Establishing boundaries can take a concerted effort, but it will go a long way toward preserving your emotional health.

First, we'll spend some time describing how to bring more mindfulness to your conversations. A mindful approach to listening and talking will serve you well in all types of communications, whether with a partner, a medical professional who is attending to your child, or someone you know more casually. Next, we'll offer tips for letting others know what you need, either on a regular basis or when a change in your child's health condition requires your family to quickly shuffle the usual routine. Finally, we'll present some tools your child can use to communicate about their illness with people they don't know well.

MINDFUL LISTENING AND TALKING

Most of us communicate in ways we learned from our family of origin. These habits are deeply ingrained and culturally bound. Take a moment and think about what it was like to grow up in your family. What was the communication like? How did your caregivers communicate with you? With each other? How much did your culture or religion influence how people communicated with each other in your family? How much do these experiences affect how you communicate now with your family and in other relationships?

Listening and talking are important skills that become even more important when you have a child with a chronic illness. We have all had the experience of being in a conversation and afterward wondering, "What did he say?" During conversations our attention can wander and cause us to lose focus. We have other things on our minds that get in the way of giving our undivided attention. Also, strong emotions make it difficult to listen to others. We may find ourselves daydreaming or zoning out.

At other times when we are listening, we find ourselves waiting for the other person to finish speaking so that we can jump in with our opinions and thoughts. Have you ever finished someone's sentence? We have all interrupted someone when they are speaking, without intending to be rude. It is natural to be thinking about what you want to say next when someone else is talking, and you may fear that if you don't say what's on your mind right now, or ask that question immediately, you'll forget what you want to say. However, when we focus too much on what we want to say, we may miss what the person is trying to say to us. We may jump to conclusions or be listening only for information relevant to our agenda and not be present to what the other person is communicating. This can cause us to miss important information and thus be detrimental to our relationships. This may be particularly problematic when we are speaking to medical professionals about our child's care.

When we are listening, we have to pay attention to not only what is actually being said but also to the other person's nonverbal communication. As the expression goes, "Actions speak louder than words." Nonverbal communication involves facial expressions, tone of voice, and body language. When we don't notice the nonverbal part of communication, we may miss certain information unless we are paying attention with senses other than hearing. Having a child with a chronic illness compounds the number of distractions. You may miss nonverbal behavior because you have so many thoughts and reminders swirling through your head and you are busy doing a multitude of things.

Certain nonverbal behaviors, such as eye contact, vary across cultures. In the United States, good eye contact typically means that you are interested in the person and in the conversation. Not maintaining eye contact may be interpreted as a lack of confidence, or a lack of interest, on the speaker's part. Some sources define "good eye contact" as looking at the speaker's eyes for 60% to 70% of the time a person is talking;[1] others note that the average preferred length of eye contact is a little over 3 seconds[2] before looking away briefly. However, in certain Middle Eastern cultures eye contact is much less common and considered less appropriate. In Asian, Latin American, and African cultures, extended eye contact can be viewed as a challenge to authority. When communicating with others, always consider how this and other types of body language might be understood differently from how you understand them.

Sometimes we struggle with listening because we may be experiencing some form of emotional detachment from the person who is speaking to us. As a defense mechanism, we disconnect emotionally because we don't want to hear what they have to say, or we find it too overwhelming or anxiety provoking. Shutting down and not listening to the person protects us from others' powerful feelings and thoughts. You have room in your head only for your own thoughts and feelings, and even that may mean a crowded space. Parents have reported experiencing this detachment when doctors were discussing diagnosis, treatments, and prognoses.

In mindful communication, it is important to be in tune and honest with yourself. We can be distracted, overwhelmed, stressed, and physically and emotionally exhausted. Dealing with a chronic illness can make these feelings more intense. If you are in a state in which you believe your mind, heart, and body are in another space and you just are not up to communicating, pick another time to connect with someone. If you are not able to give someone your full attention at a particular moment, it is perfectly acceptable to ask them to reschedule a time to talk. Doing this accomplishes two things. First, it will help them understand that you value what they are going to say. Second, it models how to be assertive, tell others what is needed, and set boundaries.

There are times when you need to pay attention no matter what is going on; this is where mindful listening can help. According to Jon Kabat-Zinn, *mindfulness* is "paying attention in a particular way, on purpose, in the present moment, and nonjudgmentally."[3] As we described in Chapter 2, mindfulness encourages us to pay attention to our present thoughts, feelings, and bodily sensations. When we are not being mindful, we may be distracted by thoughts of the past (this is where depression, remorse, and regret live) or thoughts of the future (this is where anxiety and worry live).

We can learn to listen mindfully to others. When we do so, we are less distracted by our own thoughts and feelings and more open to hearing what others are saying to us. We also retain information better. Listening mindfully looks like this (B. Sandweiss, personal communication, March 2017):

- We pay attention to the person speaking without interrupting them, without getting defensive about what is being said, and without the need to always be correct or make a point.
- We are patient and give ourselves time before responding to what was said.
- We engage in nonverbal behaviors, such as nodding, maintaining eye contact and smiling as culturally appropriate, and keeping an open posture.
- We paraphrase, or repeat back what someone has said in our own words. This shows the other person that you have been listening to what they are saying; it also clears up any potential misunderstandings. This point is helpful when asking

our children to do something. To ensure understanding, have them paraphrase your words back to you.

Because your life has added stress and responsibility given your child's medical diagnosis, it is now more important than ever to learn how to listen fully and mindfully to others. One of the great benefits of mindful listening is that it helps develop and increase *empathy*, the ability to understand another person through their perspective and point of view. It is like walking in another person's shoes. It allows you to understand their life experience and circumstances. Being empathic doesn't mean you have to agree with what others say; it means you can acknowledge that someone has a different viewpoint or experience. Expressing empathy toward a person with a chronic illness is incredibly important. Oftentimes children with chronic illnesses will express to family and others that no one understands them or knows what they are going through.

So, how do you teach your friends and acquaintances to listen mindfully when *you* are speaking? Unfortunately, this is one of those areas where you can only control what you can control. You are in charge of your own actions and no one else's. You may have to teach by example, hard as that can be. You will have to accept that others may never fully understand what it is like to be the parent of someone who has diabetes, asthma, Crohn's disease, leukemia, and so on. If they never have the intimate experience that is primary caregiving, they may understand your child's illness only on a factual level. To be a mindful listener and talker, and to model this behavior for others, you need to be proactive in several ways, which we'll describe now.

Choose Carefully How Much Information to Share and With Whom

Have you ever known someone whom you listen to all the time (the good, the bad, and the ugly), but they appear not to be present to you when you are speaking? They always have a story similar to yours. These people are commonly referred to as "toppers." Toppers always need to "top" or one-up your story, as in "If you think you have it bad, let me tell you the time . . .," or "The same thing happened to me (or someone else they know) and let me tell you . . .," and so on. These people aren't listening mindfully. They like to hear themselves talk, are too focused on themselves, or like to be the center of attention. They are typically irritating, draining, and frustrating. They are not someone you would turn to when you need to discuss your feelings, thoughts, and struggles with having a child with a chronic illness. Relationships should nurture us, not drain us. If you interact frequently with someone you know is a topper, consider limiting your conversations with them to nonpersonal topics.

The same advice applies to sharing on social media. Social media provides a forum for people to post their opinions about anything and everything. These opinions can sometimes cause hurt feelings and lead to arguments between you and others as well as between you and the people who comment on your posts. At the same time, social media can be a helpful platform for disseminating and updating information about your child quickly, so that you can avoid repeating the same story over and over. It can be a great resource for asking for favors such as running errands, getting referrals, and requesting prayers. If you choose to share about your child on social media, know that they may have strong feelings about how much information you post about them. This may be particularly true for the tweens and teens, ill or not. During this stage of development privacy is very important to them, and they do not want to be perceived as different. We suggest you discuss with your child how they feel about you posting updates regarding their medical status. Respect their privacy and wishes. Discuss with them why you are posting to social media (saves time, helps with errands) and work out a plan that is comfortable for everyone.

Both on and off your social media accounts it may be helpful to make a list of your family and friends with whom you feel
comfortable sharing information regarding your child's illness and
how much to share. We all have inner and outer circles in our lives.
You can make lists of individuals who are "Supportive Family and
Friends Who Get It" and "People Who Need to Know Minimal
Information Only." You may also want to assign another family
member or friend to handle the communication pathways to give
you a rest from calls, texts, and such.

Pause and Respond (Don't Just React)

All of us could learn to take a pause before speaking. This can be as
simple as taking a breath. A meaningful pause slows your thoughts
down. It also slows the process of communication, which helps
when the topic at hand is sensitive and the discussion may become
heated. Pausing allows you to pay attention to what is going on
within you and to what the other person is saying. Jumping in, or
speaking for the other person interrupts the flow of the conversation
and may feel irritating and invalidating to the other person. When
we don't pause, we also might be more likely to react by saying
something we regret. Pausing teaches us to respond and not to react
to what people are saying. Responding is what we do when we have
truly heard what the other person has said. When you quiet your
powerful emotions you are able to reply in a more thoughtful and
composed manner, and your listener can more easily take in your
message.

Responding rather than reacting requires some work up-front.
Often, simplifying your environment helps. Spend some time each
day without your phone, tablet, or laptop. Turn off the television,
computer, and video games. These increase the level of "noise" in
your head and can serve as barriers to listening. You may need to

prepare yourself for some conversations ahead of time, especially when you have to deliver or possibly listen to sensitive, uncomfortable, or bad news. Gather your thoughts, and pay attention to what you are feeling and thinking and to what your body is saying. This is being mindful and staying in the present moment. Perhaps you would like to pause for a meditation, to take some deep breaths, or do relaxation exercises. Taking a short pause helps with decluttering the mind, which allows room for not only your thoughts but also others' feelings and perspectives. You do not have to meditate long for it to be effective; 5 to 10 minutes a day can very beneficial. The reality is we spend that amount of time, and sometimes even more, on other activities that have fewer proven benefits, like checking social media.

Think About Your Words

Words are very powerful. We are constantly speaking and interacting with each other. Conversations can sometimes appear to be automatic. People ask, "How are you?" and it seems more of a courtesy than a genuine expression of interest. Similarly, we may respond in an immediate and reflexive way with "I'm fine," without much thought and effort on our part to say how we really are. We do not take the time to examine ourselves and ask ourselves, "Am I really fine?" Of course, the response to such a question may vary, depending on who is asking and our relationship with that person. A response we give to the cashier at the grocery store is different from a response we give to our significant other. For the neighbor we see out on a walk, we may have a few moments of leisure to respond honestly while also not going too far into the weeds.

At some times, we speak *at* others through text and social media. If you feel very comfortable with your mobile device, you may be able to type faster than you can speak! You've probably experienced someone else's failure to think about, or be mindful of, the impact of what they are saying in email and text conversations with you. When we communicate electronically, we are detached from what we are saying because we don't have to look at the person and see their reactions. You may even forget from time to time how your words affect your relationships and your well-being.

Think about a time you said something and then caught yourself but were too late. We have all put our foot in our mouth. Words can be forgiven, but they are not often forgotten. Once those words exit your mouth, pen, or fingertips, it's really hard to take them back. How many of us have said to our children, "Use your words" when they are upset or acting out, and how many of us use our words to the best of our ability so that what we say to others is kind, helpful, thoughtful, and intelligent? This is where mindful talking can be helpful.

Mindful talking, similar to mindful listening, is being in the present moment with our words and speaking from a place that does not include hostility, lying, gossip, cursing, or being argumentative. Mindful talking asks us to be attentive to what we are saying so that we cultivate relationships and understand why we say certain things. When you speak mindfully you may notice things happening in your body before, during, or after you speak. You may recognize certain parts of your body tighten up before or during a conversation. Before speaking, or while speaking, your mouth may get dry (commonly known as "cotton mouth"). When this happens it is a good idea to turn your attention to what emotions you are feeling, such as anxiety or frustration. As you are speaking you may become aware of your posture; your nonverbal behaviors, such as your use of personal space; how you are using your body; the temperature of your skin; and your tone of voice. If you suspect your emotions often get in the way when you want to talk rationally, we recommend reviewing the exercise we provide in Worksheet 9.1, "Mindful Listening and Talking Exercise."

WORKSHEET 9.1. Mindful Listening and Talking Exercise

Practicing your mindful listening skills with people you already know and trust can be a helpful preparation exercise. Next time you have a meal with a family member or close friend, or you're otherwise at leisure to talk a few minutes, try this exercise.

1. Agree to take turns speaking for 3 minutes without the other person interrupting.
2. When it is your time to speak, don't get caught up on a particular subject. Speak about whatever comes to your mind for 3 minutes.
3. If you run out of things to say in the 3 minutes, that is okay. Explore what silence feels like for you. Notice your thoughts or any body sensations, such as muscle tension or feelings in your gut.
4. While speaking, you can also pause throughout the 3 minutes to gather your thoughts.
5. When your time is up, switch and allow the other person to speak for 3 minutes without interruption. Do this several times back and forth.
6. When you are finished, take turns sharing what your experience of mindfully listening to the other person was like. You may ask yourself and each other:
   - Did I feel like interrupting?
   - Did I want to jump in and offer my opinion?
   - What was my nonverbal behavior like?
   - How difficult was it for me to just listen?
   - What was sitting in silence like?
   - Did I find my mind wandering while the other person was talking?
   - What physical sensations did I experience?
   - Were there any other barriers to me listening mindfully?

What are some things you can do to be more of mindful speaker? The first step is probably something your parents taught you: Think before you speak. We break it down specifically here (B. Sandweiss, personal communication, March 2017):

- When someone asks you a question or engages you in a conversation, you do not have to respond immediately; in fact, you are not obligated to reply at all, if you don't want to. Take a mindful pause, as noted above, to help you decide what you want to do.
- Ask yourself, "Can what I'm saying be misinterpreted?" This may be especially true if you are emailing or texting someone and you are in a hurry. Despite placing emojis in your emails and texts, your reader may misinterpret what you are saying.
- Ask yourself before you speak, "Will my words be helpful or harmful to the person, the relationship, the conversation as a whole?" In a world of "Like" buttons and places to comment (on social media), we feel compelled to comment on everything. On some social media platforms, people seem determined to twist everything into an argument or a debate. Before you speak, text, email, tweet, or post a comment on social media, think of a traffic light: Stop, Think, and then *Go*.
- Choose your words carefully. Once the words leave your mouth, you may never get a second chance with someone or something. You cannot un-say something.
- Speak from your heart. Words are meant not only to convey thoughts but also to build trust and relationships with others, diminish conflict, and connect with others and ourselves. When we speak from our heart, we can demonstrate more compassion to others.
- If someone believes they are being humorous when, in fact, what they are saying is hurtful, insulting, or disrespectful,

giving them the benefit of the doubt can be helpful. That's just how some people are. We aren't going to change others.

To speak mindfully is to be aware of when to talk and when to be silent. Silence can be difficult; it often feels awkward or uncomfortable. However, silence can be as loud or soft as words can be. Saying nothing says a lot. Choosing to remain silent can be an invitation for the person who's speaking to step back, apologize, or rephrase their question or statement. It can also show others that you are open to hearing their thoughts and that you want to be thoughtful in your responses when they do approach you.

Being a mindful communicator involves being aware of your tone of voice, inflections in your speech, how slowly or quickly you are talking, and how intense your voice is. Perhaps your tone does not match the words you are saying. When this happens, it can communicate an entirely different message to the other person. Maybe there is a particularly strong emotion you are dealing with that can affect your tone or rate of speech. When it comes to parenting children with chronic illnesses, your emotions can run the gamut. Perhaps you have just received your child's bloodwork or some other results from a diagnostic test, or maybe you just had an argument with your significant other regarding a scheduling issue. The possibilities are endless. We may displace our negative emotions on others, like a partner or a best friend, because they may be safer than taking our emotions out on others, such as our boss, the doctor, or the surgeon. If we speak in a harsh tone, and come across as short with others, it is important to own that; acknowledge what we are experiencing in the present moment; and approach the person to apologize, clarify, and talk things through.

Here is something we ask you to keep in mind before you speak. Use the word THINK, with each letter in the word meaning something to help us communicate better with others. This can be used in conversations, online, and in texts. Ask yourself (and teach your children) to consider each letter and what it represents:

T – Is it true?
H – Is it helpful?
I – Is it inspiring?
N – Is it necessary?
K – Is it kind?

See Worksheet 9.1, "Mindful Listening and Talking Exercise," for more ideas on how to practice mindful listening and speaking.

LETTING OTHERS KNOW WHAT YOU NEED

You don't have to have large groups of people in your life to call on for support. In fact, by now you most likely recognize that it's better to have a few people you can rely on daily or on a rotating basis to help with your child's basic needs, rather than managing a whole roster. But when it comes to support for you, or for the family as a whole, it also can be valuable to have others on hand from your broader support circles who can step in. The value of social support has even been measured scientifically, and the literature is unanimous on its benefits. For example, research shows that feeling that you have social support can make you less likely to feel anxiety, depression, and hopelessness.[4] In one study, social support for parents also was associated with better health outcomes for children with cystic fibrosis.[5] In another study, mothers of chronically ill children and children with disabilities consistently spoke of the importance of emotional support, that is, being able to talk about their difficulties with someone who is sympathetic. Although they expected to be more likely to receive this kind of help from family members, the understanding of neighbors and friends was also rated as highly important. In fact, they asserted that emotional support from families was more important than material and functional support, although that, too, was needed.[6]

Groups you are a part of already, such as your religious/ spiritual community, can often step in to provide you this type of social support; indeed, for many such organizations support for members is part of their mission. This support can take the form of assistance with daily needs, such as providing prepared meals, or rides to and from appointments; emotional help, including hospital visits and supportive listening; and spiritual help, such as prayer partners, community intercessions for the child and family, and healing rituals and services. Each community—even non–faith-based communities, such as a club or sports team—may have different ways of disseminating these types of support. Finding out more about what your own community offers can be a gift, not only to you but also to others who express their faith, or simply their care and friendship, through acts of service.

Your community cannot provide support, however, if you don't tell them what is going on. For example, if you want clergy to visit you or your child in the hospital, they need to know where you are and when to come. Accessing help and support requires that leaders such as deacons, rabbis, board members, or coaches know what is going on with you and what you need. These leaders can both mobilize support from within the group and connect you to outside services that they may be aware of. Childhood chronic illness isn't as uncommon as we sometimes think, so it is likely that others in your community are struggling with similar demands (see Chapter 3 for more information about support groups). Let people know what you need, and allow yourself to receive the help that is offered. This can be humbling, no doubt, but allowing people to provide much-needed help creates a special bond.

Equally important is to not take services you don't want or need. Some offerings may do more harm than good, and some practices you won't find supportive. It is appropriate to reject these things and be frank about what would be most helpful. People will be looking to you for guidance as to what is most useful, so you should take them at their word and tell them honestly what you need.

You can keep family and friends updated on your child's illness through organizations such as CaringBridge (**http://www. caringbridge.com**). Their free website, run by a nonprofit organization, allows you to communicate with others any news or updates regarding your loved one and coordinate help at the same time. This reduces phone calls and other forms of communication and saves you from having to repeat the same story about your ill loved one and answer the same questions over and over. Having to repeat this information is exhausting, stressful, and time consuming, and your time and energy are needed elsewhere. CaringBridge allows you to maintain privacy by inviting only those you want to have access to it and being able to approve or reject anyone who requests access; it also has customization features to meet your needs.

Another helpful website that fosters communication is Lotsa Helping Hands (**http://www.lotsahelpinghands.com**). This free website facilitates support for caregivers. When you create a community on the website, you can make a "help calendar" where you can post things you need assistance with, such as transportation for medical appointments, meal requests, or visitation requests. People who connect with you through this site can easily find ways to help you, and it sends reminders and helps coordinate logistics so nothing gets missed. There is a section called "Announcements," which allows others to be in the know about what is going on, and a "Well Wishes" section, where people can post words of encouragement, prayers, and other messages. You can have multiple people manage this website so you do not always have to carry the responsibility of updating and posting yourself. Check out the CaringBridge and Lotsa Helping Hands websites and see what suits you and your needs best.

Asking for help, or simply asking for distractions, such as a cup of coffee with a friend, does not mean you are weak or losing control of your life. By communicating your needs to others, you are *taking* control. You acquire strength in learning how to ask for help and to assert your needs. Do not expect others to guess or know what your needs are. When you do, you are asking others to act as mind readers about your situation, feelings, wants, and desires, and when they do not guess correctly, anger and resentment can build.

Relationships are reciprocal, so it's always nice if you are able to send a thank-you message or return the favor for someone else; however, most people will neither ask nor expect anything from you in return for their help. No one is keeping score. If they are, that is not a healthy relationship.

NEXT STEP: HELP YOUR CHILD SET HEALTHY BOUNDARIES WITH OTHERS

You are the advocate for your child with chronic illness. Depending on their age, you need to protect them (as much as possible) from individuals who do not think before they speak or do not chose their words carefully. Obviously you cannot be with your child 24/7, so you need to empower them by teaching them to advocate and speak up for themselves. They may have their illness for the rest of their lives, so they should have the tools to speak up for themselves and respond to individuals who are careless in their communication.

In our therapy practices we have noticed that children often have trouble managing their own emotions when communicating, and they struggle just as their parents do with setting boundaries and expressing their needs to others. For children—who have fewer years' experience relating to others than adults do—making people understand them, even people on their medical team, who are supposed to "know better," can be a challenge. One of Frank's patients, a 16-year-old girl with ulcerative colitis, said the following:

> I hate when people look at me. I feel like they are judging me. I hate having to sit in my hospital with all the doctors and nurses around my bed talking about me and staring at me. I feel like I'm an experiment or something. I feel they look at me in pity. Don't look at me and don't feel sorry for me!

For children and adolescents with a chronic illness, educating others about their illness and about how they wish to be treated can be exhausting if done day in and day out. Here are a few ideas to help them be mindful and proactive in their communications:

- Teach them that people who say insensitive things may do so for many reasons. Talk with them about situations they've been in where people genuinely wanted to help versus those times when others are speaking out of impatience or meanness. Can they recognize the difference?
- Prepare your child in advance for awkward interactions about their illness. For instance, rehearse with them how to give a few facts about their condition to others who seem genuinely curious or who want to help. You can supply them with a business card, as we mentioned in Chapter 4, or a "cheat sheet" to help them rattle off a few facts when they need to. Explain that such rehearsed responses help them save their energy for people they do want to engage with!
- Teach your child to respond to annoying but well-meaning comments about his illness with, "Are you offering to help me with something?" This opens the conversation rather than shutting it down. You can also teach your child to have a few

responses ready about what helps and what doesn't help when he is having symptoms or not feeling well. Ideally, the other speaker will be grateful for the information and be able to offer real help in the future.

- Humor is sometimes a great way to respond to mindless communicators. It can help to practice some snappy comebacks with your child—not to hurt others' feelings but to gently remind them to think before speaking. For example, if your child has asthma and coughs a lot, her teachers (either out of annoyance or genuine concern for others in the class) may ask, "Are you contagious?" Your child can have a response ready, such as "Not unless you can catch asthma from other people."

- As we mentioned earlier, silence is a perfectly acceptable response in many situations. Let your child know that a non-answer is okay sometimes. Just because someone asks a question doesn't mean your child has to answer it. Have him list people he loves or whose relationship he values. Might silence be the best option sometimes, with these people? Can he continue to have a good relationship with that person as long as the conversation stays away from health topics?

- Teach your child to check in with herself periodically and decide how to use her energy. A nonanswer to someone who speaks without thinking is perfectly okay if your child is feeling too tired, physically or emotionally, to respond. Choosing not to respond can be an act of self-care. Remember, a non-response is a response!

CHAPTER 10

WHEN YOUR JOURNEY INCLUDES HOSPITAL STAYS

Going to the hospital to have a medical procedure is nerve-racking. Lying flat on your back on a gurney makes you feel vulnerable and small—even if you're an adult. You want to curl up on your side for some level of protection, but you can't. You know you must lie quietly and not move, and possibly be "under" for awhile. Even a minor outpatient procedure that is not part of an ongoing illness makes most of us feel a certain loss of control. We may also mourn the activities we miss during the recovery period. It helps when surgeons and anesthesiologists have a warm, reassuring demeanor or when they help us laugh about our situation. And it really helps when friends or family are there to take us home and help us recover. Ultimately, though, being in the hospital can make us feel alone and scared.

Fortunately, it doesn't have to be that way for your child. Although you can't guarantee she won't ever feel alone, scared, and vulnerable at certain moments, you can do a lot to help minimize these feelings. In this chapter we'll discuss steps you can take to prepare your child, your family, and yourself for hospitalization and procedures. We'll provide tips for gathering information ahead of time about the location where your child's procedures and recovery will occur, who will care for them, what the procedures will involve, and how your child will feel afterward. Whether you are preparing her for an overnight hospital stay, a magnetic resonance imaging (MRI) or other type of scan, or an invasive procedure, the basic steps are the same: Gather information; tell your child about what is going to happen; prepare, by visiting the place if possible; help your child practice her coping skills; and review what to do before, during, and after. We have put together a cheat sheet—Worksheet 10.1, "Getting Ready for Hospitalization, Scans, or Invasive Procedures"— that outlines these basic steps.

Also in this chapter we will describe some strategies for taking good care of yourself while your child is in the hospital and for helping him cope with being away from school and friends. You will learn about situations where you can communicate with hospital staff or coach him to communicate in ways that will develop his sense of confidence. Last, we describe comfort care. Using the expertise of the comfort care team offers one more way you can take action and feel supported in your parenting efforts, not only in the hospital but in all of your child's medical treatment.

Hospitalization is one of the most daunting experiences that children with a chronic illness may need to endure, and it affects the entire family. While hospitalized, your child is taken out of their familiar environments—away from family and the people they know and trust—and put in a clinical setting surrounded by strangers, perhaps for the first time in their life. Daily routines are disrupted, and enjoyable activities have to take a pause. Your child will miss school and possibly fall behind if the hospitalizations are frequent or long term. Away from contact with friends, they may feel isolated and have a sense of being "defective" or "different." So many things involved in a hospital stay are unknown, from simple daily routines (like having breakfast); to complicated medical procedures; to meeting countless new people who provide care, monitoring, and follow-up. Some of this is outside of what you can control as a parent, but some of it you can help manage. For example, there are various steps you can take to help your child feel more in control. You can also teach them valuable lessons about coping with change and new situations. This all starts with gathering information.

GATHERING INFORMATION

Your child will get most of the information about their treatment from you, mostly through questions about an upcoming hospitalization.[1] Having enough and the right kind of information will lower stress for both you and him.[2] Create a plan for gathering information from as many sources as time and circumstances permit without neglecting time with the family. Decide what medical meetings or conversations you will have individually and those you will have together as a family. Write down the questions you plan to ask so you will be sure to cover all bases during conversations with his health care providers. It is easy in the moment to forget what you are supposed to be asking, especially when you are getting new information. Suppose your doctor starts talking about her concerns regarding his condition; this could raise your anxiety to the point you might forget to ask about what actual procedures are going to be performed. When dealing with this kind of information it may seem trivial to ask if it is possible to bring a sleep toy or other comfort object for his hospital stay, but keep in mind how important such an item is to your child. Make the commitment to come up with all the questions you and he can think of; then, no matter how small or unimportant one of these questions may seem, ask all of them and *write down the answers.*

Possible Questions to Ask

Questions that you ask your health care provider should address the purpose of the hospitalization and what the doctors hope to learn. If they provide written materials, be sure you understand exactly what they say, and ask for clarification if necessary. We have a few suggestions of questions to ask ahead of the hospital visit:

- Is the purpose of the hospitalization to learn more about my child's illness, or to provide a specific treatment or intervention?
- What procedures will they have to undergo? What are the specific steps involved? What bodily changes and medical equipment will they wake up with after surgery, such as an IV port, a colostomy bag, and so on?
- What pharmacological and nonpharmacological measures do you use to reduce pain for routine procedures (blood draws, heel sticks, IV insertion, vaccinations, port access) and more invasive procedures?
- Are any tests required before the hospitalization? If so, what are they, what specifically is involved (for example, is blood taken from a finger prick or intravenously), and when will they occur? Do I need to make special appointments for these, or will someone else coordinate them for us?
- What, exactly, will happen on the day of admission? For instance, will my child first go to a room or directly to one of the procedures that's expected to be performed?
- Will your facility have a certified child life specialist (CCLS, discussed in more detail later) available when we arrive?
- Can I preregister and do all the paperwork ahead of the admission day?
- What pain-easing measures will be taken after the surgery and when we go home?

While asking these pragmatic medical questions, don't forget about your child's own fears and concerns. Try to anticipate some of the topics your child will be interested in:

- Will I be able to stay with her? For how long, and for what procedures?

- Will she be able to bring a favorite stuffed animal or another treasured toy?
- Can she sleep in her own pajamas, or will she need to wear hospital garb during the stay?
- Can her brothers and sisters come to visit? Extended family? Friends? Other people she knows in the community (teachers, coaches, neighbors, etc.)?
- What play opportunities are available for her in the hospital during outpatient and inpatient visits, in waiting areas, and before and after procedures?
- Does your facility use positioning for comfort (see below)?
- Will she have a private hospital room, or will she be sharing a room with one or more children?

Along with your health care providers, the internet can also be a great source of information, especially if you have a choice of hospitals or health care providers for your child's care. Virtually all hospitals have a web presence, and their excellence in care can be researched through online communities and rating systems (refer back to Worksheet 2.1, "Using the Internet Mindfully," if you need to). Be careful, though, to not overload or burden yourself with too much information when researching your and your child's questions. It is not necessary to uncover every possible piece of information or read every individual review of a hospital or doctor. Get what you need, and then get off the computer.

Learn What Your Child's Experience Will Be Like

Children need concrete information about what they are likely to experience, so find out what your child will see, hear, feel, taste, and smell while in the hospital. Will they need to swallow something? If so, what will it feel and taste like? How will their body be different after any procedures—will there be ports or IVs or other tubes attaching them to machines? What will the ports or machines be doing, and how long will they be used? As we discuss later on, there may be videos and photos online that can help you show and acquaint your child with some sense of where they are going and what things will look and sound like.

Many health care facilities offer the opportunity to use what are called "comfort positions." That means that during an examination or procedure you can hold your child either in your lap or in some other position, so she can feel more comfortable and comforted. Having to lie down can make a child feel especially vulnerable and may lead her to thrash or fidget, which may interfere with what the health care worker needs to do. A comfort position gives her that close physical contact with you while at the same time letting the procedure be completed properly and quickly. A CCLS is your best ally in figuring out what will work best for the particular exams or procedures that must be done.[3]

PREPARING YOUR CHILD—AND YOURSELF

Children fare better when they have a positive attitude toward their hospital stay. When you introduce the subject of hospitalization, be sure to emphasize how it is going to be helpful to your child. Have the doctors had trouble arriving at a diagnosis? Explain that they will get more information in the hope of getting a clearer picture of the condition so that they can treat it more effectively. Is your child getting worse or experiencing a particularly intense flare-up of their illness? Tell him that he will get the rest and quiet he needs in the hospital far better than at home, and the doctors will be right there to make sure he will get what he needs medically.

When do you tell your child they are going into the hospital? That can depend on their individual temperament as well as their developmental level. Having enough time to prepare gives some children a sense of control and the time to ask the questions they need to feel ready to go into this new, strange, and perhaps frightening world. This may be especially true for teens. For other children, especially younger ones, too much lead time just results in more time to develop anxiety as they anticipate the coming event. You can refer back to Chapter 4 for additional tips on talking with your child about their medical treatments and procedures.

Tour the Hospital

Some hospitals provide an opportunity to tour the hospital before admission so you can see exactly where your child will be during his stay. This can be an opportunity for him to see the exact room where he may be staying, meet some of the staff, and possibly even meet some other children who are in the hospital, or planning to be soon. It's also a great time to ask questions. Touring the hospital can help reduce your child's fear of the unknown, as he sees the beds he'll sleep in and learns about the daily routines. Social interactions like this and getting tangible information before a hospital stay can go a long way to reduce his anticipatory stress (and yours!).

Seeing the space and the layout will help both of you generate more questions, and you may be surprised at the kinds of questions your child asks once he sees where he will actually be staying. Asking questions gives him a sense of control and increases his confidence that he will get what he needs during the hospital stay. Don't worry if he is asking a lot of questions or asks questions that you think may seem unimportant to the medical staff. Listening to young patients has helped hospitals and health care providers focus on what aspects of the environment—from access, to activities, to the friendliness of the staff—can be most helpful in giving children a more emotionally positive hospital experience.[4]

Can a Certified Child Life Specialist Help?

As we mentioned earlier, be sure to check to see if the hospital has a CCLS. These professionals have a bachelor's or master's degree in child development, psychology, or a related field, with special hospital-based training in evaluating families and providing support for an upcoming hospitalization. Because of their background in child development, they are attuned to differences in what children need at different times in their lives and can assess a child's developmental level, which may or may not conform to her age. They can also evaluate her stress level and coping skills, and provide games and different kinds of play, including medical play, that will help her understand the situation better, recapture a sense of control, express feelings, and just have fun.

Sometimes children, especially younger children, do not take in or understand information fully when it is presented only on a cognitive, or verbal, level. CCLS staff members often have access to play materials, videos, and storybooks that can be helpful in familiarizing your child with what's going to happen. Some types of play also give children the opportunity to express the emotions that they may be feeling about going to the hospital or even other aspects of their life that may be causing them stress and anxiety. Helping them express these feelings as well, no matter what their cause, can help them adjust better and be more willing to cooperate with staff, which will lead to better outcomes overall.

In the support of parents, CCLS are often the professionals who assess whether a child needs some anti-anxiety medication before a procedure and whether parents are suitably prepared and calm to accompany their child. The CCLS can be a support for the parents during a procedure so that the parent can be calm with their child. CCLS staff also coach parents so they can be effective and empowered.

The CCLS can assist you with your own stress levels after the procedure and after you return home, by offering tools and suggesting a parent support group, among other things. Some hospitals even have programs to help siblings better adjust and get the support they need. The CCLS can provide a comprehensive program suited to your family that can show everyone how to cope better and integrate the disruption into daily life as smoothly as possible. With this kind of developmentally appropriate and individually designed preparation, children fare much better during their hospital stays.[5]

IN THE HOSPITAL

A lot has changed since the "bad old days" when parents of hospitalized children were seen as little more than germ carriers and thus were confined to visiting for only a handful of hours each week. Fortunately, today's medical practitioners understand children's needs and what makes for a better hospital stay as well as a medically successful one. Because of this heightened awareness of how children are affected emotionally, many hospitals make efforts to create spaces that are more kid friendly, with play areas filled with toys, and some train their staff to be more playful, for example, wearing bright clothing or even dressing up as clowns!

Most hospitals allow parents to room with their children during their stay, either in the same bed or on a cot. This option, of course, needs to be balanced with the needs of your other children and the flexibility of each parent's schedule. Remember that taking care of yourself is as important as taking care of your child. Some hospitals and treatment centers may also provide a separate room where you can spend the night and thus be nearby should you be needed. Some studies have suggested that parents may get better sleep in separate but nearby rooms. If you do decide to room with your child, you can ask for some adjustments to the room to allow yourself better quality sleep—for example, ask if nightly inter-ruptions (for example, nurse visits) can be kept to a minimum. If nothing else, bring earbuds, so you can listen to calming music or white noise, and consider sleep masks for yourself and your child, if feasible.[6]

Remember to eat as healthily as possible. Make the best choices you can from the hospital vending machines, if necessary. Some hospitals have cafes that provide a greater variety of options. You can always ask a friend or delivery service to bring you groceries or a local take-out meal.

Allow yourself to take breaks. When your child is sleeping or engaged with medical personnel, take a nap, catch up on emails or phone calls, or even go home, or back to work, for awhile. You don't have to be at your child's side every single moment. Make a schedule with your child so he knows when to expect you.[7] Sticking to a schedule you and he have created together will help him feel a real sense of your support even when you cannot be there. Just be sure to show up or check in when you say you will; that sense of regularity helps children relax, knowing they can rely on you, but it also can cause anxiety if you fail to be there.

You should establish and maintain open lines of communica-tion with the hospital staff, especially as test results come in or the conditions of your child's illness change. This includes making sure their nurse, or the charge nurse in the unit, has all your contact information, including cell phone numbers, and knows how best to reach you. Continue updating your (and your child's) under-standing of what is going on and what the test results mean so you can both actively participate in treatment decisions. Giving them a voice in this process—within acceptable parameters, of course—empowers them to feel they are not completely at the mercy of the situation. It invites greater cooperation, too, which contributes to the success of medical interventions.[8] Adolescents in particular respond well to being included as an integral participant in the planning for and execution of their treatment.[9] Continue to ask questions until you feel clear about what is happening and can share it with your child in a way they can understand. If they have difficulty with any staff members, try to keep in mind that all members of the medical team care about the well-being of your child and are doing their best. By all means, advocate for your child—they need to know you will fight for their needs!—but also model for them how to advocate in a respectful way.

Dealing With Boredom and Homesickness

In addition to the various procedures they may have to undergo, the most prevalent issues your child will likely face in the hospital are feelings of boredom and homesickness. While in the hospital, they are cut off from friends, school, and their familiar routines. Your presence is probably the best antidote for homesickness, but maintaining your child's familiar routines as much as you can throughout their hospitalization can help significantly.[10] For example, you can incorporate aspects of your bedtime ritual into the hospital routine. If there is a particular time of day that you usually check in with them—the drive home from an after-school program, say, or at dinner—make a plan for that kind of check-in, whether by phone or in person, that works with the schedule in the hospital. Younger children, 4- to 6-year-olds, seem to struggle more with different fears associated with their hospital stay,[11] although children of all ages have mentioned practical issues, such as disrupted sleep and the lack of privacy.[12]

Being out of school can feel like a holiday for some children; however, for chronically ill children, who may have had more regular hospitalizations, being out of school so often can affect not only their academic and cognitive development but also their social-emotional growth. Finding ways to help your child stay connected to friends and on top of homework can ease their future reentry into school while also helping to alleviate boredom and homesickness. We explored this topic in detail in Chapter 8.

Fortunately, there now are numerous ways to bridge these physical distances. We believe the hospital is not a place to enforce limits on screen time or use of electronic devices, unless there is a medical reason for doing so. For younger children, access to videos and conversations with friends helps pass the time and keeps them engaged so that boredom does not take over. For older children, especially teens, being in contact with friends and engaging with social media can be of vital importance in easing the sense of loneliness and difference from their peers they may feel as a result of their illness. The use of computers, cell phones, or tablets can provide a distraction, enhance their connection to the external world and to home, facilitate support from friends and family, and make the whole experience feel more normal.

Being able to play in the hospital, whether with digital games or old-fashioned toys and board games, can be very beneficial for children. Play is a continuation of normal life, which has been disrupted by the hospital stay. It reduces homesickness and helps children feel more competent and confident. Children also use play to express their feelings and become familiar with the unknown, thereby reducing fear and allowing them to communicate their concerns to others. Through play, children exert control over their circumstances and increase their comfort level, as well as preserve their mental well-being and self-esteem. They learn positive coping strategies and develop autonomy and self-direction skills that enhance the effectiveness of their hospital stay. Lowering a child's stress and anxiety can also decrease the need for sedation and may lead to shorter recovery times. By providing fun and enlivening experiences, play also connects children to the part of their lives that isn't controlled by their illness, making life more normal and less defined by their medical condition.[13]

Balance Rest and Activity—And Check in Often

For some children, a hospital stay can be a time of rest and renewal. A balance between activity and rest is important, even for children who don't feel sick during their hospitalization. Privacy and being able to retreat to their room after time in the play activity area helps children find that balance. This kind of withdrawal from activities can be a means of coping with the overwhelming sensations and feelings that can come up. She may also need rest after a procedure, physical therapy session, or other intervention that may be part of her hospital stay. Some hospitals also have visual stimuli in the children's area, such as an aquarium, that don't require a lot of energy but provide enough distraction to pass the time in a way that children find soothing.[14] Teens in particular value their privacy and will want time apart from the hustle-and-bustle of a typical hospital department.

Remember, you and your child are partners in dealing with the challenging conditions, dislocation, lack of control, and confusion she may be feeling throughout the hospital stay. Check in regularly with how she is doing, what her current concerns are, and what is and is not being helpful. Teenagers may not be as willing as younger children to share their vulnerable feelings, for fear of seeming like a baby. Talking with your teen about what you would be feeling if you were going through what she is can reassure her that her feelings are perfectly okay.

Simply affirming and validating your child's distress will go a long way toward soothing her emotional discomfort and helping her find a way to deal productively with the situation. And if you have made a mistake, by perhaps misunderstanding what she wants, or steering her in the wrong direction, don't be afraid to apologize and ask for her ideas about what might work better. You are your child's ally and support, but when children proactively participate in their health care, they will enjoy better outcomes.

Long-Term Stays

If your child must be in the hospital repeatedly, or is required to stay for long periods of time, you will need to find a careful balance between being at the hospital to support him and being at work or home with your other children. You may need to become more trusting of his relationships with the hospital personnel most involved in his care. However, setting up a regular visiting schedule, creating a system whereby you and your coparent or partner take turns being at the hospital and at home, making sure that siblings and even friends have an opportunity to visit, and other similar routines will help normalize his stay while ensuring that the responsibility does not fall too heavily on one person.

Online communities of children experiencing similar circumstances can provide an opportunity for your child to connect with others who understand. Plus, creating regular YouTube, Facebook, or Instagram updates can give older children a creative outlet and a way to continue to feel connected to the larger world. The key strategy is to make these interim experiences as "normal" as possible! Using video chat apps such as FaceTime and Skype also allows him to connect with others by seeing friendly, familiar faces and to continue to be a part of the outside world.

Being in the hospital during birthdays or holidays can be especially disappointing and upsetting, but be assured that the CCLS and nursing staff at the hospital work hard to create fun and appropriate activities to make these times less distressing. Make sure they know about your child's birthday. Coordinate with them and bring in your own family's special treats and traditions so your child can feel like the holiday or birthday party came to him. A treat could be a single favorite ornament from the family Christmas tree; a "Happy Birthday" banner; or a small electric menorah for Chanukah, instead of one with candles. Bring whatever is particularly special to him, and see his face light up!

In an Emergency

Not all hospital stays can be anticipated. If your child suddenly suffers an acute worsening of their illness or experiences some other life-threatening condition, they may end up going straight from the ER to a hospital bed. You have no time to plan coping strategies or what to bring, or to include your child in the decisions—suddenly, you are just thrown into it!

Asking questions and making sure you understand the purpose of the hospitalization so that you can explain it to your child will be your key task, along with soothing them and providing the support they need. If your child is older, including them in some of these conversations and decisions can help them take ownership of what can be a scary and unpredictable situation and will help them make the best adjustment possible by increasing their sense of control. If the child is younger, ask if there is a CCLS or social worker available to help explain the situation in ways that will make more sense to them.

Often, people are left waiting in the ER until a bed opens up; try to use that time proactively. Even if your child can't come with you, can you visit the floor where he will be staying ahead of time, so you can give him a description? Take pictures with your phone to show him what his floor and room will look like. Get a list of what he wants you to bring from home. In essence, you can still go through much of what is outlined for planned hospitalizations, just earlier than you expected and in a much shorter time. The uncertainty and unpredictability of a sudden hospitalization can increase a child's distress at any age! Remember to cast it in a positive light and reassure him that you will be there to help make the accommodations he needs to feel comfortable, listen to his conflicting feelings, and soothe his distress.

When You Have to Travel

As medical care continues to become more complex, special clinics have arisen across the country, providing state-of-the art care for specific conditions. Perhaps your hometown area doesn't have a lot of medical centers that address children's medical needs, or perhaps your child has been diagnosed with a rare condition that only a few centers have expertise in handling. Although it's good to know there is a place that can handle your child's needs, having to travel can make obtaining medical care a logistical challenge. If you have other children, will they come with you? If not, where will they stay while you are gone? How will you and the other parent(s) juggle work, home, and family responsibilities?

Traveling for specialized medical care can also create financial strain because the costs of transportation, accommodations, and meals are added to the usual expenses of health care and daily life. Be sure to check with the facility you will be using to get any advice about resources they offer. Organizations such as Ronald McDonald's House Charities (**https://rmhc.org**) provide places to stay for families with a child having treatment in nearby facilities. The Genetic and Rare Diseases Information Center, a division of the National Institutes of Health, offers a list of free or low-cost services that may help you get started looking for financial help (**https://rarediseases.info.nih.gov/guides/pages/118/help-with-travel-costs**).

You will also need to make sure the medical facility has all the records they need to treat your child. In the Resources for Your Journey we discuss in more detail traveling with a child who has a chronic illness.

DEALING WITH MEDICAL PROCEDURES

As medical science pushes against the boundaries of what is currently known, the types and numbers of diagnostic and treatment procedures one may encounter continue to increase. It may not be possible to prepare your child for every type of medical procedure (and an exhaustive examination of them would certainly take more than this book to cover!). For all procedures, the basic principles remain the same: Get information, rehearse, and plan coping strategies.

Once you have found out the specific procedure your child needs and what it entails, you will both have a better sense of what will happen. As we mentioned above, you can then help prepare her by going through the process; talking about what it might be like for her, including what she will see, hear, smell, taste, and feel; and planning ways for her to cope. What does she think will cause stress, and how can you anticipate what she might need? This may involve bringing certain items from home, like a special toy or stuffed animal for a younger child or an older child's favorite portable game system; family pictures; or other objects that she is used to having around her. As you rehearse what might happen, you can help her develop coping skills.

Remember, though, even your best efforts may not succeed in lowering your child's distress. This is not a failure on your part or hers. Trust that everyone involved, including your child, is doing the best they can under the given circumstances. That said, know that if she tends to be anxious, all types of out-of-the-ordinary events are likely to trigger higher than average distress. We recommend getting the help of a mental health professional with expertise in preparing for medical procedures. With this type of support, your child can find ways to lower her anxiety on a daily basis and learn how to cope better all around.[15]

Coping Skills

With a little help and guidance, children can access a wide range of simple coping strategies to help them with their upcoming medical procedures:

- *Distraction.* Whether something is painful, boring, or just uncomfortable, there are many distraction techniques that invite the child to focus on something other than what they are experiencing. These distractions might include reading a book, watching a video, or, especially for teens, listening to their favorite music. Painful procedures are especially good candidates for these strategies. If the part of the child's body (the site for the procedure) can be kept out of sight, children who are focusing on something else may not actually be aware of what is going on with their arm or leg.
- *Humor and sarcasm.* Finding something to laugh about, or poke fun at, can help children (especially teens) distance themselves from their experience.
- *Relaxation exercises.* These exercises are particularly helpful when facing painful or uncomfortable procedures or those that require long periods of stillness and cooperation. Relaxation techniques are similar to distraction, but because they help the body become more relaxed the child is better able to cooperate; is likely to feel less pain; and will have increased tolerance for other types of discomfort, such as a difficult

position they may have to hold for the duration of the procedure. Simple ways to relax include focusing on the breath (by
counting breaths, counting by odd or even numbers, or just
following one's breath in and out) or consciously focusing on
tense areas of the body and relaxing them deliberately.

• *Soothing mental images.* Developing a mental image of a
soothing place, like being at the beach or some other natural
setting that your child finds relaxing and enjoyable, can also
help a child relax. Ask your child to think of a place they like
to be, and they can "visit" this place during the procedure, their
"calm" or "happy" place. Help them develop a vivid mental
picture by inviting them to imagine a whole range of sensations, including sights and sounds, sensations on their skin,
and even smells and tastes if they are present in the visualized
setting. The stronger the image, the more effective it will be
when things get difficult.

These coping skills can and should be practiced as part of your preparation for the procedure. Practicing these skills ahead of time, in a
calm state, is important. Children can incorporate these techniques
more effectively when they have had time to practice at least a week
in advance of their procedure, rather than at the last minute.[16]

Developing Confidence and a Sense of Control

Rehearsing with a surrogate is another way to help children develop
a sense of control and reduce distress. This involves using an alter
ego to walk through the sequence of events, giving him the opportunity to accompany his teddy bear or a friend his age through the process. You can also use an imaginary character from a favorite book.
Asking questions as he rehearses the process can also help bring
out what he may be experiencing: "What do you think (Teddy Bear

or your friend) is feeling when they do this?" "What do you think they need?" and "What do you think might help them?" Then you can also make suggestions, like "Do you think they might find the breathing exercise we practiced helpful?" This kind of rehearsal can, especially for younger children, increase their sense of control when they have very little and their confidence in their ability to handle these difficult situations. Fictional characters and superheroes can also be enlisted as support; invite him to imagine what his favorite hero would say about his ability to go through this experience, or pretend that your child has whatever superpower he believes would help him here.

Teenagers can similarly be encouraged to imagine what it will be like for them and be proactive in planning coping strategies. Watching a video that features a teen, which may be available through the health facility's website, seems to be especially helpful.[17]

Breaking down the event into smaller, more manageable steps, with some form of reward planned for each step, can be beneficial. Helping your child focus only on the very next thing, giving them time to adjust between steps, giving them a high five when each step is completed, and letting them say when they are ready for the next step goes a long way toward developing their sense of control and building confidence in their ability to cope. Your reassurance that you are available to help them and believe in their ability to handle the situation will also help them when they falter or fear that they can't handle something. Short sentences that they can say to themselves, such as "This is hard, but I can handle it," also may be helpful. Just be aware that as a parent you may often underestimate the level of distress your child is feeling, so be sure to check in and let them know that it is okay to feel whatever they are feeling and that sharing it can help them feel better.

Providing your child a choice between appropriate alternatives, such as choosing whose lap to sit on, whose hand to hold, which song she can sing, or whether or not she wants to view the procedure as it is being performed can all help build that sense of control. Just remember, once a meltdown happens, choice becomes just one more stress, and the immediate need is for some kind of soothing. Planning and rehearsing choices ahead of time may be helpful in keeping potential meltdowns in check.

Meaning and Support

Finding meaning in an experience also helps people cope. Understanding the positive purpose of a particular procedure can give children that sense of meaning, which will make the difficulties part of a larger story of how they are working together with the medical team to achieve the best possible outcome.

Of course, the number-one coping mechanism for most children is the presence and emotional support of you, their parent. Even teenagers may experience a stronger-than-usual desire to have their parents with them, despite their growing maturity. For teens, friends, along with family and parental support, can also be helpful in coping.

Above all, we advise that you learn to let go of whatever meanings *you* want your child to find in their experience. Just be okay with whatever is going on for them, so they can honestly share their feelings with you and you can figure out how to deal with it together.

Magnetic Resonance Imaging (MRI) or Functional Magnetic Resonance Imaging (fMRI)

MRI scans can be challenging for anyone, from the narrow tube your body must enter to the loud banging from the machine. Movements that involve only a few millimeters can ruin the scan, so keeping the body completely still is extremely important. For people who are claustrophobic, this procedure can be downright scary!

If your child must have an MRI, make sure you know where it will happen and what is required. Consider asking the following questions:

- Have the radiologists had special training in how to explain the process to children so as to lower their anxiety?
- If your child is not having a functional MRI (fMRI), which requires the person to be awake, and he is very young, will the team consider sedation? Explore the pros and cons of sedation with his medical team. There are side effects, and the possibility of waking in the middle of the scan, which could be scary.
- Will a contrast—a substance taken into the body that helps improve the visibility of the interior of the body—be used? If so, find out exactly what will be required.

There are some very helpful preparation options that you can look for:

- Is an open MRI available? These machines have larger openings as an alternative to the narrow tube and may be helpful for children who struggle with claustrophobia.
- Is an MRI simulator available? While introducing the child to an MRI simulator, the medical staff explain what to expect and use the simulator to mimic the sounds made by the actual machine, relating them to objects he may be familiar with, such as a car horn. He will be able to touch the machine and handle the earphones and foam cushions that are used to inhibit movement during the scan. A simulator can reduce the need for sedation for even young children who need an MRI.[18]
- Are videos and pre-MRI coaching available? Videos will help your child see and hear the machine and may show children his

own age going through it. Coaches go through a step-by-step explanation of the procedure and let children handle the equipment. Here again, a CCLS can be an important resource for coaching your child for an MRI or fMRI, and give him a chance to practice his coping strategies. Coaching has been shown to increase the success rate for scans, even for fMRI scans.[19]

- Can he choose whether he goes in head or feet first? You may be able to sit next to the machine and keep physical contact with a part of his body not in the machine, like a foot or hand.

- Using digital recordings, including favorite music, a guided meditation suitable for his age, or an engrossing story, can help him stay calm, relaxed, and still.

- Find out if the facility has an MRI Heroes Kit (**https://www. siemens-healthineers.com/en-us/magnetic-resonance-imaging/ mri-heroes-kit**), which was developed as a collaboration among Marvel Comics, Siemens (a maker of imaging equipment), and the Weill Cornell Imaging Center at New York–Presbyterian Hospital in New York City. It includes a DVD and a comic about Captain America's nervousness about getting an MRI and how Iron Man supports and encourages him to make it through the scan.[20] The kit is a concrete example of how superheroes, stuffed animals, or other fantasy or fictional characters your child connects with can be used to reduce anxiety and bring out his strength and ability to handle what at first seems like a daunting procedure.

Invasive Procedures

When your child is facing an operation or another type of invasive procedure, preparation is again key. Remember to use simple words and a neutral tone with younger children—they can take things very literally, so think it through carefully! For example, when hearing

"IV," a child may think of poison ivy, so describe a small tube that is the best way to deliver medicine. Or a child may think a "dressing change" means they will have to get undressed. Explain how this actually refers to putting on a new, clean bandage.[21]

In addition to the suggestions we make in Worksheet 10.1 ("Getting Ready for Hospitalization, Scans, or Invasive Procedures"), here are some specifics with regard to medical procedures, especially those that require anesthesia:

- Engage teenagers in whatever choices are available to them: what day they want the procedure to be scheduled on, whether it will be done as an inpatient or outpatient, and so on. They will be more cooperative and better at following through with after-care if they have some say in the matter.
- Note the time frames we suggest in Worksheet 10.1 and make adjustments according to your child's maturity level and tendency to be anxious. Very young children won't need as much preparation as older children, who will want to practice their coping strategies ahead of time.
- Figure out "jobs" for your child every step of the way, and make it your job to remind them and keep them on task.
- Your other main job is to provide comfort and emotional support, even for your oh-so-independent teen. You can also remind them of their ability to cope well with challenges.

The process involves moving from a hospital room, or pre-op room, into an induction room where anesthesia will be administered, then into the operating room and, finally, waking up in recovery. Although each of these transitions can raise anxiety, the most challenging moment tends to be the actual induction of anesthesia.[22]

Because of the chemicals released in the body, high levels of anxiety at induction can affect the anesthesia induction itself, making it less effective.[23] It can also result in higher levels of post-operative pain, lead to a longer recovery time, and increase the intensity and duration of any maladaptive behaviors, such as acting out.[24,25] Keeping your child's anxiety levels down is crucial. In extreme cases, a child might have to be restrained, making the whole experience even more traumatic.[26] Although medications can be used to reduce anxiety, they take some time to be effective and may have other adverse effects.

To prepare for invasive procedures, consider the following:

- Engage the staff to help prepare your child and develop her coping strategies. For example, if they can allow her to handle the mask that will be used to administer the anesthetic, this can reduce anxiety.[27]
- The CCLS can steer you toward any materials that would be helpful, as well as any programs the facility offers to prepare children for such procedures.
- Address your child's specific fears. What worries her the most: pain or concern about the illness? Separation from you? Waking up during the procedure or even dying?
- Assess your own anxiety and usefulness in the induction room: What will it be like for you to see your child go limp? Don't hesitate to pass this job off to a warm and trusted medical person if you feel it will be too challenging for you.
- If you can distract your child, help her stay focused on her "job," and avoid being overly reassuring, your presence may be a benefit.
- Hand-held video games can be effective in keeping your child distracted.
- Be sure to be present in the recovery room when she wakes up, to soothe and reassure her. Even older children and teens can feel vulnerable.

After the procedure, be aware there may be some regressive or acting-out behaviors as your child's body reacts to the physical trauma it has experienced. Be patient and supportive, and these behaviors should decrease in a reasonable time.

Dealing with postoperative pain is difficult, especially with young children, and many parents may undermedicate for many reasons. We have some advice in this regard:

- Ask for face pain scales or other age-appropriate visual aids to help your young child communicate how they feel.[28]
- Clarify from the doctor exactly how much, and on what schedule, pain medication should be given. It is important to give the medication regularly in order to prevent pain.
- Discuss any other concerns, such as addiction, with your medical team to make sure you are not operating under false assumptions.[29]

Adequately treating your child's pain supports their healing and will improve their recovery.

WORKSHEET 10.1. Getting Ready for Hospitalization, Scans, or Invasive Procedures	
Step	**Actions**
1. Get information	• Write down your questions, and ask all of them. • Include any questions your child wants to ask. • Find out what you can bring from home that may comfort your child. • Make sure you understand, step by step, exactly what will happen.

WORKSHEET 10.1. **Getting Ready for Hospitalization, Scans, or Invasive Procedures (*Continued*)**

Step	Actions
2. Tell your child	According to their age • 0 to 5 years: 1 or 2 days in advance • 6 to 11 years: at least 5 to 7 days • 12 and up: 7 to 10 days or more, so they have time to reflect and make choices How to tell them • Share the positive purpose. • Be careful with literal-minded children to use nonscary language.
3. Preparation is key!	• Get coaching from a CCLS and other trained staff. • Visit the place ahead of time and meet the professionals who will be involved, if possible. • Help your child understand the step-by-step process. • Use a simulator, if available and appropriate. • Watch videos/read storybooks and use other visual materials that show children going through the procedure. • Practice coping strategies to promote calm and relaxation and reduce anxiety. • Make sure the child knows what their "job" is each step of the way. • Clarify what choices are available and engage with them in making choices they want. • Clarify when you can be present and what kind of contact you can have with them.

(continues)

Step	Actions
WORKSHEET 10.1. Getting Ready for Hospitalization, Scans, or Invasive Procedures (*Continued*)	
4. During and after the procedure	• Stay in the present, focused on the immediate situation or task and on your child's "job." • Be there when you say you will be, or make sure a mutually agreed-on person—whether friend, family member, or professional member of the team—will be. • Be ready to soothe, calm, and comfort your child while you congratulate them on a job well done!

Note. CCLS = Certified Child Life Specialist.

NEXT STEP: LEARN ABOUT COMFORT CARE

Comfort or supportive care, also known as "pediatric palliative care" (PPC), can provide comprehensive support to a family dealing with a child's chronic illness. In addition to addressing various symptoms resulting from the illness, its treatment or the medications used, PPC can address all of the psychological and other effects we have discussed in this book, including helping you access respite care, community resources, and other therapeutic approaches.

Children are not just little adults. Illnesses affect children's bodies differently, and these effects change as a child grows.[30] Illnesses in children can be unpredictable. Your child may need home-based care, or at the very least some kind of long-term, holistic approach that addresses the many ways in which your family's life is affected. For all of these reasons, it makes sense to introduce PPC early.[31]

How Do I Know My Child Needs It?

If your child's medical condition is complex, you can ask for a referral to PPC, as we described in Chapter 7. This also works if your child, or any member of the family, including yourself, is suffering from pain, other physical symptoms, or emotional distress that is not under control. Even if you just need more help understanding your child's health condition, or additional support coordinating his care, such a referral could be helpful. Begin by asking for a consultation with a pediatric palliative care specialist.[32] You may also use the terms "supportive care" or "comfort care" depending on what is used in your area.

What Does Pediatric Comfort Care Address?

Comfort care for children is designed to reduce distress, both emotional and physical, in order to enhance the quality of life not only for the ill child but for the whole family. It can include

- dealing with pain and other physical symptoms, including functional limitations;
- addressing psychological and emotional issues in the family, including depression, anxiety, and grief support for everyone;
- reducing the impact of the illness on work, school, and financial and housing stability;
- respecting and helping to incorporate spiritual and religious beliefs and practices into the child's care;
- supporting cultural beliefs and traditions to strengthen the family's ties to their community;
- having the ability to coordinate care across settings, assess the family's needs (and address them), and create an individualized, comprehensive plan that keeps your preferences in mind; and

- engaging the family members as full and equal partners in creating an appropriate plan, including shared decision making on all aspects of care.

The World Health Organization (WHO) describes the purpose of PPC as being for the "active, total care of the child's body, mind and spirit, and also involves giving support to the family."[33] WHO joins the American Academy of Pediatrics (AAP), the Association for Children's Palliative Care (ACT), and the National Hospice and Palliative Care Organization (NHPCO) in support of both palliative care and disease treatment, starting at diagnosis, in order to help with the physical, psychological, and social distress of the whole family and to provide that care wherever needed, in hospitals and clinics, community health centers, or in the child's home.[34]

As we've discussed, finding appropriate child care is extremely difficult, and the unceasing challenges of your child's care can lead to your own exhaustion and illness. A PPC team can point you to local resources that can provide the respite you need.

What Kind of Physical Symptoms Can a Comfort Care Team Help With?

There are many physical symptoms that cause distress in ill children and can further complicate their healthy response to treatment. Nausea and vomiting, or a loss of appetite, can keep a child from eating enough to maintain her health and weight. Children can suffer shortness of breath, seizures, and neurological irritability that results in crying, agitation, or muscle spasms. Perhaps the worst of these is pain; no parent wants to see their child in continual pain.[35]

Many children, especially younger ones, have difficulty explaining their pain, such as where it is coming from and how severe it is. Pediatric specialists have specific, age-appropriate techniques to help clarify children's pain so that it can be addressed most effectively. Finding the right medication at the right dose is also trickier with children. They process medications differently, and swallowing pills may be hard. Pediatric specialists are well versed in alternate administration techniques, such as pills that dissolve easily and quickly.[36] They know how to adjust the environment to lessen the experience of pain, such as the light and room temperature, providing pleasant scents, guided relaxation, and soothing music. They may use massage, art therapy, and other nonmedical interventions.[37] In addition, they have a wealth of nonmedical ways to address symptoms, like avoiding disagreeable foods and odors; sucking on a mint to alleviate nausea and vomiting; sitting up, opening the window, or turning on a fan to help with shortness of breath; and using relaxation techniques.[38] They know how to communicate so children understand what is going on and can help them express their feelings.

Who Might Be on a Comfort Care Team?

The team will take some time getting to know you and your circumstances and then will work with you to create an individualized plan. Some participants could include

- a pediatric palliative care specialist, who has the expertise to appropriately address your child's physical symptoms;
- a nurse practitioner, who can manage symptom care as well as care for the whole family, with the skills to guide the family through the complexity of care both at the hospital and at home;
- a nurse coordinator, who has knowledge of resources in the hospital and the community as well as experience working with agencies that provide nursing care, equipment, and therapies for children, and will help the team members work together;

- a social worker, who can help you access counseling and other community resources; or
- a CCLS, discussed in detail earlier in the chapter, who specializes in addressing the developmental needs of all the children in the family through a variety of games, videos, and other approaches.[39]

Other professionals can be brought on board to address physical limitations your child may have, help him articulate his feelings through the expressive arts, help you integrate your spiritual beliefs and practices into your life, manage stress and provide pain relief through massage, create healthy meal plans, address potential medication interactions, provide support for transitions from hospital to home, and set up necessary medical regimens.[40]

Who Pays for Comfort Care?

The good news is that this type of care is covered by many insurance companies. In addition, public plans such as a State Children's Health Insurance Program (SCHIP) and Medicaid, which we addressed in Chapter 3, often supply them as well. Social workers can help find financial resources in the community, and they are familiar with agencies that may provide services not covered by insurance on a sliding scale or at a minimal rate.

Addressing all the ways your child's illness is affecting everyone in the household can lower stress across the board, leading to better outcomes for your ill child, his well siblings, and, especially, for you and any copilots.

CHAPTER 11

THE JOURNEY THROUGH DEATH AND BEYOND

No parent wants to even think about the end of their child's life. Parents tend to be optimistic about their child's chances of surviving even catastrophic illness, because to consider the alternative goes against all the hopes and dreams they hold for him. In one study, more than half of the parents interviewed after their child died from cancer said they believed at the time of diagnosis that the child would surely live.[1] There may come a time, however, when the adverse effects of treatment are so severe, or potentially lethal themselves, that continuing them becomes counterproductive.

Children's deaths tend to be harder to predict than those of adults. They may happen suddenly and leave no time to focus on the quality of the child's remaining life or for the family to enjoy that precious but limited time. Not addressing head-on the possibility of an abrupt, unexpected death may result in a storm of regret about what did or didn't happen. Research shows that after their child's death, parents regret 50% of cancer-directed treatment—that is, treatment directed at curing the cancer—because of the severe side effects it caused.[2] In one study of parents who lost a child to a chronic illness, although only about half the children died at home, almost all—nearly 90%—of the parents viewed home as the best place to die.[3] This supports the idea that when a child dies at home, parents and siblings are able to process their grief in a healthier manner.[4]

MAKING IMPOSSIBLE DECISIONS

If you find yourself facing the terrible decision to end treatment that is meant to cure your child, please know that this is *not* the same thing as hastening your child's death. The American Academy of Pediatrics makes very clear that the purpose of foregoing life-sustaining treatment is to enhance the child's—and, therefore, the whole family's—quality of life for the time that remains and to help the child die with dignity, without pain or distress.[5] Although some states have legalized physician-assisted death for adults facing terminal illness, it is not considered an acceptable practice with children and is not legal anywhere in the United States.

You may be familiar with hospice or palliative care—a practice that focuses on lessening pain and easing other symptoms for the patient to reduce their suffering. Although this type of care has been studied at length and has clear protocols for adults, it isn't used in the same way with children. As we described in Chapter 10, palliative care referrals for children can happen simultaneously with curative and life-sustaining treatment, and both types of care are then continued through the end of life. This is a very different approach from that used with adults. Thus, the choice to end curative or life-sustaining treatment for a child is not necessarily so that she can receive appropriate end-of-life care but rather to enhance her quality of life and relieve the distressing side effects of treatments than can be lethal in and of themselves.[6] Children may sometimes outlive estimates of their longevity after such treatment is removed because they can then focus on their overall health, gain weight perhaps, and enjoy time with family and friends.

Some of the decisions you may be looking at include

- which treatments to continue or discontinue;
- whether to bring treatment to the child at home, treat him in a recognized hospice, or continue treatment at the hospital; and
- whether and under what circumstances to introduce a "do not resuscitate" order (DNR), that is, an order not to resuscitate the child should he stop breathing or his heart stop beating.

Hospice represents a philosophy of support for end-of-life care, a plan of care built on this idea, or a place that delivers the care. The comfort care team can now transition to focusing on end-of-life care, supporting the family in the spiritual distress and bereavement that is just beginning, as well as providing expertise on the dying process itself, as they continue to address pain and other distressing symptoms.[7]

Hospice care at home often includes expert nursing care up to 24 hours a day; close collaboration and communication with the primary care team and any specialists or agencies involved with the child's care; and emotional, psychological, social and spiritual support not only for the ill child but also for the siblings, parents, and any other family members.

Social support provided by a comfort care team includes respite care for overly burdened parental caregivers.[8] Unfortunately, there are few hospice residences that have the expertise to handle children, and there may not be sufficient numbers of in-home caregivers with pediatric expertise to enable full-time treatment at home.[9] The options in your community may affect which choices are available; the comfort care team can guide you about what would work best for your child and your family.

Perhaps you have been having conversations all along with your child's comfort care team about the course of treatment and its effects, how well her symptoms are being managed, and the impact of her illness on everyone in the family. It may not be too difficult, then, to begin discussing the when and where of end-of-life care as a "what-if" type of talk. Such a conversation can happen well before action must be taken. Doing this helps you be proactive, giving your child the greatest chance of maximum enjoyment of what may be a limited life span. Parents are often soothed by the knowledge that they did their best to provide their child with the best life they could, even though she died. The earlier these conversations start, the more likely you will be to make an informed decision to ensure the best possible death, as strange as that may sound.

Who Should Be Included in the Decision-Making Process?

You probably have no idea how to talk about end-of-life issues with your children, both ill and healthy, and you may be reluctant to burden your sick child with a decision that seems beyond their years. Surprisingly, though, research tells us that children as young as 10, or even 6, in some studies, can engage meaningfully in such a decision-making process. They know the treatments they've had, they remember the options offered, and they understand the consequences, both short- and long term, of the decisions they have made. Relationships seem to be a core part of their thinking process; they naturally include their affection for people in their circle, the preferences of their care team and loved ones, and a desire to help others. They also have a desire to reduce their own suffering, wanting it to be over now that a cure is not possible. They may have witnessed others dying while connected to various machines at a hospital and realize they want something different for themselves.[10]

Children at this stage may be invited to participate in what are known as "Phase 1 studies." These studies focus on determining the safety of potential new drugs, before their effectiveness has been explored, that are not necessarily expected to improve the child's health. Motivated to help others, some children choose to take part in such studies, but it's important to fully understand what the potential side effects might be because continued suffering is not the goal. You and your child both need clear information, including facts and opinions from your care team. It may be helpful to review our discussion of clinical trials in Chapter 3. Taking time to think and reflect will help all of you be at peace with the decisions you make.[11]

It is important to understand how your child's stage of development affects how they see the process of death and dying. Very young children do not understand death as a permanent condition. They may be more afraid to be separated from their parents in the present than they are worried about a final and permanent separation. Children in elementary school may know that death lasts but may be confused about other aspects of dying. They may have fears about what happens after death, worrying, for example, that they won't go to heaven because they were "bad."

Adolescents have a more adult understanding of death. They may be more open to conversations about death and feel very sad over the loss of their future. Despite being aware of their shortened life span, they still may want to prepare and plan for events they won't participate in, such as filling out applications for college, as a way to feel more normal and aligned with their peers. It is their way of living as much of that life as they can, even though they won't be able to complete the process.[12] Psychologists, family therapists, and other child development experts can help children express their emotions and have developed ways to address these things that match a child's level of understanding. They can help stimulate these conversations with your child directly and coach you on how to do it yourself.

What Do End-of-Life Conversations Look Like?

If you have been talking with your child all along about her treatment, its effects, and how she is doing, you've probably already touched on some of these topics. The best conversations happen over a period of time, in lots of different situations. Talking with your child regularly can provide a good foundation for moving toward more sensitive subjects.[13] There are two ways to create space for these conversations: the direct method and the indirect method. With the direct method, you initiate a conversation with your child. You may be hesitant to do this, because you don't want to burden her or you may be afraid that she will be so distressed you won't be able to comfort her. Your reluctance to use the direct method may also be because of the feelings you have when you think about your child dying.

With the indirect method, you respond to something your child says, does, or suggests by his face and body language. The danger of relying on the indirect method is that you may miss his cues. With so much on your mind, you may not have the presence of mind to sit, closely observe, and listen to him. For both these reasons, his perspective may be easily misinterpreted.[14]

Whichever method you choose, leaving space for your child to ask questions, and taking care to pause, invites them to voice their concerns so you can address them. You may wish to review the process of mindful talking and listening we discussed in Chapter 9. When your child asks a question about death or dying, be sure to find out where the question is coming from. Are they having a symptom that is bothering them and wondering if that means they are about to die? Did they hear someone say something, which they may have misunderstood? Did they see something—for example, at the hospital—that involved another child, and they are wondering if they are in the same or a different boat from that other child? Knowing where the question is coming from lets you address their particular concern.

Start by asking your child what they already know or think about the issue. Then you can give the information that fits best with their worries. Usually, if you give them only the information they need, they will be quite satisfied. If your family follows a particular spiritual path or religion, this may be a time to explore what that means for your child. Even if your family does not adhere to a particular belief, children hear things from friends that may confuse them. These can be opportunities to share with your child your own deeply held beliefs, as well as to explore with them their understanding of spirituality, the connection they have with you and the rest of the family, and what they think happens after death.

Children often take in a lot more than we realize; they hear other people's conversations, and they sense the emotional energy in the home. You may think you are protecting your child by not talking about these things, but chances are he is picking up on tension and hints of change. Unless he can understand their relevance to him, his illness, and the family, he is likely to get more upset and worried.

Including children in religious or spiritual rituals that have meaning for them is especially important at this time. Children continue their development even though they are sick, and the suffering they experience, although it takes away a certain childhood innocence, can at the same time enable them to develop a wisdom beyond their years. You may be surprised at their level of awareness and understanding.

What Gets in the Way of These Conversations?

If you are the primary caregiver, you may be so involved with your ill child's life, guiding and supporting her, as well as taking care of her medical and other physical needs, that you feel you intuitively know what she wants. And most of the time, you are probably right! But that intense involvement may make it hard for you to see when her preferences differ from yours. This is especially true when the child is very young.

It's likely that even thinking about your child's possible death can overwhelm you with emotion, making it difficult to even touch on the topic with her. This is completely understandable! Just know that this can also make it difficult for you to know the difference between what you want, and what your child wants, when they are not the same. We know you have the best of intentions, and you have been doing an amazing job taking care of your child. You don't want to give up too soon, and sometimes you may need to encourage your child to get past a temporary loss of hope. But be aware that putting off end-of-life conversations also helps you avoid your own feelings of grief and loss. As death becomes inevitable, you may have to think about whether you will be able to cope with your own sadness and at the same time focus on supporting what your child wants, which is sometimes called the "voice of the child."[15] All of us have limitations on the level of emotion we can handle and the types of situations that arouse these strong feelings. If you know what you can and can't do, you will be better able to create the right situation so your child can figure out what they want.

If you have a partner and are struggling with emotions, perhaps the partner would be able to have a talk like this with the child. Members of your child's care team also know how to help them express their thoughts and feelings about what is going on, using age-appropriate questions and other approaches. If you're afraid that you won't know how to comfort your child should their own strong emotions come up, these same team members can coach you with simple suggestions. Just being with your child, affirming the feelings they are having, whether fear, sadness, or something else, can go a long way toward providing comfort. Younger children in particular may grieve intensely for a short period and then want to get busy with some of their usual activities.

In addition to helping your child cope, find someone you trust—a friend, family member, or a professional—with whom you can talk about your feelings. Talking about your feelings (provided you do not think about them constantly) can ease your distress and clear the way for you to better understand what your child needs.[16] Naming your fears, even just saying them out loud, may seem counterintuitive, especially if you've been brought up to believe that speaking what you are afraid of will cause the thing you fear to happen. We want to emphasize that science supports the practice of sharing your feelings—especially the distressing ones—as part of your self-care.

COMING TO THE END OF THE ROAD

The unthinkable has happened—your child has died, and you are left to cope with the unimaginable. You may be caught in despair; you may be frozen in shock. Even if you had some warning of impending death, the reality is so much starker than what you ever could have envisioned. You may be convinced that you lack the strength to survive this. This event has marked you, forever changed your relationship to the world, to life. Such a loss is not something that you get over; instead, this is the beginning of a new journey that will last the rest of your life.

Your child has died, but the love you have for her has not, and you will carry her in your heart as long as you draw breath. And yet, and yet . . . as time goes on, you will reengage with life. If you have other children, you will continue to care for them, to be their parent. You will find joy again, and happiness, and all the other qualities that make life so precious. You may even find that you savor these qualities more now that you are so vividly aware how fleeting they really are. Friends will move on, and even some family members may move on, but you will always remember. Your child mattered. Her life was meaningful, and you will hold on to that meaning until the very end.

The Effects of Death on the Living

The death of a child upends our understanding of the natural order of things, where parents die before their children, not vice versa. Parents invest their hopes and dreams in their children and sometimes see them as a continuation of their own story. A child's death challenges parents' fundamental understanding of themselves, the world, and their place in it, and may shatter basic assumptions about how life works.[17] If your child dies, you may start wondering about the meaning of life and question the purpose of your own. If you've focused your time and energy on caring for your sick child, you feel the loss not only of the child, and your connection with him, but also the loss of your role as his caregiver. It should not be surprising that parental grief, especially in the short term, is marked by an emotional intensity found in few other areas of life.

How Are Parents Affected as Individuals?

Such an early death so violates the parental role of protection and care that you may find yourself experiencing profound guilt about your child's death, even though you did everything you could. You may be incapable of functioning for periods of time, literally unable to work or even get out of bed and carry out typical household tasks. It's common to have difficulty eating or sleeping. You may even question whether life is worth living, or feel that you're "going crazy," that the pain you experience is almost physically unbearable.[18] Early stages of grief can be characterized by disbelief, confusion, and a sense of unreality, of living a nightmare from which you have yet to wake up. You may have intense periods of emotional release, usually characterized by tears but sometimes showing up as angry explosions. Especially after a long period of intensive caregiving, you are physically and emotionally exhausted and may at first be disoriented and confused about how to readjust to life without your deceased child.[19] Mothers in heterosexual couples appear to report more intense symptoms than those fathers.[20]

As time moves forward, and years go by, the outward expression of grief may lessen, but for most parents the experience of grief does not go away. Your friends and family members may not even be aware of your vivid sense of pain and loss, and this can make you feel very isolated. Despite the appearance that you have moved on, the emotional tie to your child persists, and always will.[21] Grief usually comes in waves of intensity for many years after the loss, often triggered by important dates, anniversaries, and family or life events.

> When I was young I noticed that there was always one day a year when Mom was not herself. She seemed distraught, closed the door and stayed in her bedroom all day. When I got older, I understood: It was the day Jessica died.
> —Older brother of a 3-year-old who died of cancer

Over time, you may focus less on your child as she was in illness and death and remember more the times when she was happy and enjoying life. For many, the greatest fear is that the child will be forgotten.[22]

It may make sense here to include some discussion of Elisabeth Kübler-Ross's famous work, the "stages of grief," in response to a diagnosis of a fatal disease. The five stages are Denial, Anger, Bargaining, Depression, and Acceptance (DABDA). Kübler-Ross spoke to people who themselves were dying and organized the descriptions of their experience into these five emotional categories.[23] Others have applied the DABDA stages to the experience of grief after a death, which may or may not be accurate. Another caveat is that the process of moving into one stage and out of another isn't as easy to define as the stages might suggest. Grief is highly individual and messy. It's entirely possible to go through the stages in order, and then in reverse. You may get stuck in one stage or another, or even cycle through all the stages in one day, or one hour. In the paragraphs that follow, we take a closer look at each of Kübler-Ross's stages.

Denial has been given a bad rap. It actually protects you against knowing something that will get in the way of carrying out necessary tasks. When you wake up, there may be a moment when you forget your child has died, and you experience a feeling of normalcy that is hard to find when you are fully aware of that reality. Denial can help you put aside your grief temporarily, so you can make funeral arrangements, care for your other children, or continue to work. Perhaps you didn't think your child would die, and you regret some opportunity missed. But a certain amount of denial helped you be there for your child without being swallowed up by your own sorrow. Give yourself a pass; you did the best you could. That is all anyone can do.

Anger is a common response to loss, though not one that is often acknowledged. Anger is disruptive, and challenging, but it also feels powerful. Anger says, "This is wrong; this child should not have died." Perhaps anger will be the primary emotion you feel. It protects you from the vulnerable feelings of pain and loss. Just remember not to vent that anger on your remaining loved ones, those who did their best caring for your child, or those who are reaching out in compassion to try to be helpful, even if they do it clumsily. Try not to let your anger isolate you at a time when you most need human connection.

Bargaining looks different after loss than for the people Kübler-Ross spoke with. For her subjects, bargaining was an attempt to put off death; in grief, it takes the form of thoughts about what could have, or should have, been done. "If only we had caught it sooner," "If only we had not done that last intervention," "If only . . . if only . . . if only. . . ." There is no way to change what has happened, and yet the mind reaches back, looking for something that could have changed the outcome. You may get obsessed with thoughts like these and even experience moments when you feel you could, if you wished hard enough, bring your child back. These kinds of thoughts make up some of the "magical thinking" that often happens after loss. Even though you know it won't really work, you may find yourself falling down this little rabbit hole. Perhaps it helps us keep our loved ones with us, in the present.

Depression as Kübler-Ross discussed it is really a deep sadness. It fits with cultural expectations, and for many it is the most long-lasting response to the death. Not being able to go to work, lying in bed all day, having trouble eating and sleeping—these classic symptoms of depression are very common for parents who have lost a child. If months go by and you find yourself stuck in a place of depression, it may be helpful to consult with a professional for individual counseling or try a support group. Talking with others who also are struggling with such a loss is an incredibly helpful and comforting way to understand what has happened and figure out how to live with it. We share a couple of these groups in the Resources for Your Journey.

Acceptance is in some ways the most painful of Kübler-Ross's stages. There can be a sense, when the loss has become part of life's landscape and grief is not so intense, that your child has been lost to you again, somehow. Active grief keeps the person vividly in our minds and imaginations; accepting that loss can feel like giving up. But acceptance does not mean an end to grieving the loss of your child. Acceptance can, of course, be momentary. It can also last for a time, giving you more energy to focus on living your life. This can be your opportunity to honor your child and integrate your love for him into your daily routine, such as building a legacy, which we talk about later in the chapter.

Many people have unusual experiences when grieving. You may sense your child nearby, just in another room, only a few feet away. Out in the world, you may catch a glimpse of the back of someone's head that looks exactly like her, or you may see her in others' faces or even think you see her being put into someone else's car. If such experiences disturb you, do talk to someone about them, but this does not mean you are going crazy! It is simply one of the ways humans respond to the loss of a loved one. Only if you become convinced that your child is actually alive—and that perhaps others are hiding her from you—should you be concerned. In such a case, seek professional help promptly.

How Does Grief Affect a Couple?

The most important thing about grief is to remember that each person's way of grieving is different. One of you may be sunk in sadness while the other is angry all the time. One of you may be efficiently handling things, in some level of functional denial, while the other can barely get up in the morning. We urge you not to compare what you are doing and feeling with what your partner does or feels, or draw any conclusions from the differences. "Why aren't you sad?" the sad one might say; "Why aren't you angry?" the other one might snap back. You and your partner are different people, and you both may cope with this loss differently. Remember that your partner also loved your child, and trust that you are each handling your loss in the best way you know how.

The research on whether the death of a child leads to divorce is somewhat mixed. It was once taken for granted that the chances of divorce were much higher after such a loss, but recent literature has also suggested that relationships can survive and even grow stronger after the death of a child.[24] If you and your partner have struggled throughout your child's illness, you may cope with loss by being emotionally distant and not communicating with each other, and this will increase the chances of a permanent separation. Being flexible with each other's grieving styles, and accepting the differences even though they may be confusing, will help you get through it together.

Open communication will help you and your partner connect while you're grieving. Some partners want to talk with each other about the loss, even though that can temporarily make the feelings stronger. Over time, the pain can become less powerful as a result. For others, sharing grief becomes too overwhelming, too painful, for one or both of you. In that case, again, don't judge if you both feel differently. If you need to talk, and your partner is not available, find a good friend to share your feelings with. Giving your partner the space he needs helps you both walk through it together, though separately.

If you feel the need to "be strong" for your partner, remember that this usually backfires. As we discussed in Chapter 5, your partner may be relieved to know that you are going through the same things she is. If you find it difficult to sit with your partner's pain, remember that you can't fix it. Just be present.

Emotional support can be communicated in many ways, not just in words. If you can be a source of stability and security for both of you, an increased closeness and deepening of your relationship may occur. If you choose not to talk about the loss, stay connected in other ways. Establish activities and rituals centered around the memory of your child, such as the legacy project we mentioned earlier and discuss further at the end of the chapter.[25]

What About the Child's Siblings?

Brothers and sisters of the deceased child are often described as "the forgotten mourners."[26] As a parent, you may be struggling with your own sense of loss, and you may not be as present to your other children and their grief process as you would like. They may feel abandoned, and guilty that they are still alive, especially if they felt intense sibling rivalry, had strong negative attitudes toward their sibling, or had engaged in arguments or exchanged harsh words. These kinds of incidents may haunt surviving children. Younger children may even feel personally responsible for the death, as if their thoughts and actions could actually have caused it.

Remember, too, that children's understanding of death is greatly influenced by their own developmental stage. When Carol's husband died, her son was only a baby, and would never remember his father. Even at that age, though, he sensed that someone important had left his life. First, he had nighttime fears about her leaving. As a toddler, seeing other families in preschool, he began to ask about his own father. When she told him his father had died, he wondered "When he's through dying, will he come to my house?" He could not conceive of anything as permanent as death. Not until he was 6 or 7 did he begin to understand. When she went to pick him up at school one day, the teacher pulled her aside and asked if anything was going on at home, because he had been acting up at school quite a bit. When Carol looked at the calendar, she realized it was the anniversary of his father's death. At home, she asked her son if he was sad that his father had died. At that, he began to cry intensely for about 10 minutes. Then he got up and went to play a video game. Even though he had strong feelings, he was ready in that moment to move on much more quickly than a typical adult would be.

Be sure that there is someone available to talk one-on-one with your other children. First, be honest with yourself about your own ability to sit calmly with a child and share what has happened to his sibling. If you feel you wouldn't be able to contain your own feelings well enough—and this is completely understandable!—recruit your partner, an extended family member, or even a child development specialist from your child's medical team. Whoever ends up having the conversation could also be coached by any team member who knows the ins and outs of talking with children of different ages in helpful ways.

Avoid euphemisms. Remember that young children can take things very literally! Telling a young child a sibling went "to sleep" may leave her frightened at bedtime that she will go to sleep and not wake up. Be careful about talking too much about heaven as a place the child "is." An impressionable sibling may decide the best course is to try and follow her, sometimes leading to actual suicidal type behavior. Be sure to ask questions about what the sibling understands, what her fears or worries are. This is an opportunity to emphasize that the death was not her fault, that we all have angry moments with people we love, and that is normal, but angry words, thoughts, and actions in and of themselves don't kill other people. There are many good books for children of all ages that talk about death; we list some in the Resources for Your Journey at the end of this book. Be sure to review any book you want to share with your child beforehand, so you know what to expect and can determine whether it feels appropriate to your family and culture.

Depending on your children's age and maturity, you may want to offer them some choices as to how they wish to say goodbye to their sibling. Your cultural background and religious tradition may determine whether or not you have an open casket at the wake or viewing. If this is the first death your children have experienced, be sure to prepare them for what they will see and give them the choice of whether or not they want to see their sibling this way. For some people, children included, seeing the person at peace can be profoundly comforting; for others, the same sight may be horrifying.

Whether or not to include children in funerals or other memorial services depends again on their age, maturity, and desire to attend. If you have a baby or young child that you feel will be hanging on you and taking away from your ability to experience the comfort such a service can provide, find someone with whom he has a good connection to attend to him at home or in another space near the service, such as a side room. Older children may wish to join you, but be prepared: If the service goes past their ability to participate meaningfully and they become fidgety and restless, have someone standing by to take them somewhere else with a game or puzzle that you have brought with you. Teens are usually mature enough to engage with these traditions, but do ask them if they want to attend, in case they are simply not prepared to go through it at that time, or in public. As you develop other rituals and projects of remembrance in the family, all the children will have more opportunities to share their thoughts and feelings about their sibling's death, and you can continue to work through your grief as a family. Also, remember that those developmental specialists you have worked with during your child's illness can help you figure out how to help your children say goodbye to their deceased sibling and whether and how to include them in services or other rituals.

Be aware that older children, in particular those who had been involved in caring for the sick child, may feel the loss of that role as well; they may also attempt to step in with younger siblings, aware of your distraction. This can be very helpful for the younger children and adaptive for the family in the short term. Be careful, however, that the older sibling doesn't end up saddled with more responsibility than they can really take on long term; that could hamper their own development.[27]

How you handle your own grief can have a huge impact on your surviving children's well-being. If you are highly anxious, you may be tempted to be overprotective, possibly interfering with your remaining children's ability to take risks and develop a healthy level of independence. Honoring the departed child with rituals and other acts of memory-making provides the whole family with a way to share the loss, but take care not to idealize your deceased child or make a shrine that somehow sets him apart from the rest of the family. Your remaining children may become jealous or resentful of their departed sibling and feel incapable of living up to the ideal he now represents. This can lead to either feelings of inadequacy and depression, called "acting in," or anger expressed as rebellion and behavior problems, termed "acting out."

Naturally, you will look to your other children to fulfill some of the hopes and dreams your departed child represented.[28] Just be aware of how you are doing that. Make sure you recognize the differences between her and the remaining children. If she was musically gifted, or particularly mature or intelligent, there may be other ways to commemorate those gifts than expecting your remaining children to follow in her footsteps, especially when they have different abilities and ways of expressing who they are.

What Do People Find Most Helpful When Grieving a Child?

Support groups, as we described in Chapter 3, provide an avenue for each member of the family to explore the grief process with peers who are experiencing a similar loss. Young children in particular, whose understanding of death may still be forming, benefit from the kinds of expressive arts therapies that are used in such groups for the younger participants. Teens, with their rising sense of independence, may not want to rely too heavily on their parents during this time. For everyone, sitting with others who understand the magnitude of the loss you have suffered, because they have experienced it themselves, provides a context of safety and unspoken connection that can ease the pain. As time moves on, and the outward signs of grief abate, friends and family forget the need for support, but the group understands.[29] A member of one of Carol's widows and widowers group once asked, "What do I say when my friends ask me if I'm still going to 'that support group'?" She was happy to supply the perfect comeback: "Tell them he's still dead!"

Because loss of meaning and purpose is such a big part of the grief over the loss of a child, finding ways to create and support meaning, both of life in general and of the particular child's life, can help the family in developing a fresh sense of its life together. Here are some suggestions:

- Religious and spiritual traditions often have opportunities to memorialize the deceased child (for example, having a Catholic Mass said for them or, for those of the Jewish faith, reciting the Mourner's Kaddish), to share feelings with a broader community and to highlight the particular gifts the family and community received from having this child in their midst.
- Hold as full a memorial as you would for an adult; you may be surprised at how many people have been touched by your child's journey through illness and death.
- Some families choose to make some kind of explicit memorial to their child, whether related to the illness or to a favorite interest the child exhibited. You can invite your community to share in a fundraising project to address a local need that connects with your child's life, contribute to research on the disease, or provide care to others who suffer from it.
- Find special ways to honor birthdays and other anniversaries; this helps keep the connection with your child alive in a growth-promoting way.[30]

- Recognize that anniversaries and holidays are coming, and be proactive in taking care of yourself and your family. These are especially difficult in the first year. Sometimes, being away from home or planning something brand new is the best way to help everyone deal with a painful reminder.

You may even find, over time, that you experience personal growth with an expanded ability to empathize with others and a new sense of yourself as competent, strong, and resilient in the face of what many say is life's biggest challenge. You may even discover a deeper understanding of your values and priorities and appreciation of what really matters in life.[31]

NEXT STEP: BUILDING YOUR CHILD'S LEGACY

With the death of your child, one journey has ended, but a new one has begun. Your journey will be painful, challenging, and lifelong, but it can also provide a basis for resilience and growth, as you readjust your priorities with the clarity of knowing what is important to you and find ways to stay connected to your deceased child.

Many families decide to create a legacy project as a remembrance to the child who has died. Perhaps you can all participate in an art project, memorializing special moments with your child and the particular qualities she brought to life. You could create a scrapbook, highlighting special memories and milestones of her life. If you have the space, planting a tree or a rosebush can create a physical location where memories can be kept alive. Ongoing fundraising projects like walking in 5Ks to raise funds for research or institutions that care for children with the disease can become a yearly tradition. Some people may even be able to create scholarships or awards of financial support for people who exemplify some of the qualities most important to your child's life.

Create something that can change and grow over time, as the other children in the family mature and find their relationship to their departed sibling changing. Find ways to add to the project, as your relationship to your child shifts and changes over time. Be sure to find a way to include everyone. Any project should be focused on helping the new family tree grow into its future without its missing branch.

Death ends a human life, but not a relationship. You may be surprised to experience growth and change in that relationship even though your child is no longer with you physically. They are as close as your breath, one with the love that you hold for them in your heart.

CHAPTER 12

CONCLUDING THOUGHTS: BUILDING RESILIENCE ON THE JOURNEY

We are almost at the final stop of our journey together. Congratulations! Think about what you have already learned and done. Together, we have explored various tools for and ideas on how to navigate the expedition of parenting a child with a chronic medical illness. Parenting journeys never end; however, they do shift gears depending on the ages and needs of your children. Perhaps you read our book cover to cover, or maybe you focused only on selected chapters that address your immediate concerns. However you approached this book, we hope the guidance offered brings validation, hope, and confidence. Parenting a child with a chronic illness may involve detours, bumps, and curves, but it also includes clear paths where you are just cruising along. No two paths are alike.

We began this journey together, focusing on you, the parent, and the importance of taking care of yourself first so you will be able to take care of others. We explored some of the feelings that arise when your child receives a medical diagnosis. Some of these feelings are strong, and, difficult as that can be, it is important for you to experience and manage them. We stressed the importance of self-care practices and described some to cultivate, including mindfulness and gratitude. Engaging in such practices will give you more mileage in the long run. When your tank is running low, we suggested you seek the help of others and set healthy boundaries. We also provided some direction on when and how to seek mental health care.

We then proceeded to that sometimes-complicated landscape of communication. Good communication sets a foundation for all your relationships. We showed how to communicate with your child based on their age and developmental stage, when to listen, how to talk, and how to apply mindfulness to talking and listening. We shared effective communication skills to use with other parental figures, siblings, and extended family. We discussed the many professionals and systems you need to interact with on an ongoing basis. Good communication with medical and school professionals can build bridges and avoid traffic jams that block the path to your child's well-being. This includes knowing when to listen and recognizing when you need to speak up as an advocate for what your child and family need. We also suggested ways you can empower your children to advocate for themselves as they grow to adulthood. We hope that the resources we have provided can help you gain confidence moving into these areas even though they can seem daunting.

Finally, we came to the most difficult territory for children and families dealing with a chronic medical illness—coping with uncomfortable procedures, hospitalization, and possibly even death. It is likely that your child has endured procedures or tests that cause discomfort and/or pain. Using appropriate coping strategies can help make that experience less scary, overwhelming, and painful for them—and for you. Your child may go on to live the long life you dreamed for them, maintaining good health and actively managing the illness when it flares up. Or, your child's life journey may end too soon. Death ends a life, but not a relationship. Your new journey continues.

You have by now developed new skills and expertise. You have handled situations you might never have been able to imagine before your child became ill. So, what's next—where do you go from here? We invite you, first, to review the Resources for Your Journey, which provides a wealth of information about getting support for you, your child, and your family. Next, take a moment to reflect on what you have read here. Are there particular steps that you can put into practice now that would be beneficial to you, your child, or your family? You know your circumstances better than anyone else! But don't let that stop you from experimenting and trying something new. Are there sections you want to reread? Often we are ready to hear and do things differently the second time around. Talk or journal your way through the worksheets more than once and you'll see what we mean. The "Next Step" sections at the end of each chapter offer you an abundance of ideas for action steps to help you and your family cope better. Allow our book to unfold and come alive in assisting you to parent more confidently and more optimistically, wherever you find yourself on the journey.

There will be moments when you feel the need to press hard on the gas pedal; other times, you want to drive slowly or hit the brakes. Although you are in the driver's seat, it's still okay to share the ride or let someone else take the wheel. You don't have to be alone on this journey! Stay focused, stay flexible—you're building resilience. Trust yourself to be good enough. You got this!

RESOURCES FOR YOUR JOURNEY

Here we provide you with a list of important resources that we hope will make your journey easier to navigate. First is a list of organizations dedicated to research and support for people who have various medical conditions. Every website listed here was confirmed as a functioning website as of September 2020; however, we still encourage you to use the tips we offered in Chapter 2 about mindful internet use and exercise caution about information you find. Also, please note that in our fast-paced world, organizations and websites can change every day. Some organizations may refocus their efforts; for example, in future years they may prefer to focus on raising money for research whereas before they did more storytelling and local support groups.

Next we offer a series of resources to help you locate various kinds of support for your family, such as child care and assistance with schooling issues. This is followed by a listing of apps you may find helpful for organization and staying healthy. We also include an extensive list of children's books about various medical topics, including death.

It is important to emphasize that just because a resource or website is listed does not mean we as the authors or the American

Psychological Association are endorsing a particular organization, service, or product. Moreover, as much as we have tried to be inclusive of all types of diseases and other resources, we may have overlooked some. We encourage you to conduct your own research and speak to professionals and other parents for recommendations to assist you on your parenting journey. This serves as a place to start.

Finally, we discuss some tips for traveling with your child. If you don't have the means to travel as a family or to support your child's special medical needs while far from home, we encourage you to be creative. A change of scenery can lift everyone's spirits; however, we understand the complexities of traveling with a child who has a chronic illness.

CHRONIC-ILLNESS ORGANIZATIONS

American Autoimmune Related Diseases Association, Inc., https://www.aarda.org

American Cancer Society, https://www.cancer.org

American Childhood Cancer Organization, https://www.acco.org

American Diabetes Association, https://www.diabetes.org

American Heart Association, https://www.heart.org

American Juvenile Arthritis Organization, https://www.arthritis.org

American Lung Association, https://www.lung.org

American Sickle Cell Anemia Association, http://www.ascaa.org

Asthma and Allergy Foundation of America, https://www.aafa.org

Childhood Liver Disease Research Network, https://www.childrennetwork.org

Child Neurology Foundation, https://www.childneurologyfoundation.org

Children's Leukemia Research Association, Inc., https://www.childrensleukemia.org

Children's Tumor Foundation, https://www.ctf.org

Children With Diabetes, https://www.childrenwithdiabetes.com

Chronic Disease Coalition, https://www.chronicdiseasecoalition.org

Crohn's & Colitis Foundation, https://www.crohnscolitisfoundation.org

Cystic Fibrosis Foundation, https://www.cff.org

Dystonia Medical Research Foundation, https://www.dystonia-foundation.org

Elizabeth Glaser Pediatric AIDS Foundation, https://www.pedaids.org

Epilepsy Foundation, https://www.epilepsy.com

International Foundation for Gastrointestinal Disorders, https://www.iffgd.org

Invisible Disabilities® Association, https://www.invisibledisabilities.org

JDRF (formerly Juvenile Diabetes Research Foundation), https://www.jdrf.org

Leukemia & Lymphoma Society, https://www.lls.org

Lung Transplant Foundation, https://www.lungtransplantfoundation.org

Lupus Foundation of America, https://www.lupus.org

Muscular Dystrophy Association, https://www.mda.org

National Bone Marrow Transplant Link, https://www.nbmtlink.org

National Hemophilia Foundation, http://www.hemophilia.org

National Kidney Foundation, https://www.kidney.org

National Multiple Sclerosis Society, https://www.nationalmssociety.org/

National Organization for Rare Disorders, https://www.rarediseases.org

Rare Cancer Alliance, https://www.rare-cancer.org

Rare Diseases Clinical Research Network, https://www.rarediseasesnetwork.org

Spina Bifida Association, https://www.spinabifidaassociation.org

United Cerebral Palsy, https://www.ucp.org

GOVERNMENT ORGANIZATIONS

Children's Health Insurance Program (CHIP), https://www.healthcare.gov/medicaid-chip/childrens-health-insurance-program/

CHIP is a government program that provides low-cost health coverage to children of families who do not qualify for Medicaid. In some states, CHIP covers pregnant women.

Clinical Trials, https://www.clinicaltrials.gov

This site contains information on current clinical trial studies receiving U.S. government funding as well as on some supported by private industry. For information about clinical trials conducted in Europe, see https://www.clinicaltrialsregister.eu

Genetic and Rare Diseases (GARD) Information Center, https://www.rarediseases.info.nih.gov

GARD provides the public with access to current, reliable, and easy-to-understand information about rare or genetic diseases in English or Spanish.

Medicaid, https://www.medicaid.gov

Medicaid is a government program that provides health care insurance to children, elderly people, low-income families, and people with medical needs and/or disabilities.

MedlinePlus, https://www.medlineplus.gov

This agency is part of the National Institutes of Health. It is a service of the National Library of Medicine, the world's largest medical library. The site provides health information that is easy to understand in English and Spanish. All information is free, and they do not endorse any products or companies.

National Center for Complementary and Integrative Health, https://www.nccih.nih.gov

This government agency was established to conduct research on alternative or complementary medical and health care systems, practices, and products and to educate professionals and the public about them.

National Institute of Diabetes and Digestive and Kidney Diseases, https://www.niddk.nih.gov

Part of the National Institutes of Health, this agency conducts and supports research about diabetes and digestive and kidney diseases and disseminates research findings and information to the public.

Office of Dietary Supplements, https://www.ods.od.nih.gov

The goal of this branch of the National Institutes of Health is to acquire knowledge about and evaluate dietary supplements. They provide professionals and the public with the latest information about vitamins, minerals, herbal supplements, and so on.

Supplemental Security Income (SSI), https://www.ssa.gov/ssi/

This government program provides financial assistance to children under age 18 who have a medical condition that results in severe functional limitations or who have been diagnosed with a terminal condition.

U.S. Department of Education, https://www2.ed.gov

This is the U.S. government's website on all things education. Click on the "Laws" tab to learn more about the Individuals with Disabilities Education Act and the Rehabilitation Act of 1973. There are other topics you can learn about as well, such as civil rights, the Every Student Succeeds Act, and more.

Women, Infants, and Children (WIC), https://www.fns.usda.gov/wic

The WIC program aims to safeguard the health of low-income women, infants, and children up to age 5 who are at nutritional risk by providing nutritious foods to supplement diets, information on healthy eating, and referrals to health care professionals.

PARENT AND FAMILY SUPPORT RESOURCES

Band-Aides & Blackboards, https://www.lehman.cuny.edu/faculty/jfleitas/bandaides/
> This site offers stories and articles by and from the point of view of children and teens with chronic medical illnesses.

Bereaved Parents of the USA, https://www.bereavedparentsusa.org
> With chapters across the United States, this group supports parents, siblings, and grandparents who have suffered the death of a child by providing a place for them to connect and share their stories with each other in a safe environment.

Birth Defect Research for Children, https://www.birthdefects.org
> This organization provides parents and expectant parents with information about birth defects and support services for their children.

Brave Kids, http://www.hotels-oklahoma.com/bravekidsorg/
> This site provides links to specific childhood diseases, information about many resources, and suggested books.

Children's Hospital Colorado, https://www.childrenscolorado.org/conditions-and-advice/parenting/parenting-articles/toolkit/
> This site provides articles for parents on various topics related to parenting a child with a chronic illness.

Caring Bridge, https://www.caringbridge.org
> This site offers free websites so that families and friends can communicate information, photos, and videos about a loved one's medical status all in one place. It is password protected and private.

The Compassionate Friends, https://www.compassionatefriends.org
> Compassionate Friends provides emotional support to families after a child dies.

Dream Street Foundation, https://www.dreamstreetfoundation.org
> This foundation provides camping programs for children and teens with chronic or life-threatening illnesses.

GriefNet, https://www.griefnet.org

> GriefNet offers online support and information to families who are grieving.

Healthy Children, https://www.healthychildren.org

> This site, published by the American Academy of Pediatrics, offers expert advice and information for children of all ages, including specifics on safety and injury prevention, childhood illnesses and diseases, immunization information, developmental milestones, nutrition and fitness, behavioral issues, and more.

The Hole in the Wall Gang Camp, https://www.holeinthewallgang.org

> A camp for children with serious illness that was begun by actor Paul Newman.

Kids Health, https://www.kidshealth.org

> This organization is sponsored by a nonprofit children's health system and provides health information for parents and kids, including those with chronic illness.

Lotsa Helping Hands, https://www.lotsahelpinghands.com

> This website provides a central location to communicate with family and friends and to organize needed support. With the Help calendar located on the site, you can provide a place where people can sign up to help with meals, rides to appointments, and pick-ups and drop-offs for your other children and to share visiting information.

Make-A-Wish Foundation, https://www.wish.org

> This foundation grants wishes to children with critical illnesses.

Needy Meds, https://www.needymeds.org

Patient Services Incorporated, https://www.patientservicesinc.org

Rx Assist, https://www.rxassist.org

Rx Hope, https://www.rxhope.com

Rx Outreach, https://www.rxoutreach.org

The previous four sites and this one are for organizations that provide affordable options for covering medication costs.

Pull-thru Network, https://www.pullthrunetwork.org

This volunteer-based nonprofit organization is dedicated to providing information, education, support, and advocacy to families, children, teens, and adults who are living with the challenges of congenital anorectal, colorectal, and/or urogenital disorders and any of the associated diagnoses.

Rainbows for All Children, https://www.rainbows.org

This organization helps children navigate the grief process, whatever the nature of the loss, including death, separation/divorce, deportation, deployment, incarceration, or other trauma.

Ronald McDonald House Corporation, https://www.rmhc.org

This foundation provides many services for families with a child who is receiving treatment for a serious illness, such as housing for their families when the treatment facility is far from home.

Smart Patients, https://smartpatients.com

This site has an online community for patients and families affected by illness, including information on illnesses as well as contact with other patients and parents. Access support through the "Find Your Community" link.

Starlight Children's Foundation, https://www.starlight.org

Starlight Foundation delivers virtual reality headsets, books, toys, games, arts and crafts, and other items to children in hospitals and helps transform indoor and outdoor environments to make them more comfortable for children and their families.

St. Jude's Children's Research Hospital, https://www.stjude.org

The website provides information and articles for parents and children dealing with serious health issues. Click on the "Care & Treatment" tab, then on "Patient & Family Resources," to find information on all kinds of medical procedures and on help preparing children for medical treatment and procedures, broken down by age group.

CHILD CARE RESOURCES

ARCH National Respite Network, https://archrespite.org

This organization helps caregivers of people in all age groups connect with appropriate respite care across the country. It also connects to state organizations.

https://www.care.com

This site provides a tool to help users find an appropriate caregiver. It also includes a list of all kinds of illnesses.

https://www.findababysitter.org

This site is generally more for parents of typical, non-ill children, but it has a great deal of information on screening, hiring, and paying for a babysitter. It also lists links to agencies and other babysitter resources. **UrbanSitter (https://www.urbansitter.com/mobile)** is an app that offers similar tools.

https://www.greataupair.com

This site is geared toward parents of children who are not sick, but you can conduct a search of "special needs" in some areas. It provides information on hiring someone and about confidential and secure payment options. A list of medical illnesses is provided, but it is not extensive.

RESOURCES FOR GETTING MENTAL HEALTH CARE

Most of these websites have search functions to help you locate professionals in your area. In addition, a simple Google search will help you locate numerous therapist registries.

American Art Therapy Association, https://www.arttherapy.org

American Association for Marriage and Family Therapy, https://www.aamft.org

American Music Therapy Association, https://www.musictherapy.org

American Psychiatric Association, https://www.psychiatry.org

American Psychological Association, https://www.apa.org

Association for Play Therapy, https://www.a4pt.org

National Association of Social Workers, https://www.socialworkers.org

HELPFUL APPS FOR PARENTS AND CHILDREN

In the following sections we list numerous apps you may find helpful. These can be located at and downloaded from the App Store and Google Play.

Calendars, List-Maker, and Note-Taking Apps

Our patients have recommended **Cozi Family Organizer (https://www.cozi.com)** for sharing schedules, appointments, to-do lists, and shopping lists. It helps you keep all parts of a family journal in one place. Similarly, the **To Do List and Calendar (https://apps.apple.com/us/app/to-do-list-calendar/id1360537794)** contains a calendar, to-do list, reminders, planning, a sharing feature, and a feature that lets you sync it with your other devices. Other organization tools include **Evernote (https://www.evernote.com)** and **Google Calendar (https://www.gsuite.com/google/products/calendar)**. The financial app **Mint (https://www.mint.com)** monitors your bank accounts, credit card expenditures, and bill due dates.

Fitness, Nutrition, and Health Apps

Fitness Coach (https://apps.apple.com/us/app/fitness-coach/id1472638797) can be used at home or the gym. You choose a goal and the app designs a program according to your level. There are many exercises and sessions to choose from. It also tracks progress. **My Fitness Pal (https://www.myfitnesspal.com/apps)** tracks diet and exercise and helps you keep track of nutrients by entering foods from their database and scan barcodes of items you have purchased. **Nutritionix Track (https://www.nutritionix.com/app)** is a fitness-tracking app that was developed and maintained by registered dieticians. It allows you to log in your food choices, scan barcodes, and create your own custom foods. It also tracks food intake, nutrient totals, exercise, weight and weight-loss progress, calorie counts, and water intake. Meal Subscription services, such as **Blue Apron (https://www.blueapron.com)** and **Green Chef (https://www.greenchef.com)**, are great for families who still want to have home-cooked family dinners.

Medical Apps

Appointment Minder (https://play.google.com/store/apps/details?id=com.cheltenham.appointments&hl=en_NZ) is an app (compliant with the Health Insurance Portability and Accountability Act of 1996) available through Google Play with a secure login that displays your appointments on your phone. You can even confirm your appointments with this app. Alerts will pop up if something affects your appointment, like the weather, office closures, or changes in date. You will get notifications in pleasant tones. Moreover, you can access your provider's website or patient portal through this app.

    CareZone (https://www.carezone.com) manages prescriptions and dosages for every member of your family.

    ContinuousCare (https://www.continuouscare.io) allows you to keep track of appointment and medical records and ask trained health care specialists medical questions. If your provider uses **Virtual Practice for Healthcare Providers (https://play.google.com/**

store/apps/details?id=com.needstreet.health.hp&hl=en_US), you can schedule video consults and follow-ups.

Follow My Health (https://about.followmyhealth.com/) allows you to communicate securely with your health care team, schedule appointments, view test and lab reports, manage prescriptions, and manage connections with health care organizations to access your health information and interact with providers.

GoodRx (https://www.goodrx.com) helps you compare prescription drug prices. The app offers cash and sale prices, manufacturer coupons, pharmacy discounts, and other savings tips. It will tell you which pharmacies have generic drugs for less than $4.00 per refill and where certain prescriptions are free. Many of the coupons are found right in the app itself, so there is no need to print coupons out.

Health Genie (https://apps.apple.com/us/app/health-genie/id1291730862) helps you remember to schedule doctor appointments, keep track of doctors, and record your family's health concerns.

KidsDoc (https://apps.apple.com/us/app/kidsdoc-from-the-aap/id373964536) gives you the most recent information when your child has physical symptoms. It provides guidance you can use for minor illnesses. Navigation is easy because things are listed alphabetically; there is a keyword search and a body area index.

Medisafe Medication Management (https://www.medisafeapp.com) provides medication reminders, creates reports to share with your health care providers, keeps track of your whole family's medicines in one place, has various tones (including Darth Vader, Austin Powers, and "Nagging Mom") to remind you to take your medication, provides coupons and discounts to various drug stores; reminds patients to take medications on time every time even when the device is put into sleep mode, adjusts to travel and time zone changes, and gives refill reminders.

Sit or Squat (https://www.charmin.com/en-us/about-us/sitorsquat) is an app developed by Charmin that helps you locate nearby restrooms. Each location is rated. This is ideal for patients with bowel and urinary issues as well as for children who are being toilet trained.

Meditation/Mindfulness Apps

- **My Affirmations: Live Positive,** which can be found on Google Play (https://play.google.com/store/apps/details?id=com.ascent.affirmations.myaffirmations&hl=en_US) offers free daily, positive affirmations.
- **Calm** (https://www.calm.com) offers meditations, stories to help you fall asleep, breathing exercises, soothing sounds, and music.
- **Headspace** (https://www.headspace.com/headspace-meditation-app) offers hundreds of guided meditations.
- **Insight Timer** (https://www.insighttimer.com) allows you to set a timer for meditations. The app provides guided meditations, music, and meditations for children.
- **Down Dog** (https://www.downdogapp.com/web) and **Yoga for Beginners** (https://play.google.com/store/apps/details?id=net.workoutinc.yoga.beginners.free.workouts.studio&hl=en_US) offer customized yoga workouts and tips for yoga practice.

CHILDREN'S BOOKS THAT DEAL WITH MEDICAL ISSUES

The books listed here are best read with an adult caregiver who can foster a conversation about the book and discuss any thoughts and feelings that arise. They are also helpful for other family members and friends who are unfamiliar with your child's particular illness.

We encourage you to alert your libraries and schools to these books and to acquire them for their collections. The following list includes books we have used in our clinical practices with children and families as well as ones recommended to us by our patients.

AIDS

- *Alex, the Kid With AIDS*, by Linda Walvoord Girard
- *You Can Call Me Willy: A Story for Children About AIDS*, by Joan C. Verniero

Asthma

- *The ABC's of Asthma: An Asthma Alphabet Book for Kids of All Ages*, by Kim Gosselin
- *Breathe Easy: Young People's Guide to Asthma*, by Jonathan H. Weiss
- *Brianna Breathes Easy: A Story About Asthma*, by Virginia L. Kroll
- *I Have Asthma*, by Jennifer Moore-Mallinos
- *The Lion Who Had Asthma*, by Jonathan London
- *Mostly Monty: First Grader*, by Johanna Hurwitz
- *Once Upon a Breath: The Story of a Wolf, 3 Pigs and Asthma*, by Aaron Zevy
- *Taking Asthma to Camp*, by Kim Gosselin
- *Taking Asthma to School*, by Kim Gosselin

Cancer

- *The Bald-Headed Princess: Cancer, Chemo, and Courage*, by Maribeth R. Ditmars
- *The Great Katie Kate Tackles Questions About Cancer*, by M. Maitland Deland

- *Taking Cancer to School*, by Kim Gosselin
- *There's an Elephant in My Room*, by Jill Trotta Calloway
- *Upside Down and Backwards: A Sibling's Journey Through Childhood Cancer*, by Julie Greves, Katy Tenhulzen, and Fred Wilkinson
- *When a Kid Like Me Fights Cancer*, by Catherine Stier

Cerebral Palsy

- *Nathan's Wish: A Story About Cerebral Palsy*, by Laurie Lears

Crohn's Disease

- *Toilet Paper Flowers: A Story for Children About Crohn's Disease*, by Frank J. Sileo

Cystic Fibrosis

- *The Baking Life of Amelie Day*, by Vanessa Curtis
- *Cadberry's Letters*, by Jennifer Racek
- *Caleb and Kit*, by Beth Vrabel
- *Taking Cystic Fibrosis to School*, by Cynthia S. Henry

Death

- *Always Remember*, by Cece Meng
- *Ben's Flying Flowers*, by Inger Maier
- *The Dead Bird*, by Margaret Wise Brown
- *The Fall of Freddie the Leaf*, by Leo Buscaglia
- *Gentle Willow: A Story for Children About Dying*, by Joyce C. Mills
- *The Gift of Gerbert's Feathers*, by Meaghann Weaver and Lori Wiener

- *The Goodbye Book*, by Todd Parr
- *The Invisible String*, by Patrice Karst
- *Lifetimes*, by Bryan Mellonie
- *The Memory Box: A Book About Grief*, by Joanna Rowland
- *The Memory Tree*, by Britta Teckentrup
- *Remembering Ethan*, by Leslea Newman
- *Saying Goodbye to Lulu*, by Corinne Demas
- *Something Very Sad Happened: A Toddler's Guide to Understanding Death*, by Bonnie Zucker
- *The Tenth Good Thing About Barney*, by Judith Viorst
- *When Dinosaurs Die: A Guide to Understanding Death*, by Laurie Krasney Brown and Marc Brown

Diabetes

- *Diabetes Doesn't Stop Maddie*, by Sarah Glenn Marsh
- *Even Little Kids Get Diabetes*, by Connie White Pirner
- *Even Superheroes Get Diabetes*, by Sue Ganz-Schmitt
- *The Great Katie Kate Discusses Diabetes*, by M. Maitland Deland
- *Rufus Comes Home: Rufus, the Bear With Diabetes*, by Kim Gosselin
- *Sugar Was My Best Food: Diabetes and Me*, by Adair Gregory, Kyle Carney Gregory, Carol Antoinette Peacock
- *Taking Diabetes to School*, by Kim Gosselin
- *Trick or Treat for Diabetes: A Halloween Story for Kids Living With Diabetes*, by Kim Gosselin
- *Type 1 Teens: A Guide to Managing Your Life With Diabetes*, by Korey K. Hood
- *Why Am I So Tired?: A First Look at Childhood Diabetes*, by Pat Thomas

Epilepsy

- *The Great Katie Kate Explains Epilepsy*, by M. Maitland Deland
- *Mighty Mike Bounces Back: A Boy's Life With Epilepsy*, by Robert Skead and Mike Simmel
- *Taking Seizure Disorders to School: A Story About Epilepsy*, by Kim Gosselin

General

- *Ariana Rose: A Story of Courage*, by Ariana Feiner
- *The Dragon With Flames of Love*, by Deborah D. Miller
- *Little Tree: A Story for Children With Serious Medical Problems*, by Joyce C. Mills
- *The Moon Balloon: A Journey of Hope and Discovery for Children and Families*, by Joan Drescher
- *My Life By Me: A Kid's Forever Book*, by Beth Barber
- *What About Me? When Brothers and Sisters Get Sick*, by Allan Peterkin
- *When Will I Feel Better? Understanding Chronic Illness*, by Robin Prince Monroe

Heart Issues

- *Riley's Heart Machine*, by Lori M. Jones

Hospitalization and Procedures

- *The Berenstain Bears Go to the Doctor*, by Stan and Jan Berenstain

- *The Berenstain Bears: Hospital Friends,* by Mike Berenstain
- *Curious George Goes to the Hospital,* by Margaret Rey and H. A. Rey
- *Franklin Goes to the Hospital,* by Paulette Bourgeois and Brenda Clark
- *Going to the Hospital,* by Fred Rogers
- *Harry Goes to the Hospital: A Story for Children About What It's Like to Be in the Hospital,* by Howard J. Bennett
- *Lions Aren't Scared of Shots: A Story for Children About Visiting the Doctor,* by Howard J. Bennett
- *Little Critter: My Trip to the Hospital,* by Mercer Mayer
- *S is for Surgery: A Kids Surgery Book From A–Z,* by Dyan Fox
- *A Sleep Tale: My First Surgery,* by Jennifer Maziad
- *A Visit to the Sesame Street Hospital,* by Deborah Hautzig

Leukemia

- *Chemo to the Rescue: A Children's Book About Leukemia,* by Mary Brent

Organ Donation/Transplants

- *Angel Donor,* by Jennifer Gladen
- *The Gift: For Children Who Are Bone Marrow Donors,* by Sue P. Heiney and Sheldon Lamphier
- *Me and My Marrow: A Kid's Guide to Bone Marrow Transplants,* by Karen Crowe

Pain Management

- *Imagine a Rainbow: A Child's Guide for Soothing Pain,* by Brenda S. Miles

Children in Wheelchairs

- *Best Friend on Wheels*, by Debra Shirley
- *Roll With It*, by Jamie Sumner
- *Yes I Can! A Girl and Her Wheelchair*, by Kendra J. Barret, Jacqueline B. Toner, Claire A. B. Freeland

WHEN A CHANGE OF SCENERY IS IN ORDER: TIPS FOR TRAVELING WITH YOUR CHILD

For children who are not able to join their peers on school field trips, traveling with family or just changing up the local scenery can give them a sense of adventure. Sometimes the purpose of a trip isn't adventure or relaxation. Perhaps you are traveling to consult a specialist in a different area of the country for a second opinion, or you are going to a distant hospital or clinic for treatment. Sometimes these trips happen at the last minute, leaving you little time to plan. In either case, it is possible to find respite from the daily routine and feel energized, despite the extra planning and troubleshooting involved.

Logistics, Planning, and Packing—Some Checklists

If you are traveling, it goes without saying that you'll want to plan ahead. This will help you, your child, and the whole family feel more relaxed about the trip. Where will you go, and how will you get there? What kinds of activities are a good fit for your family's needs, interests, and budget?

When planning travel, begin by speaking with **your child's doctor** about whether or not they believe he is fit for the trip you are planning. Here are some questions you can ask:

- Is the destination safe and an appropriate place to bring him?
- Is it safe to use methods of transportation that involve long periods of time being confined to a small space, such as on

an airplane, train, or boat? Would a shorter trip, or travel by a family vehicle, make more sense? Talk about risks such as exposure to germs, lack of movement, dehydration, and constipation.

- How much exposure to other people or to local water/foods is okay if my child's medicine suppresses his immune system?
- Can the doctor prescribe an antibiotic to kill any bacteria or parasites contracted through water? Can you get it ahead of time just in case?
- How might the climate or weather affect my child (for example, certain medications cause greater sensitivity to the sun)?
- Are any shots required to visit the destination, and how might they interfere with my child's current medications and health?
- How can we be in contact with the medical team or with local doctors or facilities if something should come up? Does your medical team have referrals?

Besides your doctor, another good resource is the national or local **chapter of an organization dedicated to your child's illness** (if one exists) to discuss referrals to doctors and other health care providers in the area you are traveling to. These organizations can also offer invaluable tips for how to travel with your child's particular illness. Some organizations are internationally based, so it will be important to have those numbers available if you travel abroad.

Make sure you also have plenty of **medication for the trip**. Speak with your doctor and your pharmacist to see if you can get extra some medicine before your trip; also, contact your insurance company to refill medicines early if necessary. Here's a checklist for medications:

- Find out where the closest pharmacy is to your destination.
- Check insurance coverage for out-of-network providers.

- Buy travel health insurance, if needed, and medical evacuation insurance (a type of coverage that will reimburse costs should your child need to be, for example, airlifted to a hospital).
- Locate specialists in the area where you'll be traveling who can assist in an emergency.
- Be sure to put all medications in a carry-on bag, in their original bottles (for airline security checks); checked bags sometimes get lost.

We highly recommend purchasing **trip cancellation insurance** for any kind of journey that necessitates reservations—including a car trip, if you are reserving accommodations or tours ahead of time. This type of insurance covers your expenses should you have to cancel or reschedule your trip due to illness or other factors. It can provide peace of mind and take away the "What if?" of traveling with an ill child. Make sure you read everything thoroughly, including the fine print, so you know exactly what's covered.

For **airline travel,** it's important to keep medications close at hand, in a carry-on bag, as mentioned above. Some other considerations for this mode of travel include the following:

- What are the procedures for people with special medical needs or equipment?
- Does the airline need documentation ahead of time to provide special accommodations for my child?
- What foods are available on the airplane and in the airport?
- What are some helpful apps, devices, or comfort objects for managing potential delays or long waits?
- How will the timing of flights and layovers (including time zone changes) affect medication schedules or other care routines, such as rest or exercise?

- What items will help keep our personal space clean, such as sanitizers?

When **packing clothing and supplies,** in addition to weather and climate, you should take the following into consideration:

- When packing, distribute each family member's clothes across multiple bags, so if a bag is lost or delayed, you still have some clothes for everyone.
- Bring clothing layers to help cope with body temperature shifts between your hometown and your destination or changes in indoor heating or air conditioning.
- Pack a change of clothes in your carry-on bag just in case of bowel accidents, vomiting, or other mishaps.
- Be sure to tuck some plastic bags into your carry-on; they almost always come in handy (for example, to contain wet or dirty clothes).
- Estimate how much stuff you need to carry when out and about—heavy bags will drain energy levels.
- Think about finding shops where you can easily buy items such as snacks, tissues, or an extra pair of socks or underwear.
- Bring mobile entertainment options, not just for travel but in case you get stuck waiting or have to curtail a planned activity.

We also recommend enlisting the help of a **travel agent.** Their knowledge and expertise are invaluable. Travel agents have a great deal of information at their disposal that a layperson does not have. For example:

- They know when conventions are in town and accommodations might be scarce, or crowds larger.

- They are familiar with the street layouts in certain cities, so they can recommend daily routes to minimize walking or maximize proximity to clean public restrooms.
- They can set up things ahead of time for you, such as refrigerators or microwaves in your hotel room. They can let you know if rooms have safes or if the front desk at a hotel has safety deposit boxes to keep medications and other equipment secure during your stay. They can book a hotel that has handicap-accessible rooms. Check out **https://www.wheelchairtravel.org** for more information.
- They will know about the disability policies at theme parks or other sites, and what documentation is required to receive accommodations such as shorter wait times and assistive equipment.
- An agent can alert restaurant staff of dietary needs before you arrive. The restaurant staff will know which foods are safe or not, such as fruits and vegetables washed in the local water, and they can advise about bottled water availability.

In short, travel agents can help take some of the pressure and stress of planning off you. This does not mean that you are giving up control of planning your trip. Communicate clearly with a travel professional about your child and family's needs. If you encounter a problem when traveling, whether it be the wrong accommodations, flight delays or cancellations, a hotel that does not meet your expectations or is not providing what you thought was agreed to, or you need help in communicating with others on your trip, your travel professional can help. They can reach out to their contacts and make changes for you, smooth things out, and act as a resource while you are away from home. Their goal is to help make your vacation everything you want it to be, to work out any issues or problems, and to act as your advocate while you are in an unfamiliar location. You will not be able to tap into these resources if you book everything on your own or through a travel website.

Expect the Unexpected, but Don't Expect Perfection

Even when you do use a travel agent, there may still be rough patches on your trip that someone else can't smooth out for you. You will still need to advocate for your child's special needs. Also, as we've mentioned elsewhere in the book, you can be a good model of how to speak up and how to adjust in the moment. Whenever possible, you can also empower and teach your child to be a self-advocate. This skill will help them immensely, especially in the tricky social situations that can arise with travel.

Frank can personally attest to the challenges of traveling with a chronic illness:

I (Frank) will never forget the time when one of my work flights was delayed . . . and delayed . . . and delayed. I have a gastro-intestinal condition, Crohn's disease, and had been feeling well that day—until I got on the plane and we were sitting on the tarmac getting ready to take off. All of a sudden, I felt the strong urge to use the restroom. No distraction in the world was helping. I HAD TO GO! I hit the button for the flight attendant, but she quickly turned it off. I hit it again, and the flight attendant approached me. I told her that I had Crohn's disease and that I needed to use the restroom, now. She proceeded to the front of the plane and phoned the pilot. I got up and ran to the bathroom. The plane was already very delayed, so there I am sitting in the bathroom getting sick, and all I could think of is, "The passengers are going to riot since I am holding up our takeoff. How can I relax doing what I'm doing knowing I may be facing a mob scene when I leave the restroom?!"

When you are sick with Crohn's, you never know how long your restroom trip may take. After what seemed like an eternity, I finally returned to my seat. We were ready for takeoff, and again, I felt ill. This time I relied on deep breathing and some heavy praying, and thank goodness, it was enough. However, I think people would have been sympathetic, if not exactly happy, had I needed to make another mad dash down the aisle.

In a situation like the one just described, it's probably safe to assume that most people will quickly grasp the situation and give you the benefit of the doubt, even if they don't know all the ins and outs of your illness. You can teach your child this, too. Timely communication—and sometimes, being brave and just getting out of your seat even if you're not supposed to!—goes a long way toward facilitating understanding. Most people your child will encounter in life will have empathy, especially for an illness that doesn't follow social rules.

When you travel, it's easy to get excited about all the attractions. As much as you may want to do fun activities, expecting to do them *all* may not be realistic. If you push too hard, you may stress your child's body and have to call it quits anyway. Or, if you skip some activities but worry afterward about missing out, then how can you really relax and enjoy yourself? All children, not just ones with a medical condition, and all adults can get tired, hungry, and cranky while on vacation. Accept this if it happens, and the next day try to factor in extra time to take a pause or just sit quietly.

Traveling can be difficult enough without a chronic health condition in the mix. Expectations that are too high will only add to your stress. Try to be in the moment with your family—you might want to return to our mindfulness tips in Chapter 2. Take pictures. Capture moments. Your child and the rest of your family will thank you, and you will thank yourself.

If traveling simply isn't in your budget, create a "vacation" in different ways. It may be a cliché, but it's about quality, not quantity. You could visit a local museum (many have free days or offer passes through the public library). You could try out a park in a different neighborhood or just go for a long ride. Read books about places and cultures that are different from your own. Any time you designate to set apart, to make memories with those you love, can be a vacation. Enjoy it. Traveling can be good medicine!

NOTES

Here we have listed some of the key studies and other references we used in preparing this book. Many of the articles and book chapters are available online, but some content is paywalled. Where this is the case, you may be able to gain access via your public library's database subscription; alternatively, you can consult a librarian at your nearest community college or university.

THE UNEXPECTED JOURNEY BEGINS

1. Tew, K., Landreth, G. L., Joiner, K. D., & Solt, M. D. (2002). Filial therapy with parents of chronically ill children. *International Journal of Play Therapy, 11*(1), 79–100. https://doi.org/10.1037/h0088858
2. Anderson, T., & Davis, C. (2011). Evidence-based practice with families of chronically ill children: A critical literature review. *Journal of Evidence-Based Social Work, 8*(4), 416–425. https://doi.org/10.1080/15433710903269172
3. Mullins, L. L., Molzon, E. S., Suorsa, K. I., Tackett, A. P., Pai, A. L. H., & Chaney, J. M. (2016). Models of resilience: Developing psychosocial interventions for parents of children with chronic health conditions. *Family Relations, 64*(1), 176–189. https://doi.org/10.1111/fare.12104
4. Sileo, F. J. (2006). *Toilet paper flowers: A story for children about Crohn's disease.* Health Press.

CHAPTER I

1. Ray, L. (2002). Parenting and childhood chronicity: Making visible the invisible work. *Journal of Pediatric Nursing, 17*(6), 424–438. https://doi.org/10.1053/jpdn.2002.127172

2. Quittner, A. L., Espelage, D. L., Opipari, L. C., Carter, B., Eid, N., & Eigen, H. (1998). Role strain in couples with and without a child with a chronic illness: Associations with marital satisfaction, intimacy and daily mood. *Health Psychology, 17*(2), 112–124. https://doi.org/10.1037/0278-6133.17.2.112

3. Mokkink, L. B., van der Lee, J. H., Grootenhuis, M. A., Offringa, M., & Heymans, H. S. A. (2008). Defining chronic diseases and health conditions in childhood (0–18 years of age): National consensus in the Netherlands. *European Journal of Pediatrics, 167*(12), 1441–1447. https://doi.org/10.1007/s00431-008-0697-y

4. Focus for Health. (2017). *Chronic illness and the state of our children's health*. https://www.focusforhealth.org/chronic-illnesses-and-the-state-of-our-childrens-health/

5. van der Lee et al. (2007), cited in Focus for Health. (2017). *Chronic illness and the state of our children's health*. https://www.focusforhealth.org/chronic-illnesses-and-the-state-of-our-childrens-health/

6. Van Cleave et al. (2010), cited in Focus for Health. (2017). *Chronic illness and the state of our children's health*. https://www.focusforhealth.org/chronic-illnesses-and-the-state-of-our-childrens-health/

7. Mundell, E. J. (2008, Mach 23). *Rise in child chronic illness could swamp health care*. https://abcnews.go.com/Health/Healthday/story?id=4507708&page=1

8. Segerstrom, S. C., & Miller, G. E. (2004). Psychological stress and the human immune system: A meta-analytic study of 30 years of inquiry. *Psychological Bulletin, 130*(4), 601–630. https://doi.org/10.1037/0033-2909.130.4.601

9. Salleh, M. R. (2008). Life event, stress and illness. *The Malaysia Journal of Medical Sciences, 15*(4), 9–18.

10. Martini, D. R. (2008). Helping children cope with chronic illness. *Developmentor,* American Academy of Child and Adolescent Psychiatry. https://www.aacap.org/aacap/medical_students_and_residents/mentorship_matters/developmentor/Helping_Children_Cope_with_Chronic_Illness.aspx

11. American Psychiatric Association. (2013). *Diagnostic and statistical manual of mental disorders* (5th ed.). American Psychiatric Publishing.
12. Snyder, C. R., Rand, K. L., & Sigmon, D. R. (2002). Hope theory: A member of the positive psychology family. In C. R. Snyder & S. J. Lopez (Eds.), *Handbook of positive psychology* (pp. 257–276). Oxford University Press.
13. Horton, T. V., & Wallander J. L. (2001). Hope and social support as resilience factors against psychological distress of mothers who care for children with chronic physical conditions. *Rehabilitation Psychology*, *46*(4), 382–399. https://doi.org/10.1037/0090-5550.46.4.382
14. Mednick, L., Cogen, F., Henderson, C., Rohrbeck, C. A., Kitessa, D., & Streisand, R. (2007). Hope more, worry less: Hope as a potential resilience factor in mothers of very young children with type 1 diabetes. *Children's Health Care*, *36*(4), 385–396. https://doi.org/10.1080/02739610701601403
15. See Note 12.

CHAPTER 2

1. Donohue, P. K., Williams, E. P., Wright-Sexton, L., & Boss, R. D. (2018). "It's relentless": Providers' experience of pediatric chronic critical illness. *Journal of Palliative Medicine*, *21*(7), 940–946. https://doi.org/10.1089/jpm.2017.0397
2. Basaran, A., Karadavut, K. I., Uneri, S. O., Balbaloglu, O., & Atasoy, N. (2013). The effect of having children with cerebral palsy on quality of life, burn-out, depression and anxiety scores: A comparative study. *European Journal of Physical and Rehabilitation Medicine*, *49*(6), 815–822.
3. Alpert, P. T. (2014). Who's caring for the caregiver? *Home Health Care Management & Practice*, *26*(4), 266–268. https://doi.org/10.1177/1084822314521210
4. Davidson, R. J., & Kaszniak, A. W. (2015). Conceptual and methodological issues in research on mindfulness and meditation. *American Psychologist*, *70*(7), 581–592. https://doi.org/10.1037/a0039512
5. Killingsworth, M. A., & Gilbert, D. T. (2010). A wandering mind is an unhappy mind. *Science*, *330*(6006), 932. https://doi.org/10.1126/science.1192439

6. Gothe, N., Pontifex, M., Hillman, C., & McAuley, E. (2013). The acute effects of yoga on executive function. *Journal of Physical Activity and Health, 10*(4), 488–495. https://doi.org/10.1123/jpah.10.4.488

7. Streeter, C. C., Whitfield, T. H., Owen, L., Rein, T., Karri, S. K., Yakhkind, A., Perlmutter, R., Prescot, A., Renshaw, P. F., Ciraulo, D. A., & Jensen, J. E. (2010). Effects of yoga versus walking on mood, anxiety, and brain GABA levels: A randomized controlled MRS study. *Journal of Alternative and Complementary Medicine, 16*(11), 1145–1152. https://doi.org/10.1089/acm.2010.0007

8. Thirthalli, J., Naveen, G. H., Rao, M. G., Varambally, S., Christopher, R., & Gangadhar, B. N. (2013). Cortisol and antidepressant effects of yoga. *Indian Journal of Psychiatry, 55*(Suppl. 3), S405–S408. https://doi.org/10.4103/0019-5545.116315

9. Kabat-Zinn, J., Massion, A. O., Kristeller, J., Peterson, L. G., Fletcher, K. E., Pbert, L., Lenderking, W. R., & Santorelli, S. F. (1992). Effectiveness of a meditation-based stress reduction program in the treatment of anxiety disorders. *The American Journal of Psychiatry, 149*(7), 936–943. https://doi.org/10.1176/ajp.149.7.936

10. Minor, H. G., Carlson, L. E., Mackenzie, M. J., Zernicke, K., & Jones, L. (2006). Evaluation of a mindfulness-based stress reduction (MBSR) program for caregivers of children with chronic conditions. *Social Work in Health Care, 43*(1), 91–109. https://doi.org/10.1300/J010v43n01_06

11. Hölzel, B. K., Carmody, J., Vangel, M., Congleton, C., Yerramsetti, S. M., Gard, T., & Lazar, S. W. (2011). Mindfulness practice leads to increases in regional brain gray matter density. *Psychiatry Research, 191*(1), 36–43. https://doi.org/10.1016/j.pscychresns.2010.08.006

12. Lin, K. (2011, June 10). How to find good health information online. *U.S. News & World Report.* https://health.usnews.com/health-news/blogs/healthcare-headaches/2011/06/10/how-to-find-good-health-information-online

13. Mullins, L. L., Molzon, E. S., Suorsa, K. I., Tackett, A. P., Pai, A. L. H., & Chaney, J. M. (2016). Models of resilience: Developing psychosocial interventions for parents of children with chronic health conditions. *Family Relations, 64*(1), 176–189. https://doi.org/10.1111/fare.12104

14. Baumeister, R. F., & Vohs, K. D. (2002). The pursuit of meaningfulness in life. In C. R. Snyder & S. J. Lopez (Eds.), *Handbook of positive psychology* (pp. 608–618). Oxford University Press.

15. Pargament, K. I., & Mahoney, A. (2002). Spirituality: Discovering and conserving the sacred. In C. R. Snyder & S. J. Lopez (Eds.), *Handbook of positive psychology* (pp. 646–659). Oxford University Press.
16. See Note 15.
17. Barnard, L. K., & Curry, J. F. (2011). Self-compassion: Conceptualizations, correlates and interventions. *Review of General Psychology, 15*(4), 289–303. https://doi.org/10.1037/a0025754
18. See Note 17.
19. Moreira, H., Gouveia, M. J., Carona, C., Silva, N., & Canavarro, M. C. (2015). Maternal attachment and children's quality of life: The mediating role of self-compassion and parenting stress. *Journal of Child and Family Studies, 24*(8), 2332–2344. https://doi.org/10.1007/s10826-014-0036-z
20. Emmons, R. A., & Shelton, C. M. (2002). Gratitude and the science of positive psychology. In C. R. Snyder & S. J. Lopez (Eds.), *Handbook of positive psychology* (pp. 459–471). Oxford University Press.
21. See Note 17.
22. Pargament, K. I., & Mahoney, A. (2002). Spirituality: Discovering and conserving the sacred. In C. R. Snyder & S. J. Lopez (Eds.), *Handbook of positive psychology* (pp. 646–659). Oxford University Press.
23. Manninen, S., Tuominen, L., Dunbar, R. I., Karjalainen, T., Hirvonen, J., Arponen, E., Hari, R., Jaaskelainen, I. P., Sams, M., & Nummenmaa, L. (2017). Social laughter triggers endogenous opioid release in humans. *The Journal of Neuroscience, 37*(25), 6125–6131. https://doi.org/10.1523/JNEUROSCI.0688-16.2017
24. Savage, B. M., Lujan, H. L., Thipparthi, R. R., & DiCarlo, S. E. (2017). Humor, laughter, learning, and health! A brief review. *Advances in Physiology Education, 41*, 341–347. https://doi.org/10.1152/advan.00030.2017
25. Mora-Ripoll, R. (2010). The therapeutic value of laughter in medicine. *Alternative Therapies in Health and Medicine, 16*(6), 56–64.
26. See Note 25.
27. See Note 25.
28. See Note 23.
29. Skinner N., & Brewer N. (2002). The dynamics of threat and challenge appraisals prior to stressful achievement events. *Journal of Personality and Social Psychology, 83*(3), 678–692.

30. Kraft, T. L., & Pressman, S. P. (2012). Grin and bear it: The influence of manipulated facial expression on the stress response. *Psychological Science, 23*(11), 1372–1378. https://doi.org/10.1177/0956797612445312

CHAPTER 3

1. Pietrangelo, A., & Cherney, K. (2019, October 22). The effect of depression in your body. *Healthline.* https://www.healthline.com/health/depression/effects-on-body

2. Juckett, G. (2005). Cross-cultural medicine. *American Family Physician, 72*(11), 2267–2274.

3. In regard to online services, the American Psychological Association's *Guidelines for the Practice of Telepsychology* (Guideline 2, "Definition of Telepsychology") notes that email and text are "used for non-direct services (e.g., scheduling)" but also urges psychologists "to conduct an initial assessment to determine the appropriateness of the telepsychology service to be provided" and to "review . . . the most appropriate medium (e.g., video teleconference, text, email, etc.) . . . for the service delivery." See https://www.apa.org/practice/guidelines/telepsychology

4. Reviews by mental health providers of several telehealth platforms may be found at https://www.apaservices.org/practice/good-practice/winter-2020.pdf

5. Novotney, A. (2017). A growing wave of online therapy. *Monitor on Psychology, 48*(2), 48. https://www.apa.org/monitor/2017/02/online-therapy

6. Patient Protection and Affordable Care Act, Pub. L. 111-148, 42 U.S.C. §§ 18001–18121 (2010).

7. Social Security Act of 1935, Pub. L. 74-271, 42 U.S.C. §§ 301–1397mm.

8. Individuals With Disabilities Education Improvement Act of 1990, Pub. L. 101-476, 20 U.S.C. §§ 1400–1482.

9. Social Security Amendments of 1965, Pub. L. 89-97, 42 U.S.C. §§ 1395–1395kkk1 (Medicare) and 42 U.S.C. §§ 1396–1396w5 (Medicaid).

10. Mary J. Labyak Institute for Innovation. (2012). *Pediatric concurrent care* [Continuum briefing]. https://www.nhpco.org/wp-content/uploads/2019/04/Continuum_Briefing.pdf

11. Krauss, M. W., Wells, N., Gulley, S., & Anderson, B. (2001). Navigating systems of care: Results from a national survey of families of children with special health care needs. *Children's Services: Social Policy, Research, and Practice, 4*(4), 165–187. https://doi.org/10.1207/S15326918CS0404_02

12. Masumerci, M. B., & Foutz, J. (2019, June 12). *Medicaid's role for children with special health care needs: A look at eligibility, services, and spending* [Issue brief]. Henry J. Kaiser Family Foundation.

13. George, A., Vickers, M. H., Wilkes, L., & Barton, B. (2008). Working and caring for a child with chronic illness: Challenges in maintaining employment. *Employee Responsibilities and Rights Journal, 20*, 165–176. https://doi.org/10.1007/s10672-008-9065-3

14. Giridharadas, A. (2018). *Winners take all: The elite charade of changing the world*. Knopf.

15. Lukemeyer, A., Meyers, M. K., & Smeeding, T. (2000). Expensive children in poor families: Out-of-pocket expenditures for the care of disabled and chronically ill children in welfare families. *Journal of Marriage and Family, 62*(2), 399–415. https://doi.org/10.1111/j.1741-3737.2000.00399.x

16. Grineski, S. E. (2009). Parental accounts of children's asthma care: The role of cultural and social capital in health disparities. *Sociological Focus, 2*(2), 107–132, p. 109. https://doi.org/10.1080/00380237.2009.10571346

    All the discussion about social and cultural capital comes from this source.

17. See Note 16.

18. Coffey, J. S. (2006). Parenting a child with chronic illness: A metasynthesis. *Pediatric Nursing, 32*(1), 51–59.

19. See Note 13.

20. See Note 13.

21. American Autism Association. (2014). *Finding a babysitter for a special needs child* [Pamphlet].

22. Miller, V. A., & Feudtner, C. (2016). Parent and child perceptions of the benefits of research participation. *IRB Ethics and Human Research*, *38*(4), 1–7.

23. See Note 21.

CHAPTER 4

1. Where we discuss different aspects of child development in this chapter, note that we have relied on several sources, including the following:

    • Centers for Disease Control and Prevention. (2020). *Milestone tracker* [iOS and Android app]. https://www.cdc.gov/ncbddd/actearly/milestones-app.html

    • California Department of Education. (2000). *Care about quality: Ages and stages of development*. https://www.cde.ca.gov/sp/cd/Re/caqdevelopment.asp

    • Institute for Human Development, Ohio Child Welfare Training Program. (2007). *Developmental milestones chart*. https://www.rsd.k12.pa.us/Downloads/Development_Chart_for_Booklet.pdf

    • Centers for Disease Control and Prevention. (2020). *Positive parenting tips*. https://www.cdc.gov/ncbddd/childdevelopment/positiveparenting/index.html

    • Child Care Resource Center. (2020). *Your child's growth and development*. https://www.ccrcca.org/parents/your-childs-growth-and-development

2. Gibbons, M. B. (2009). Psychosocial aspects of serious illness in childhood and adolescence: Responding to the storm. In A. Armstrong-Dailey & S. Zarbock (Eds.), *Hospice care for children* (3rd ed., pp. 54–65). Oxford University Press.

3. See Note 2.

4. See Note 2.

5. Pinquart, M., & Teubert, D. (2012). Academic, physical, and social functioning of children and adolescents with chronic physical illness: A meta-analysis. *Journal of Pediatric Psychology*, *37*(4), 376–389. https://doi.org/10.1093/jpepsy/jsr106

6. Morse, J. M., Wilson, S., & Penrod, J. (2000). Mothers and their disabled children: Refining the concept of normalization. *Health*

Care for Women International, 21(6), 659–676. https://doi.org/
10.1080/073993300300340501

7. Knight, D. (2005). Beliefs and self-care practices of adolescents with asthma. *Issues in Comprehensive Pediatric Nursing, 28*(2), 71–81. https://doi.org/10.1080/01460860590950845

8. Yeo, M., & Sawyer, S. (2005). ABC of adolescence: Chronic illness and disability. *British Medical Journal, 330*(7493), 721–723. https://doi.org/10.1136/bmj.330.7493.721

9. Gibson F., Hibbins, S., Grew, T., Morgan, S., Pearce, S., Stark, D., & Fern, L. A. (2016). How young people describe the impact of living with and beyond a cancer diagnosis: Feasibility of using social media as a research method. *Psycho-Oncology, 25*(11), 1317–1323. https://doi.org/10.1002/pon.4061

10. Waldboth, V., Patch, C., Mahrer-Imhof, R., & Metcalfe, A. (2016). Living a normal life in an extraordinary way: A systematic review investigating experiences of families of young people's transition into adulthood when affected by a genetic and chronic childhood condition. *International Journal of Nursing Studies, 62*, 44–59. https://doi.org/10.1016/j.ijnurstu.2016.07.007

11. Elkind, D. (1967). Egocentrism in adolescence. *Child Development, 38*(4), 1025–1034. https://doi.org/10.2307/1127100

12. Stam, H., Hartman, E. E., Deurloo, J. A., Groothoff, J., & Grootenjhuis, M. A. (2005). Young adult patients with a history of pediatric disease: Impact on course of life and transition into adulthood. *Journal of Adolescent Health, 39*(1), 4–13. https://doi.org/10.1016/j.jadohealth.2005.03.011

13. Pozo, J., & Argente, J. (2002). Delayed puberty in chronic illness. *Best Practice & Research Clinical Endocrinology & Metabolism, 16*(1), 73–90. https://doi.org/10.1053/beem.2002.0182

14. Invisible Disabilities Association. (2020). *What is an invisible disability?* https://invisibledisabilities.org/what-is-an-invisible-disability/

15. See Note 10.

16. Lewis, P., Klineberg, E., Towns, S., Moore, K., & Steinbeck, K. (2016). The effects of introducing peer support to young people with a chronic illness. *Journal of Child and Family Studies, 25*(8), 2541–2553. https://doi.org/10.1007/s10826-016-0427-4

17. Meuleners, L. B., Binnes, C. W., Lee, A. H., & Lower, A. (2002). Perceptions of the quality of life for the adolescent with a chronic

illness by teachers, parents and health professionals: A Delphi study. *Child: Care, Health and Development, 28*(5), 341–349. https://doi.org/10.1046/j.1365-2214.2002.00283.x

18. Cramm, J. M., Strating, M. M. H., Roebroeck, M. E., & Nieboer, A. P. (2013). The importance of general self-efficacy for the quality of life of adolescents with chronic conditions. *Social Indicators Research, 113*(1), 551–561. https://doi.org/10.1007/s11205-012-0110-0

19. See Note 10.

20. Heath, G., Farre, A., & Shaw, K. (2017). Parenting a child with chronic illness as they transition into adulthood: A systematic review and thematic synthesis of parents' experiences. *Patient Education and Counseling, 100*(1), 76–92. https://doi.org/10.1016/j.pec.2016.08.011

21. Joly, E. (2015). Transition to adulthood for young people with medical complexity: An integrative literature review. *Journal of Pediatric Nursing, 30*(5), 91–103. https://doi.org/10.1016/j.pedn.2015.05.016

22. See Note 2.

CHAPTER 5

1. We extend many thanks to The Abuse Prevention Program at the Southern California Counseling Center for the inspiration for this worksheet.

2. Gottman, J., & Silver, N. (2015). *The seven principles for making marriage work* (Rev. ed.). Harmony.

3. Carol is indebted to the class on Couples Therapy given for years by Walter Brackelmanns at the University of California, Los Angeles, for the concept of the "Three Ts."

4. Hendrix, H. (1988). *Getting the love you want: A guide for couples.* Henry Holt.

5. Brown, R. T., Weiner, L., Kupst, M. J., Brennan, T., Behrman, R., Compas, B. E., Elkin, T. D., Fairclough, D. L., Friebert, S., Katz, E., Kazak, A. E., Madan-Swain, A., Mansfield, N., Mullins, L. N., Noll, R., Patenaude, A. F., Phipps, S., Sahler, O. J., Sourkes, B., & Zeltzer, L. (2008). Single parents of children with chronic illness: An understudied phenomenon. *Journal of Pediatric Psychology, 33*(4), 408–421. https://doi.org/10.1093/jpepsy/jsm079

6. Quittner, A. L., Espelage, D. L., Opipari, L. C., Carter, B., Eid, N., & Eigen, H. (1998). Role strain in couples with and without a child with a chronic illness: Associations with marital satisfaction, intimacy and daily mood. *Health Psychology, 17*(2), 112–124. https://doi.org/10.1037//0278-6133.17.2.112

7. Berant, E., Mikulincer, M., & Florian, V. (2003). Marital satisfaction among mothers of infants with congenital heart disease: The contribution of illness severity, attachment style, and the coping process. *Anxiety, Stress & Coping, 16*(4), 397–415. https://doi.org/10.1080/10615580031000090079

8. Berge, J. M., Patterson, J. M., & Rueter, M. (2006). Marital satisfaction and mental health of couples with children with chronic health conditions. *Families, Systems, & Health, 24*(3), 267–285. https://doi.org/10.1037/1091-7527.24.3.267

9. Turner, A. P., Barlow, J. H., & Wright, C. C. (2001). Residential workshop for parents of adolescents with juvenile idiopathic arthritis: A preliminary evaluation. *Psychology, Health & Medicine, 6*(4), 447–461. https://doi.org/10.1080/13548500126540

10. Davis, G. L., Parra, G. R., & Phipps, S. (2010). Parental post-traumatic stress symptoms due to childhood cancer and child outcomes: Investigation of the role of child anger regulation. *Children's Health Care, 39*(3), 173–184. https://doi.org/10.1080/02739615.2010.493763

11. Patterson, C. J., & Farr, R. H. (2011). Coparenting among lesbian and gay couples. In J. P. McHale & K. M. Lindahl (Eds.), *Coparenting: A conceptual and clinical examination of family systems* (pp. 127–146). American Psychological Association.

12. Russell, L. T., Coleman, M., Ganong, L. H., & Gayer, D. (2016). Divorce and childhood chronic illness: A grounded theory of trust, gender, and third-party care providers. *Journal of Family Nursing, 22*(2), 252–278. https://doi.org/10.1177/1074840716639909

13. See Note 12.

14. Ganong, L., Doty, M. E., & Gayer, D. (2003). Mothers in post-divorce families caring for a child with cystic fibrosis. *Journal of Pediatric Nursing, 18*(5), 332–343. https://doi.org/10.1016/s0882-5963(03)00105-2

15. See Note 12.

16. Blumberg, S. (Director). (2012). *Thanks for sharing*. Class 5 Films and Olympic Pictures.

CHAPTER 6

1. Cohen, M. S. (1999). Families coping with childhood chronic illness: A research review. *Family Systems and Health, 17*(2), 149–164. https://doi.org/10.1037/h0089879
2. Reichman, N. E., Corman, H., & Noonan, K. (2008). Impact of child disability on the family. *Maternal and Child Health Journal, 12*(6), 679–683. https://doi.org/10.1007/s10995-007-0307-z
3. Lee, M., & Gardner, J. E. (2010). Grandparents' involvement and support in families with children with disabilities. *Educational Gerontology, 36*(6), 467–499. https://doi.org/10.1080/03601270903212419
4. Hollidge, C. (2000). Well children living with diabetic siblings: Implications for emotional adjustment utilizing a psychodynamic framework. *Psychoanalytic Social Work, 7*(4), 49–74. https://doi.org/10.1300/J032v07n04_02
5. Sharpe, D., & Rossiter, L. (2002). Siblings of children with a chronic illness: A meta-analysis. *Journal of Pediatric Psychology, 27*(8), 699–710. https://doi.org/10.1093/jpepsy/27.8.699
6. Strohm, K. (2001). Sibling Project: A project in south Australia is pioneering the provision of services for siblings of children with disabilities or chronic illness—A group whose needs are only beginning to be recognized in Australia. *Youth Studies Australia, 20*(4), 48–52.
7. See Note 5.
8. See Note 6.
9. See Note 4.
10. Williams, P. D., Ridder, E. L., Setter, R. K., Liebergen, A., Curry, H., Piamjariyakul, U., & Williams, A. R. (2009). Pediatric chronic illness (cancer, cystic fibrosis) effects on well siblings: Parents' voices. *Issues in Comprehensive Pediatric Nursing, 32*(2), 94–113. https://doi.org/10.1080/01460860902740990
11. Bellin, M. H., & Kovacs, P. J. (2006). Fostering resilience in siblings of youths with a chronic health condition: A review of the literature. *Health and Social Work, 31*(3), 209–216. https://doi.org/10.1093/hsw/31.3.209

12. de Roos, S. A., de Boer, A. H., & Bot, S. M. (2016). Well-being and need for support of adolescents with a chronically ill family member. *Journal of Child and Family Studies*, *26*(2), 405–415. https://doi.org/10.1007/s10826-016-0574-7

13. See Note 6.

14. See Note 4.

15. See Note 4.

16. Branstetter, J. E., Domian, E. W., Williams, P. D., & Graff, J. C. (2008). Communication themes in families of children with chronic conditions. *Issues in Comprehensive Pediatric Nursing*, *31*(4), 171–184. https://doi.org/10.1080/01460860802475184

17. See Note 6.

18. See Note 4.

19. See Note 4.

20. See Note 6.

21. See Note 4.

22. See Note 4.

23. See Note 4.

24. See Note 11.

25. Besier, T., Hölling, H., Schlack, R., West, C., & Goldbeck, L. (2010). Impact of a family-oriented rehabilitation programme on behavioural and emotional problems in healthy siblings of chronically ill children. *Child: Care, Health and Development*, *36*(5), 686–695. https://doi.org/10.1111/j.1365-2214.2010.01085.x

26. See Note 16.

27. See Note 5.

28. See Note 11.

29. See Note 6.

30. Lee, M., & Gardner, J. E. (2010). Grandparents' involvement and support in families with children with disabilities. *Educational Gerontology*, *36*(6), 467–499. https://doi.org/10.1080/03601270903212419

31. Mitchell, W. (2007). The role of grandparents in intergenerational support for families with disabled children: A review of the literature. *Child & Family Social Work*, *12*(1), 94–101. https://doi.org/10.1111/j.1365-2206.2006.00421.x

32. Wakefield, C. E., Drew, D., Ellis, S. J., Doolan, E. L., McLoone, J. K., & Cohn, R. J. (2014). Grandparents of children with cancer:

A controlled study of distress, support, and barriers to care. *Psycho-Oncology, 23*(8), 855–861. https://doi.org/10.1002/pon.3513

33. See Note 30.

34. See Note 32.

35. Pit-ten Cate, I. M., Hastings, R. P., Johnson, H., & Titus, S. (2007). Grandparent support for mothers of children with and without physical disabilities. *Family Relations, 88*(1), 141–146. https://doi.org/10.1606/1044-3894.3601

36. Miller, E., Buys, & Woodbridge, S. (2012). Impact of disability on families: Grandparents' perspectives. *Journal of Intellectual Disability Research, 56*(1), 102–110. https://doi.org/10.1111/j.1365-2788.2011.01403.x

37. See Note 30.

38. Kelly, K. P., & Ganong, L. (2011). Moving to place: Childhood cancer treatment decision making in single parent and repartnered family structures. *Qualitative Health Research, 21*(3), 349–364. https://doi.org/10.1177/1049732310385823

39. See Note 1.

40. Boss, P., & Couden, B. A. (2002). Ambiguous loss from chronic physical illness: Clinical interventions with individuals, couples and families. *Journal of Clinical Psychology, 58*(11), 1351–1360. https://doi.org/10.1002/jclp.10083

41. See Note 30.

42. Knafl, K. A., Deatrick, J. A., Knafl, G. J., Gallo, A. M., Grey, M., & Dixon, J. (2013). Patterns for family management of childhood chronic conditions and their relationship to child and family functioning. *Journal of Pediatric Nursing, 28*(6), 523–535. https://doi.org/10.1016/j.pedn.2013.03.006

43. Cipolletta, S., Marchesin, V., & Benini, F. (2015). Family functioning as a constituent aspect of a child's chronic illness. *Journal of Pediatric Nursing, 30*(6), e19–e28. https://doi.org/10.1016/j.pedn.2015.01.024

44. See Note 1.

45. See Note 1.

46. See Note 43.

47. *That Dragon, Cancer* [Mobile app]. (2016). https://www.thatdragoncancer.com/

CHAPTER 7

1. Health Insurance Portability and Accountability Act of 1996, Pub. L. 104-191, 42 U.S.C. § 300gg, 29 U.S.C. §§ 1181–1183, and 42 U.S.C. §§ 1320d–1320d9.
2. Sabate, E. (2003). *Adherence to long-term therapies: Evidence for action.* Geneva, Switzerland: World Health Organization.
3. Rapoff, M. A. (2010). *Adherence to pediatric medical regimens* (2nd ed.). Springer.
4. Gardiner, P., & Dvorkin, L. (2006). Promoting medication adherence in children. *American Family Physician, 74*(5), 793–798.
5. Penkower, L., Dew, M. A., Ellis, D., Sereika, S. M., Kitutu, J. M., & Shapiro, R. (2003). Psychological distress and adherence to the medical regimen among adolescent renal transplant recipients. *American Journal of Transplant, 3*(11), 1418–1425. https://doi.org/10.1046/j.1600-6135.2003.00226.x
6. See Note 4.
7. Dawood, O. T., Izham, M., Ibrahim, M. I., & Palaian, S. (2010). Medication compliance among children. *World Journal of Pediatrics, 6*(3), 200–202. https://doi.org/10.1007/s12519-010-0218-8
8. Schwartz, R. (2000). Enhancing children's satisfaction with antibiotic therapy: A taste study of several antibiotic suspensions. *Current Therapeutic Research, 61*(8), 570–581. https://doi.org/10.1016/S0011-393X(00)80039-9
9. Duncan, C. L., Mentrikoski, J. M., Wu, Y. P., & Fredericks, E. M. (2014). Practice-based approach to assessing and treating nonadherence in pediatric regimen. *Clinical Practice in Pediatric Psychology, 2*(3), 322–336. https://doi.org/10.1037/cpp0000066
10. Dean, A. J., Walters, J., & Hall, A. (2010). A systematic review of interventions to enhance medication adherence in children and adolescents with chronic illness. *Archives of Disease in Childhood, 95*(9), 717–723. https://doi.org/10.1136/adc.2009.175125
11. See Note 3.
12. Patel, A., Jacobsen, L., Jhaveri, R., & Bradford, K. K. (2015). Effectiveness of pediatric pill swallowing interventions: A systematic review. *Pediatrics, 135*(5), 2014–2114. https://doi.org/10.1542/peds.2014-2114

13. Ghuman, J. K., Cataldo, M. D., Beck, M. H., & Slifer, K. J. (2004). Behavioral training for pill-swallowing difficulties in young children with autistic disorder. *Journal of Child and Adolescent Psychopharmacology, 14*(4), 601–611. https://doi.org/10.1089/cap.2004.14.601

14. See Note 13.

15. Funk, M. J., Mullins, L. L., & Olson, R. A. (1984). Teaching children to swallow pills: A case study. *Children's Health Care, 13*(1), 20–23. https://doi.org/10.1207/s15326888chc1301_4

16. Hankinson, J. C., & Slifer, K. J. (2013). Behavioral treatments to improve pill swallowing and adherence in an adolescent with renal and connective tissue diseases. *Clinical Practice in Pediatric Psychology, 1*(3), 227–234. https://doi.org/10.1037/cpp0000032

17. Kaplan, B. (2019, October 9). *How to swallow pills* [YouTube video]. https://www.research4kids.ucalgary.ca/pillswallowing
    Another helpful website is https://www.pillswallowing.com.

18. Bienvenu, O. J., & Eaton, W. W. (1998). The epidemiology of blood-injection-injury phobia. *Psychological Medicine, 28*(5), 1129–1136. https://doi.org/10.1017/s0033291798007144

19. Broome, M. E., Bates, T. A., Lillis, P. P., & McGahee, T. W. (1990). Children's medical fears, coping behaviors, and pain perceptions during a lumbar puncture. *Oncology Nursing Forum, 17*(3), 361–367.

20. McMurtry, C. M., Riddell, R. P., Taddio, A., Racine, N., Asmundson, G. J. G., Noel, M., Chambers, C. T., & Shah, V. (2015). Far from "just a poke": Common painful needle procedures and the development of needle fear. *The Clinical Journal of Pain, 31*(10 Suppl.), S3–S11. https://doi.org/10.1097/AJP.0000000000000272

21. See https://onevoice4kids.com/

22. Wolfram, R. W., & Turner, E. D. (1996). Effects of parental presence during children's venipuncture. *Academic Emergency Medicine, 3*(1), 58–64. https://doi.org/10.1111/j.1553-2712.1996.tb03305.x

23. Uman, L. S., Chambers, C. T., McGrath, P. J., & Kisely, S. (2005). Psychological interventions for needle-related pain and distress in children and adolescents. *Cochrane Database of Systematic Reviews.* https://doi.org/10.1002/14651858.CD005179.pub4

24. Birnie, K. A., Noel, M., Parker, J. A., Chambers, C. T., Uman, L. S., Kisely, S. R., & McGrath, P. J. (2014). Systematic review and meta-analysis of distraction and hypnosis for needle-related pain and

distress in children and adolescents. *Journal of Pediatric Psychology,* *39*(8), 783–808. https://doi.org/10.1093/jpepsy/jsu029

25. DeMore, M., & Cohen, L. L. (2005). Distraction for pediatric immunization pain: A critical review. *Journal of Clinical Psychology in Medical Settings, 12*(4), 281–291. https://doi.org/10.1007/s10880-005-7813-1

26. See Note 20.

27. Skinner, E. A., & Zimmer-Gembeck, M. J. (2007). The development of coping. *Annual Review of Psychology, 58,* 119–144. https://doi.org/10.1146/annurev.psych.58.110405.085705

28. Morrison, M. (2016, May 10). *Dr. Amy Baxter: Buzzing her way out of the ED and into business.* https://feminem.org/2016/05/10/dr-baxter-buzzing-way-ed/

CHAPTER 8

1. Lum, A., Wakefield, C. E., Donnan, B., Burns, M. A., Fardell, J. E., & Marshall, G. M. (2017). Understanding the school experiences of children and adolescents with serious chronic illness: A systematic meta-review. *Child: Care, Health and Development, 43*(5), 645–662. https://doi.org/10.1111/cch.12475

2. See Note 1.

3. See Note 1.

4. See Note 1.

5. Where we discuss different aspects of school and chronic illness in this chapter, note that we have relied on several government sources, including the following:
   - https://www.ada.gov
   - https://sites.ed.gov/idea/
   - https://www.hhs.gov/ocr/office/about/rgn-hqaddresses.html

6. Individuals With Disabilities Education Act of 1990, Pub. L. 101-476, renamed the Individuals With Disabilities Education Improvement Act, codified at 20 U.S.C. §§ 1400–1482.

7. Rehabilitation Act of 1973, Pub. L. 93-112, 29 U.S.C. §§ 701–7961.

8. Lee, A. M. I. (n.d.). *The 13 disability categories under IDEA.* Understood. https://www.understood.org/en/school-learning/special-services/special-education-basics/conditions-covered-under-idea

9. The Understood Team. (n.d.). *What is an IEP?* Understood. https://www.understood.org/en/school-learning/special-services/ieps/what-is-an-iep

10. The Understood Team. (n.d.). *The difference between IEPs and 504 plans.* Understood. https://www.understood.org/en/school-learning/special-services/504-plan/the-difference-between-ieps-and-504-plans

11. Lee, A. M. I. (n.d.). *The difference between special education advocates and attorneys.* Understood. https://www.understood.org/en/school-learning/your-childs-rights/dispute-resolution/the-difference-between-special-education-advocates-and-attorneys

12. See Note 11.

13. See Note 11.

14. *School Accommodation (504) Plan and Inflammatory Bowel Diseases (IBD).* (2016). [Fact sheet]. Crohn's & Colitis Foundation. https://www.crohnscolitisfoundation.org/sites/default/files/2019-07/school-accommodation-12-16.pdf

15. See Note 10.

16. See Note 10.

17. See Note 14.

18. A'Bear, D. (2014). Supporting the learning of children with chronic illness. *Canadian Journal of Action Research*, *15*(1), 22–39. https://doi.org/10.33524/cjar.v15i1.143

19. See Note 18.

20. Anthony, A. (2017, August 3). The robot that staves off loneliness for chronically ill children. *The Guardian.* https://www.theguardian.com/technology/2017/aug/13/robot-to-help-sick-children-norwegian-start-up

21. Wilkie, K. J., & Jones, A. J. (2008). *Link and learn: Student connecting to their schools and studies using ICT despite chronic illness* [Paper]. Australian Association for Research in Education annual conference, Brisbane, Australia.

22. Newhart, V. A. (2019). *Are they present? Homebound children with chronic illness in our schools and the use of telepresence robots to reach them* [Doctoral dissertation, University of California, Irvine]. ProQuest Information & Learning.

23. U.S. Department of State, Family Liaison Office. (n.d.). *Home-schooling and online education.* https://www.state.gov/family-liaison-office/education-and-youth/homeschooling-and-online-education/
24. Woodie, H. (n.d.). *Homeschooling teens who have a chronic illness.* Blog, She Wrote. https://blogshewrote.org/homeschooling-kids-with-chronic-illness/
25. See Note 24.
26. See Note 24.
27. Kearney, C. A., Lemos, A., & Silverman, J. (2004). The functional assessment of school refusal behavior. *The Behavior Analyst Today,* *5*(3), 275–283. https://doi.org/10.1037/h0100040
28. Kearney, C. A. (2006, December). Solutions to school refusal for parents and kids: Pinpoint and address reinforcers of the child's behavior. *Current Psychiatry,* *5*(12), 67–78.
29. Kearney, C. A. (2003). Bridging the gap among professionals who address youths with school absenteeism: Overview and suggestions for consensus. *Professional Psychology: Research and Practice,* *34*(1), 57–65. https://doi.org/10.1037/0735-7028.34.1.57
30. See Note 27.
31. Kearney, C. A. (2001). *School refusal behavior in youth: A functional approach to assessment and treatment.* American Psychological Association.
32. Torma, S., & Halsti, A. (1975). Factors contributing to school refusal and truancy. *Psychiatria Fennica,* *76*, 209–220.
33. Timberlake, E. M. (1984). Psychosocial functioning of school phobics at follow-up. *Social Work Research & Abstracts,* *20*(1), 13–18. https://doi.org/10.1093/swra/20.1.13
34. Weiss, M. G., Ramakrishna, J., & Somma, D. (2006). Health-related stigma: Rethinking concepts and interventions. *Psychology, Health & Medicine,* *11*(3), 277–287. https://doi.org/10.1080/13548500600595053
35. MamaBear. (2020). *MamaBear* [Mobile app]. Google Play Store, App Store.
36. Carlton, M. P. (2020, May 5). *Federal partners in bullying prevention: Empowering schools to change behavior and attitudes.* https://www.stopbullying.gov/blog/categories/federal-partners-bullying-prevention

37. Americans With Disabilities Act of 1990, Pub. L. 101-336, 42 U.S.C. §§ 12101–12213 (2000).
38. U.S. Department of Education, Office for Civil Rights. (2000, July 25). *Prohibited disability harassment: Reminder of responsibilities under Section 504 of the Rehabilitation Act of 1973 and Title II of the Americans With Disabilities Act.* https://www2.ed.gov/about/offices/list/ocr/docs/disabharassltr.html
39. Stop Bullying. (2018, January 7). *Laws, policies, & regulations.* https://www.stopbullying.gov/resources/laws

CHAPTER 9

1. Zandan, N. (n.d.). Eye contact—A declining communications tool? *Quantified Communications.* https://www.quantifiedcommunications.com/blog/eye-contact-a-declining-communications-tool/
2. Binetti, N., Harrison, C., Coutrot, A., Johnston, A., & Mareschal, I. (2016). Pupil dilation as an index of preferred mutual gaze duration. *Royal Society Open Science, 3*(7). https://doi.org/10.1098/rsos.160086
3. Kabat-Zinn, J (1994). *Wherever you go, there you are: Mindfulness meditation in everyday life.* Hyperion.
4. Bayat, M., Erdem, E., & Kuzucu, E. G. (2008). Depression, anxiety, hopelessness, and social support levels of the parents of children with cancer. *Journal of Pediatric Oncology Nursing, 25*(5), 247–253. https://doi.org/10.1177/1043454208321139
5. McCubbin et al. (1983), cited in Charron-Prochownik, D., & Kovacs, M. (2000). Maternal health-related coping patterns and health and adjustment outcomes in children with Type 1 diabetes. *Children's Health Care, 29*(1), 37–45. https://doi.org/10.1207/S15326888CHC2901_3
6. Saadah, N., Hajar, S., & Islam, M. R. (2014). Coping strategies among mothers of chronically ill children: A case study in Malaysia. *Journal of Social Service Research, 40*(2), 160–177. https://doi.org/10.1080/01488376.2013.866613

CHAPTER 10

1. Gordon, B. K., Jaaniste, T., Bartlett, K., Perrin, M., Jackson, A., Sandstrom, R., & Sheehan, S. (2010). Child and parental surveys about pre-hospitalization information provision. *Child: Care, Health and Development, 37*(5), 727–733. https://doi.org/10.1111/j.1365-2214.2010.01190.x
2. Al-Yateem, N., Issa, W. B., & Rossiter, R. (2015). Childhood stress in healthcare settings: Awareness and suggested interventions. *Issues in Comprehensive Pediatric Nursing, 38*(2), 136–153. https://doi.org/10.3109/01460862.2015.1035465
3. Beickert, K., & Mora, K. (2017). Transforming the pediatric experience: The story of child life. *Pediatric Annals, 46*(9), e345–e351. https://doi.org/10.3928/19382359-20170810-01
4. Ekra, E. M. R., & Gjengedal, E. (2012). Being hospitalized with a newly diagnosed chronic illness: A phenomenological study of children's lifeworld in the hospital. International *Journal of Qualitative Studies on Health and Well-Being, 7*, 1–9. https://doi.org/10.3402/qhw.v7i0.18694
5. Burns-Nader, S., & Hernandez-Reif, M. (2016). Facilitating play for hospitalized children through child life services. *Children's Health Care, 45*(1), 1–21. https://doi.org/10.1080/02739615.2014.948161
6. Franck, L., Wray, J., Gay, C., Dearmun, A., Alsberge, I., & Lee, K. A. (2014). Where do parents sleep best when children are hospitalized? A pilot comparison study. *Behavioral Sleep Medicine, 12*(4), 307–316. https://doi.org/10.1080/15402002.2013.801347
7. DeMaso, D. R., & Snell, C. (2013). Promoting coping in children facing pediatric surgery. *Seminars in Pediatric Surgery, 22*(3), 134–138. https://doi.org/10.1053/j.sempedsurg.2013.04.004
8. Tapp, H., Shade, L., Mahabaleshwarkar, R., Taylor, Y. J., Ludden, T., & Dulin, M. F. (2017). Results from a pragmatic prospective cohort study: Shared decision making improves outcomes for children with asthma. *Journal of Asthma, 54*(4), 392–402. https://doi.org/10.1080/02770903.2016.1227333
9. See Note 7.
10. Thurber, C. A., Patterson, D. R., & Kiomi-Mount, K. (2007). Homesickness and children's adjustment to hospitalization: Toward

a preliminary model. *Children's Health Care, 36*(1), 1–28. https:// doi.org/10.1080/02739610701316753

11. Salmela, M., Aronen, E., & Salanterä, S. (2011). The experience of hospital-related fears in 4- to 6-year-old children. *Child: Care, Health and Development, 37*(5), 719–726. https://doi.org/10.1111/ j.1365-2214.2010.01171.x

12. Spirito, A., Stark, L. J., & Tyc, V. L. (1994). Stressors and coping strategies described during hospitalization by chronically ill children. *Journal of Clinical Child Psychology, 23*(3), 314–322. https://doi.org/ 10.1207/s15374424jccp2303_9

13. See Note 5.

14. See Note 4.

15. See Note 7.

16. Children's Hospital Colorado. (n.d.). *Parent toolkit: Helping your child cope with medical procedures.* https://www.childrenscolorado. org/conditions-and-advice/parenting/parenting-articles/coping-with-medical-procedures/

17. Capurso, M., & Ragni, B. (2016). Psycho-educational preparation of children for anaesthesia: A review of intervention methods. *Patient Education and Counseling, 99*(2), 173–185. https://doi.org/ 10.1016/j.pec.2015.09.004

18. de Bie, H. M. A., Boersma, M., Wattjes, M. P., Adriaanse, S., Vermeulen, R. J., Oostrom, K. M., Huisman, J., Veltman, D. J., & Delemarre-Van de Waal, H. A. (2010). Preparing children with a mock scanner training protocol results in high quality structural and functional MRI scans. *European Journal of Pediatrics, 169*(9), 1079–1085. https://doi.org/10.1007/s00431-010-1181-z

19. Leroux, G., Lubin, A., Houdé, O., & Lanoë, C. (2013). How to best train children and adolescents for fMRI? Meta-analysis of the training methods in developmental neuroimaging. *Neuroeducation, 2*(1), 44–70. https://doi.org/10.24046/neuroed.20130201.44

20. Dechter, F. (2015, July 1). *Conquering children's fears of MRI with the help of superheros.* Radiological Society of North America. https:// www.rsna.org/news/2015/july/conquering-childrens-fear-of-mri

21. Beickert, K., & Mora, K. (2017). Transforming the pediatric experience: The story of child life. *Pediatric Annals, 46*(9), e345–e351. https://doi.org/10.3928/19382359-20170810-01

22. Carlsson, R. N. E., & Henningsson, R. N. (2018). Visiting the operating theatre before surgery did not reduce the anxiety in children and their attendant parent. *Journal of Pediatric Nursing, 38*, e324–e329. https://doi.org/10.1016/j.pedn.2017.09.005

23. Goldschmidt, K., & Woolley, A. (2017). Using technology to reduce children's anxiety throughout the perioperative period. *Journal of Pediatric Nursing, 36*, 256–258. https://doi.org/10.1016/j.pedn.2017.04.006

24. See Note 7.

25. Lang, E. V., Viegas, J., Bleeker, C., Bruhn, J., & van Geffen, G-J. (2017). Helping children cope with medical tests and interventions. *Journal of Radiology Nursing, 36*(1), 44–50. https://doi.org/10.1016/j.jradnu.2016.11.005

26. Perry, J. N., Hooper, V. D., & Masiongale, J. (2012). Reduction of preoperative anxiety in pediatric surgery patients using age-appropriate teaching interventions. *Journal of Perianesthesia Nursing, 27*(2), 69–81. https://doi.org/10.1016/j.jopan.2012.01.003

27. MacLaren, J. E., & Kain, Z. N. (2008). Development of a brief behavioral intervention for children's anxiety at anesthesia induction. *Children's Health Care, 37*(3), 196–209. https://doi.org/10.1080/02739610802151522

28. Harris, T. B., Sibley, A., Rodriguez, C., & Brandt, M. L. (2013). Teaching the psychosocial aspects of pediatric surgery. *Seminars in Pediatric Surgery, 22*(3), 161–166. https://doi.org/10.1053/j.sempedsurg.2013.05.005

29. Zisk Rony, R. Y., Fortier, M. A., Chorney, J. M., Perret, D., & Kain, Z. N. (2010). Parental postoperative pain management: Attitudes, assessment, and management. *Pediatrics, 125*(6), e1372–e1378. https://doi.org/10.1542/peds.2009-2632

30. Center to Advance Palliative Care. (n.d.). *Pediatric vs. adult palliative care.* https://getpalliativecare.org/whatis/pediatric/adult-vs-pediatric-palliative-care/

31. Ullrich, C., & Morrison, R. S. (2013). Pediatric palliative care research comes of age: What we stand to learn from children with life-threatening illness. *Journal of Palliative Medicine, 16*(4), 334–336. https://doi.org/10.1089/jpm.2013.9518

32. National Institute of Nursing Research. (2015, July). *Palliative care for children: Support for the whole family when your child is living*

with a serious illness (NIH Publication No. 15-NR-8003). https://www.ninr.nih.gov/sites/files/docs/NINR_508cBrochure_2015-7-7.pdf

33. World Health Organization. (n.d.). *WHO definition of palliative care*. https://www.who.int/cancer/palliative/definition/en/

34. Monterosso, L., Kristjanson, L. J., Aoun, S., & Phillips, M. B. (2007). Supportive and palliative care needs of families of children with life-threatening illnesses in western Australia: Evidence to guide the development of a palliative care service. *Palliative Medicine, 21*(8), 689–696. https://doi.org/10.1177/0269216307083032

35. Yu, J. A., Schenker, Y., Maurer, S. H., Cook, S. C., Kavlieratos, D., & Houtrow, A. (2019). Pediatric palliative care in the medical neighborhood for children with medical complexity. *Families, Systems, & Health, 37*(2), 107–119. https://doi.org/10.1037/fsh0000414

36. Palliative Doctors. (n.d.). *Hospice and palliative care for children*. https://palliativedoctors.org/start/child

37. See Note 32.

38. Palliative Doctors. (n.d.). *Medical treatments for pain relief*. https://palliativedoctors.org/start/treatments

39. Center to Advance Palliative Care. (n.d.). *The pediatric palliative care team*. https://getpalliativecare.org/whatis/pediatric/the-pediatric-palliative-care-team/

40. See Note 32.

CHAPTER I I

1. Hechler, T., Blankenburg, M., Friedrichsdorf, S. J., Garske, D., Hübner, B., Menke, A., Wamsler, C., Wolfe, J., & Zernikow, B. (2008). Parents' perspective on symptoms, quality of life, characteristics of death and end-of-life decisions for children dying from cancer. *Klinische Pädiatrie, 220*(3), 166–174. https://doi.org/10.1055/s-2008-1065347

2. See Note 1.

3. See Note 1.

4. McSherry, M., Kehoe, K., Carroll, J. M., Kang, T. I., & Rourke, M. T. (2007). Psychosocial and spiritual needs of children living with a life-limiting illness. *Pediatric Clinics of North America, 54*(5), 609–629. https://doi.org/10.1016/j.pcl.2007.08.002

5. See Note 4.
6. American Academy of Pediatrics, Committee on Bioethics and Committee on Hospital Care. (2000). Palliative care for children. *Pediatrics, 106*(2), 351–357. https://doi.org/10.1542/peds.106.2.351
7. Yu, J. A., Schenker, Y., Maurer, S. H., Cook, S. C., Kavlieratos, D., & Houtrow, A. (2019). Pediatric palliative care in the medical neighborhood for children with medical complexity. *Families, Systems, & Health, 37*(2), 107–119. https://doi.org/10.1037/fsh0000414
8. International Children's Palliative Care Network. (n.d.). *What is children's palliative care?* http://www.icpcn.org/about-icpcn/what-is-childrens-palliative-care/
9. Monterosso, L., Kristjanson, L. J., Aoun, S., & Phillips, M. B. (2007). Supportive and palliative care needs of families of children with life-threatening illnesses in western Australia: Evidence to guide the development of a palliative care service. *Palliative Medicine, 21*(8), 689–696. https://doi.org/10.1177/0269216307083032
10. Hinds, P. S., Drew, D., Oakes, L. L., Fouladi, M., Spunt, S. L., Church, C., & Furman, W. L. (2005). End-of-life care preferences of pediatric patients with cancer. *Journal of Clinical Oncology, 23*(36), 9146–9154. https://doi.org/10.1200/JCO.2005.10.538
11. See Note 10.
12. See Note 4.
13. See Note 4.
14. Kars, M. C., Grypdonck, M. H. F., de Bock, L. C., & van Delden, J. J. M. (2015). The parents' ability to attend to the "voice of their child" with incurable cancer during the palliative phase. *Health Psychology, 34*(4), 446–452. https://doi.org/10.1037/hea0000166
15. See Note 14.
16. See Note 14.
17. Albuquerque, S., Narciso, I., & Pereira, M. (2018). Posttraumatic growth in bereaved parents: A multidimensional model of associated factors. *Psychological Trauma, 10*(2), 199–207. https://doi.org/10.1037/tra0000305
18. Wender, E., & The Committee on Psychosocial Aspects of Child and Family Health. (2012). Supporting the family after the death of a child. *Pediatrics, 130*(6), 1164–1169. https://doi.org/10.1542/peds.2012-2772

19. Meert, K. L., Thurston, C. S., & Thomas, R. (2001). Parental coping and bereavement outcome after the death of a child in the pediatric intensive care unit. *Pediatric Critical Care Medicine, 2*(4), 324–328. https://doi.org/10.1097/00130478-200110000-00007

20. Wijngaards-de Meij, L., Stroeve, M., Schut, H., Stroebe, W., van den Bout, J., van der Heijden, P., & Dijkstra, I. (2005). Couples at risk following the death of their child: Predictors of grief versus depression. *Journal of Consulting and Clinical Psychology, 73*(4), 617–623. https://doi.org/10.1037/0022-006X.73.4.617

21. Rogers, C. H., Floyd, F. J., Seltzer, M. M., Greenberg, J., & Hong, J. (2008). Long-term effects of the death of a child on parents' adjustment in midlife. *Journal of Family Psychology, 22*(2), 203–211. https://doi.org/10.1037/0893-3200.22.2.203

22. See Note 18.

23. Gregory, C. (2020, June 25). *The five stages of grief: An examination of the Kübler-Ross model.* https://www.psycom.net/depression.central.grief.html

24. Albuquerque, S., Pereira, M., & Narciso, I. (2016). Couple's relationship after the death of a child: A systematic review. *Journal of Child and Family Studies, 25*(1), 30–53. https://doi.org/10.1007/s10826-015-0219-2

25. See Note 14.

26. See Note 18.

27. See Note 18.

28. See Note 21.

29. Kazak, A. E., & Noll, R. B. (2004). Child death from pediatric illness: Conceptualizing intervention from a family/systems and public health perspective. *Professional Psychology: Research and Practice, 35*(3), 219–226. https://doi.org/10.1037/0735-7028.35.3.219

30. See Note 24.

31. See Note 24.

INDEX

ABOUT THE AUTHORS

Frank J. Sileo, PhD, is a New Jersey–licensed psychologist, an award-winning author, and a national and international speaker. He is the founder and executive director of The Center for Psychological Enhancement, LLC, in Ridgewood, NJ. He graduated cum laude from Iona College with a bachelor of arts degree in psychology and received his doctorate in counseling psychology from Fordham University. He is the author of 12 children's books that have been translated into four languages.

Dr. Sileo has maintained a private practice since 1995. He works with children, adolescents, adults, and families. He specializes in the treatment of chronic illness in children and adults. Since 2010, Dr. Sileo has consistently been recognized as one of "New Jersey's Top Kids' Docs." He is a member of the American Psychological Association and the New Jersey Psychological Association. He was the founding chairperson of the Task Force on Health Psychology through the New Jersey Psychological Association. Dr. Sileo has taught at Fordham University and St. Thomas Aquinas College.

His research has been published in journals and presented at conferences in the United States and Canada. He is often the go-to psychologist for the media because of his insights into a variety of psychological topics, health issues, and parenting. Dr. Sileo has been quoted in newspapers, magazines, and websites, including *The New York Times*, *The Chicago Tribune*, *Parents*, *Family Circle*, *USA Today*, *Psychology Today*, WebMD, CNBC, and *The Boston Globe*. He has been a radio guest on WCBS, Radio Disney, and numerous podcasts. He has also appeared on television on Fox 5 News and Caucus NJ on PBS. He speaks to local and national organizations, schools, businesses, nonprofit organizations, hospitals, and medical practices.

Dr. Sileo was diagnosed with Crohn's disease in 1989. It has been his goal to bring hope and awareness of the disease to all.

You can find more information regarding Dr. Sileo at https:// www.drfranksileo.com, and you can follow him on Twitter (@drfranksileo), Instagram (@drfranksileo), and Facebook (fb.com/drfranksileo).

Carol S. Potter, MFT, is a Licensed Marriage and Family Therapist in Los Angeles, California. She graduated from Harvard University cum laude with a bachelor of arts degree in social relations and received her master of arts in marriage and family therapy in 1997 from the Phillips Graduate Institute in Chatsworth, California. Her MFT training includes working with children and adolescents in school settings; working with individuals, families, and couples; and facilitating groups focused on adolescent issues, bereavement, and anger management, with significant advanced training utilizing strength-based (postmodern) approaches to therapy. She has completed the American Association for Marriage and Family Therapy–Certified Training in Family Therapy and the American Association of Couples and Sex Therapists' training in couples and sex therapy, and she has received the Institute for Mindfulness and Psychotherapy's certificate in Mindfulness and Psychotherapy. She also cocreated the "Best Practice Parenting" program for the Southern California Counseling Center.

Her writing has appeared in *Lear's*, *Redbook*, and *PGI's Progress Journal*, which published her original research on adolescent girls. For her work on behalf of women survivors of domestic violence she was honored as Woman of the Year by Sojourn, a shelter for survivors and their children, in 1994.

Prior to becoming a marriage and family therapist, Ms. Potter spent 25 years in the entertainment industry. She is most remembered for playing Cindy Walsh, one of TV's most beloved mothers, on the hit show *Beverly Hills, 90210*. The show continues to have a worldwide and current following. While appearing on *90210*, she wrote an advice column for *16* magazine. Advocates for Youth, which focuses on adolescent sexuality and health, invited her to write the introduction to their booklet for parents.

Ms. Potter lost her husband to cancer after the birth of her son Christopher, a story that was chronicled in *People* magazine. You may find more information about Ms. Potter on her website: https://www.carolpotter.net, and follow her on Instagram (@carolpotter90210) and Twitter (@CarolSP90210).